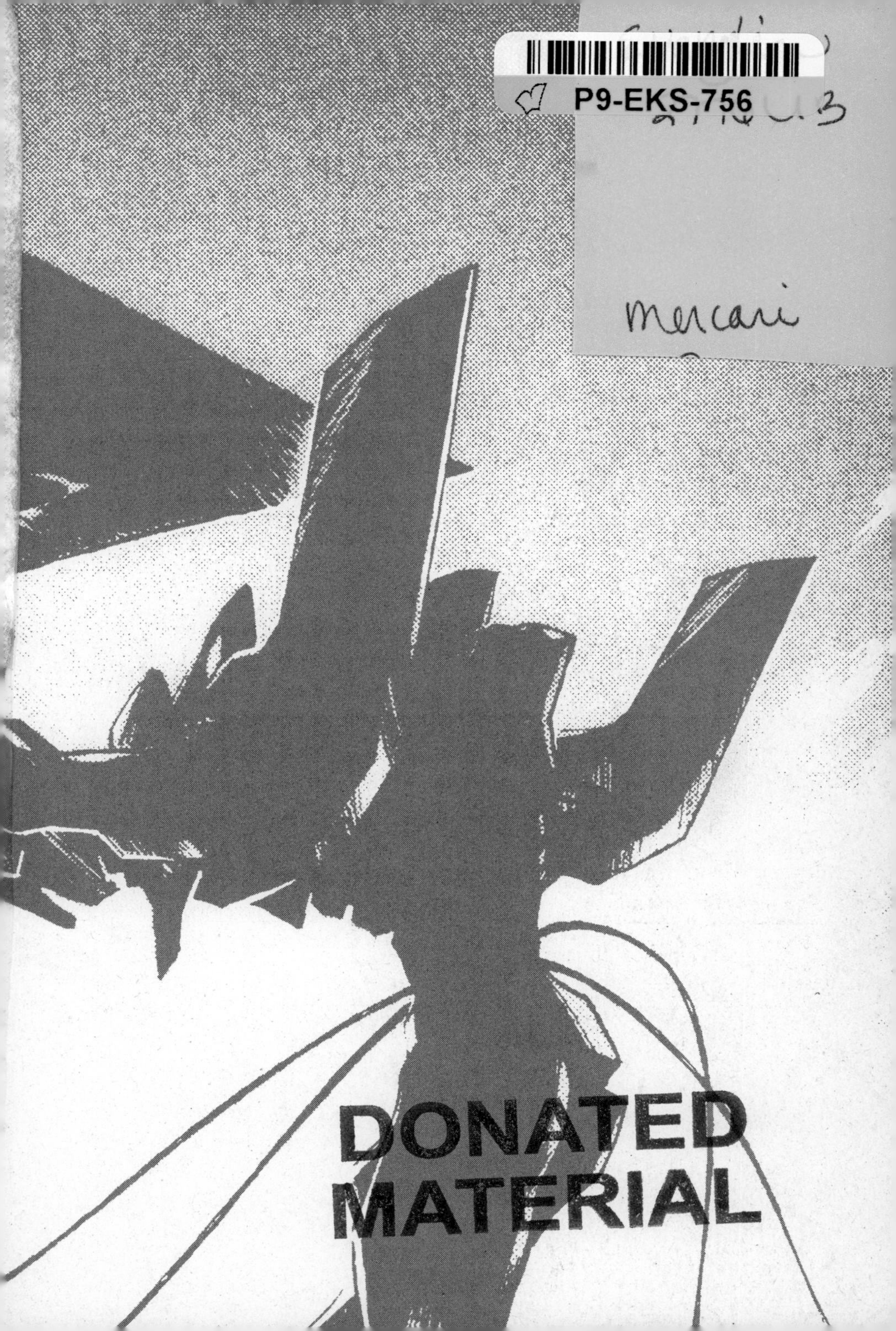

NEON GENESIS EVANGELION

Volume 2

Story & Art by
Yoshiyuki Sadamoto
Created by
GAINAX

Neon Genesis EVANGELION
Vol.2

CONTENTS

This volume contains NEON GENESIS EVANGELION Book Two #1 through #5 in their entirety.

Story & Art by Yoshiyuki Sadamoto
Created by GAINAX

English Adaptation by Fred Burke

Translation/Lillian Olsen
Touch-Up Art & Lettering/Wayne Truman
Cover Design/Hidemi Sahara
Editor/Carl Gustav Horn
Assistant Editor/Annette Roman

Managing Editor/Hyoe Narita
Editor-in-Chief/Satoru Fujii
Publisher/Seiji Horibuchi

First Published in 1995 by KADOKAWA SHOTEN PUBLISHING CO., LTD. Tokyo. English translation rights arranged with KADOKAWA SHOTEN PUBLISHING CO., LTD., Tokyo.

For the purposes of publication in English, the artwork in this publication is printed in reverse from the original Japanese version.

Printed in Canada

Published by Viz Communications, Inc.
P.O. Box 77010
San Francisco, CA 94107

10 9 8 7 6 5 4 3 2 1
First printing, December 1998

Vizit us at our World Wide Web site at www.viz.com and our Internet magazine, j-pop.com, at www.j-pop.com!

NEON GENESIS EVANGELION GRAPHIC NOVELS TO DATE

NEON GENESIS EVANGELION VOL. 1
NEON GENESIS EVANGELION VOL. 2

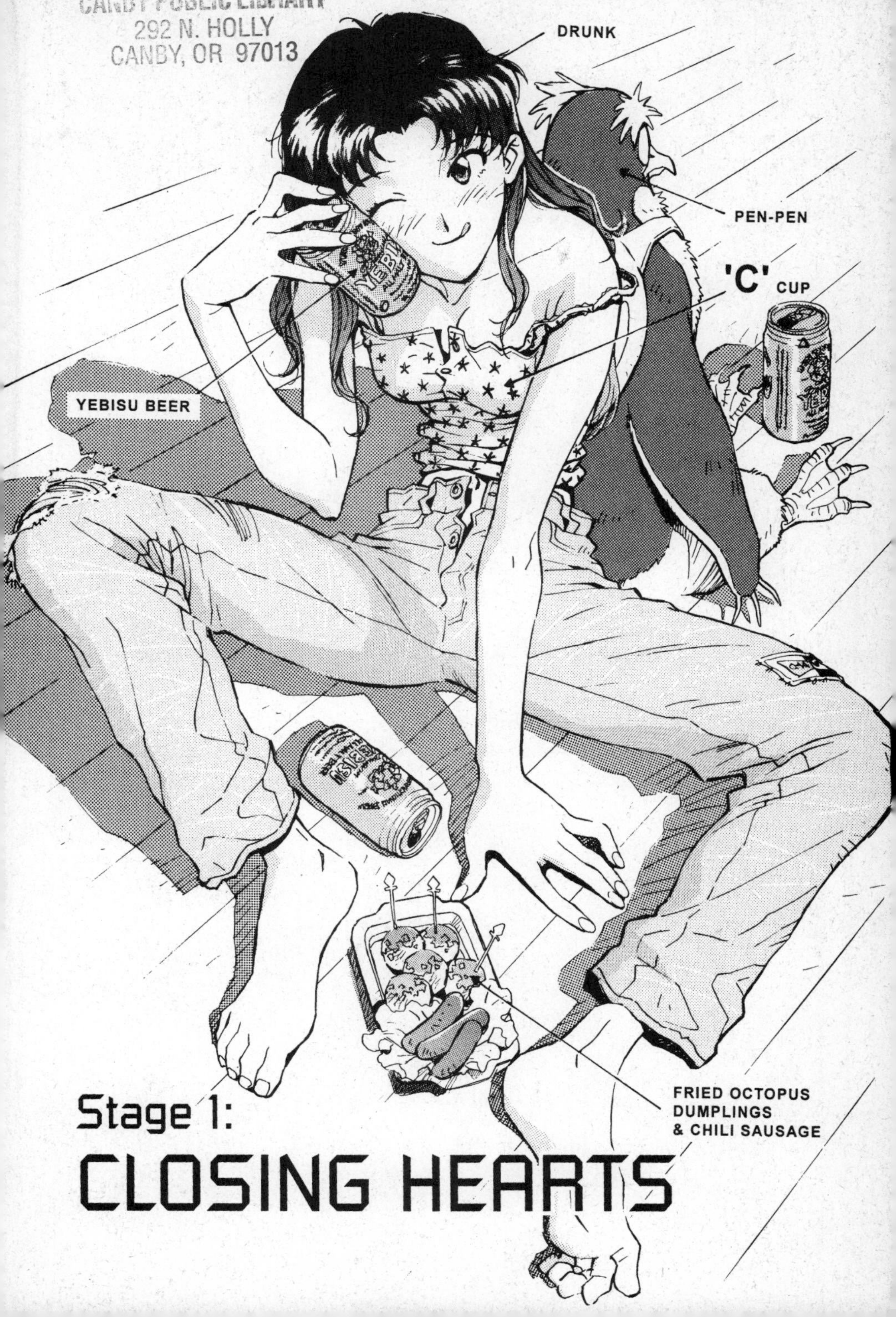
DRUNK
PEN-PEN
'C' CUP
YEBISU BEER
FRIED OCTOPUS
DUMPLINGS
& CHILI SAUSAGE

Stage 1:
CLOSING HEARTS

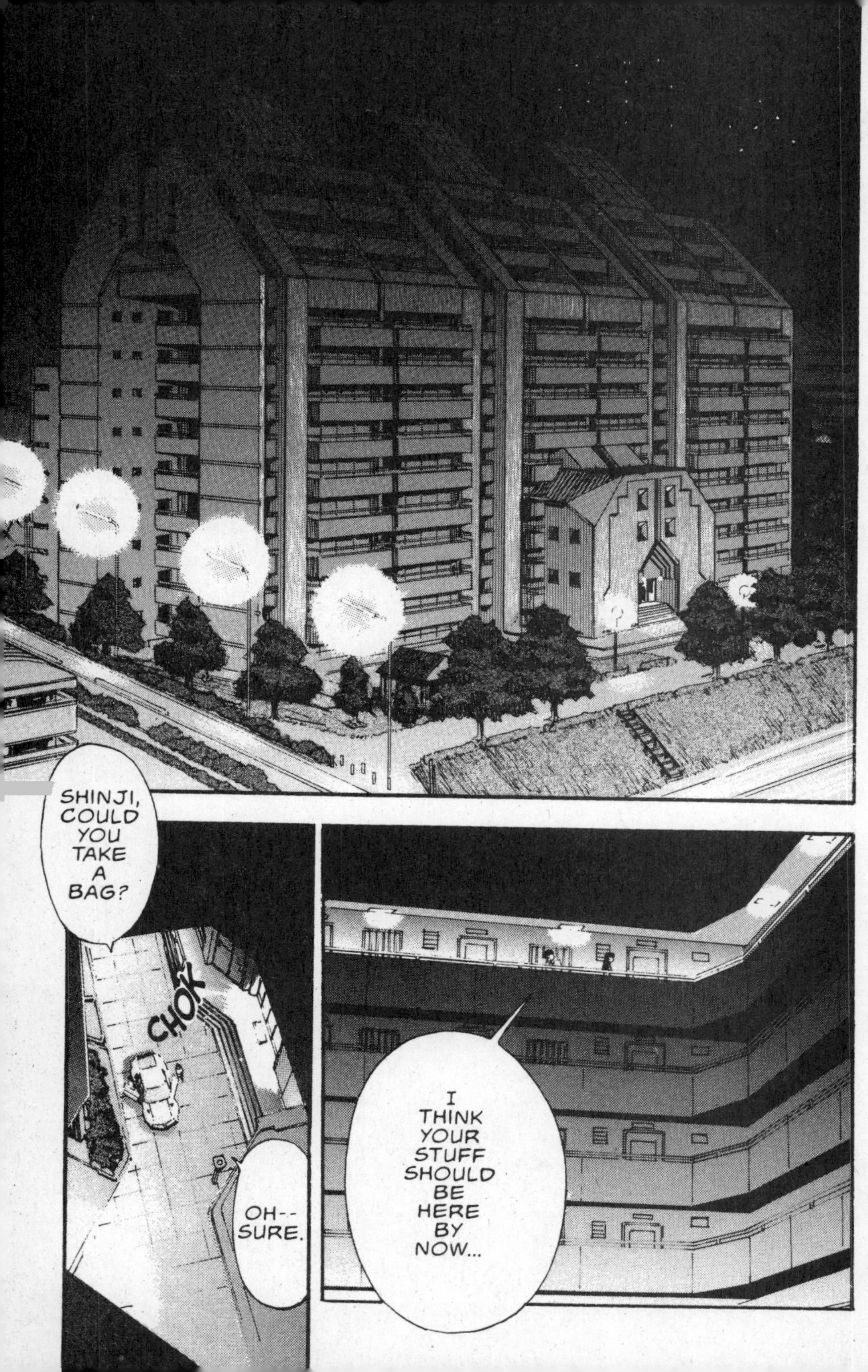
SHINJI, COULD YOU TAKE A BAG?
CHOK
OH-- SURE.
I THINK YOUR STUFF SHOULD BE HERE BY NOW...

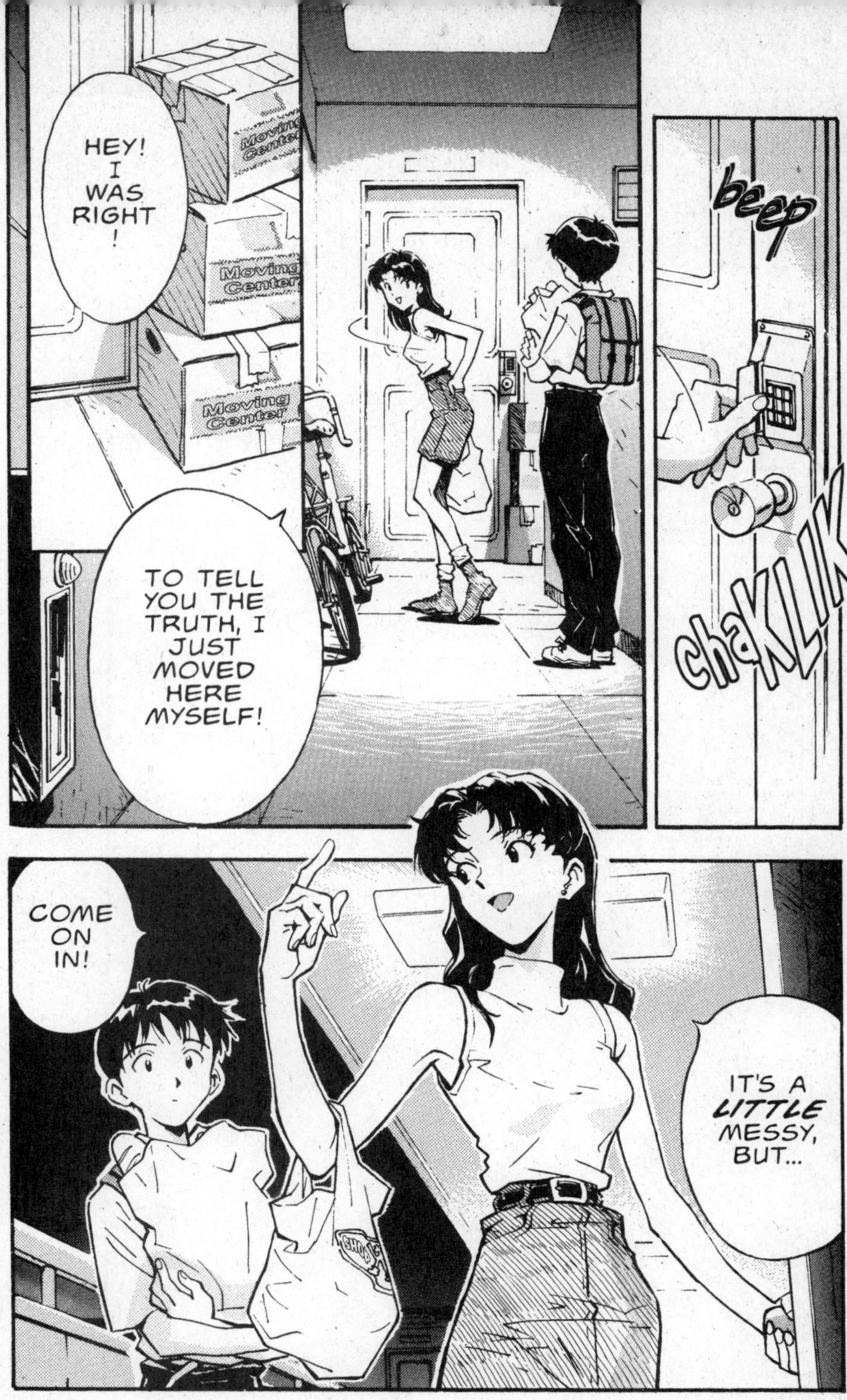
HEY! I WAS RIGHT!
TO TELL YOU THE TRUTH, I JUST MOVED HERE MYSELF!
beep
chaKLIK
COME ON IN!
IT'S A LITTLE MESSY, BUT...

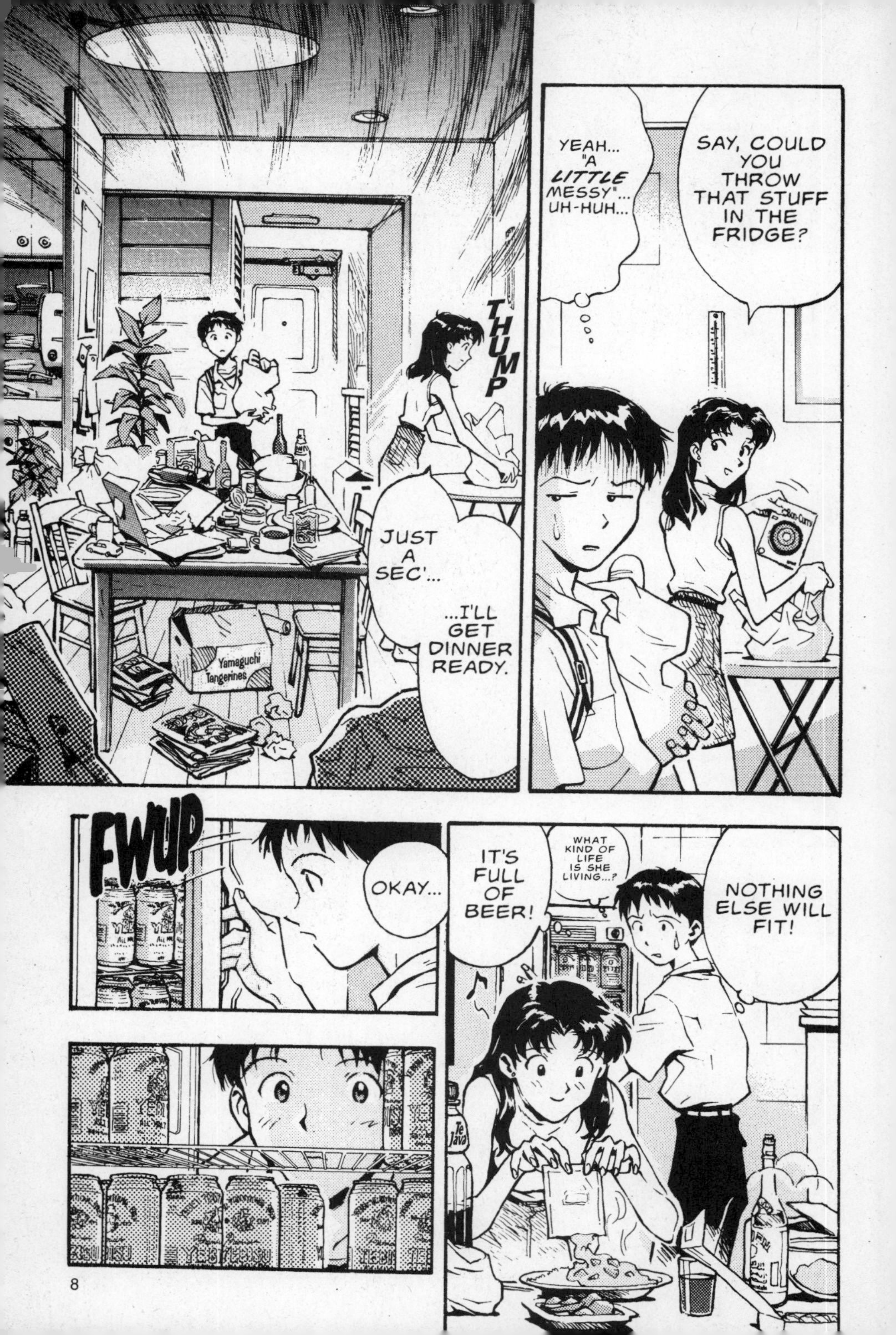

THUMP
JUST A SEC'...
...I'LL GET DINNER READY.
Yamaguchi Tangerines
YEAH... "A *LITTLE* MESSY"... UH-HUH...
SAY, COULD YOU THROW THAT STUFF IN THE FRIDGE?
FWUP
OKAY...
IT'S FULL OF BEER!
WHAT KIND OF LIFE IS SHE LIVING...?
NOTHING ELSE WILL FIT!

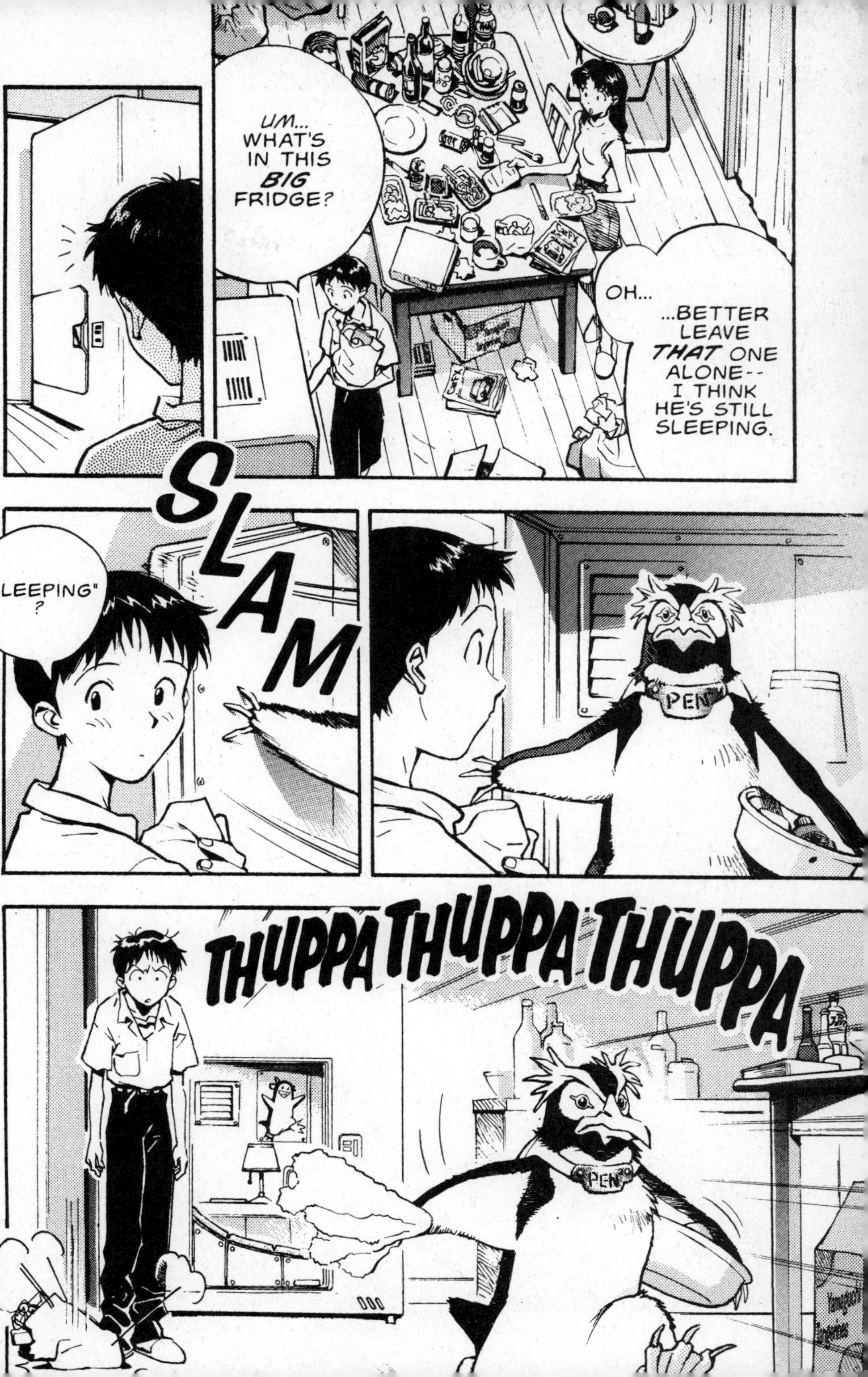

UM... WHAT'S IN THIS BIG FRIDGE?
OH...
...BETTER LEAVE THAT ONE ALONE-- I THINK HE'S STILL SLEEPING.
SLAM
"SLEEPING"?
PEN
THUPPA THUPPA THUPPA
PEN

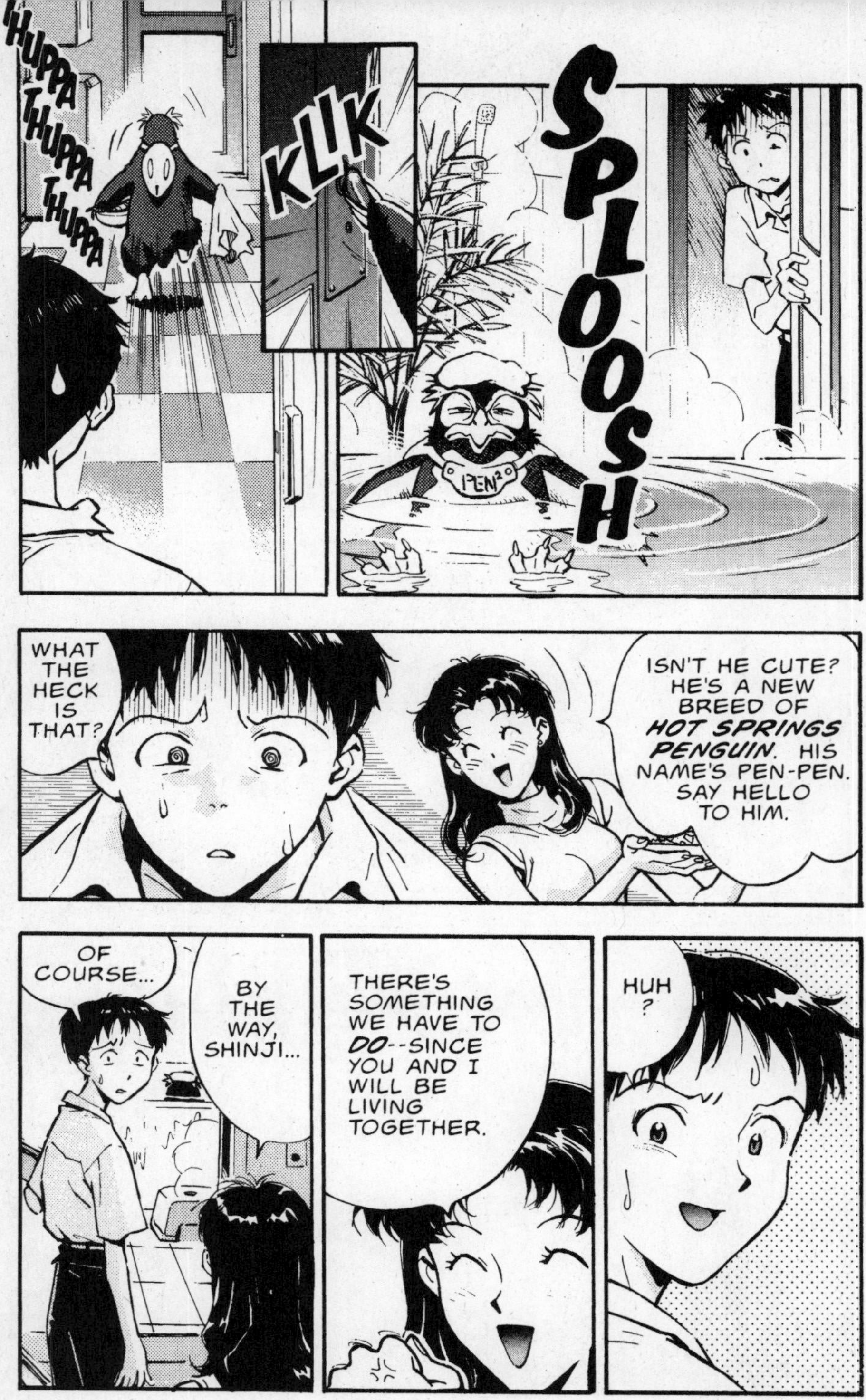
THUPPA THUPPA THUPPA THUPPA
KLIK
SPLOOSH
WHAT THE HECK IS THAT?
ISN'T HE CUTE? HE'S A NEW BREED OF HOT SPRINGS PENGUIN. HIS NAME'S PEN-PEN. SAY HELLO TO HIM.
OF COURSE...
BY THE WAY, SHINJI...
THERE'S SOMETHING WE HAVE TO DO--SINCE YOU AND I WILL BE LIVING TOGETHER.
HUH?

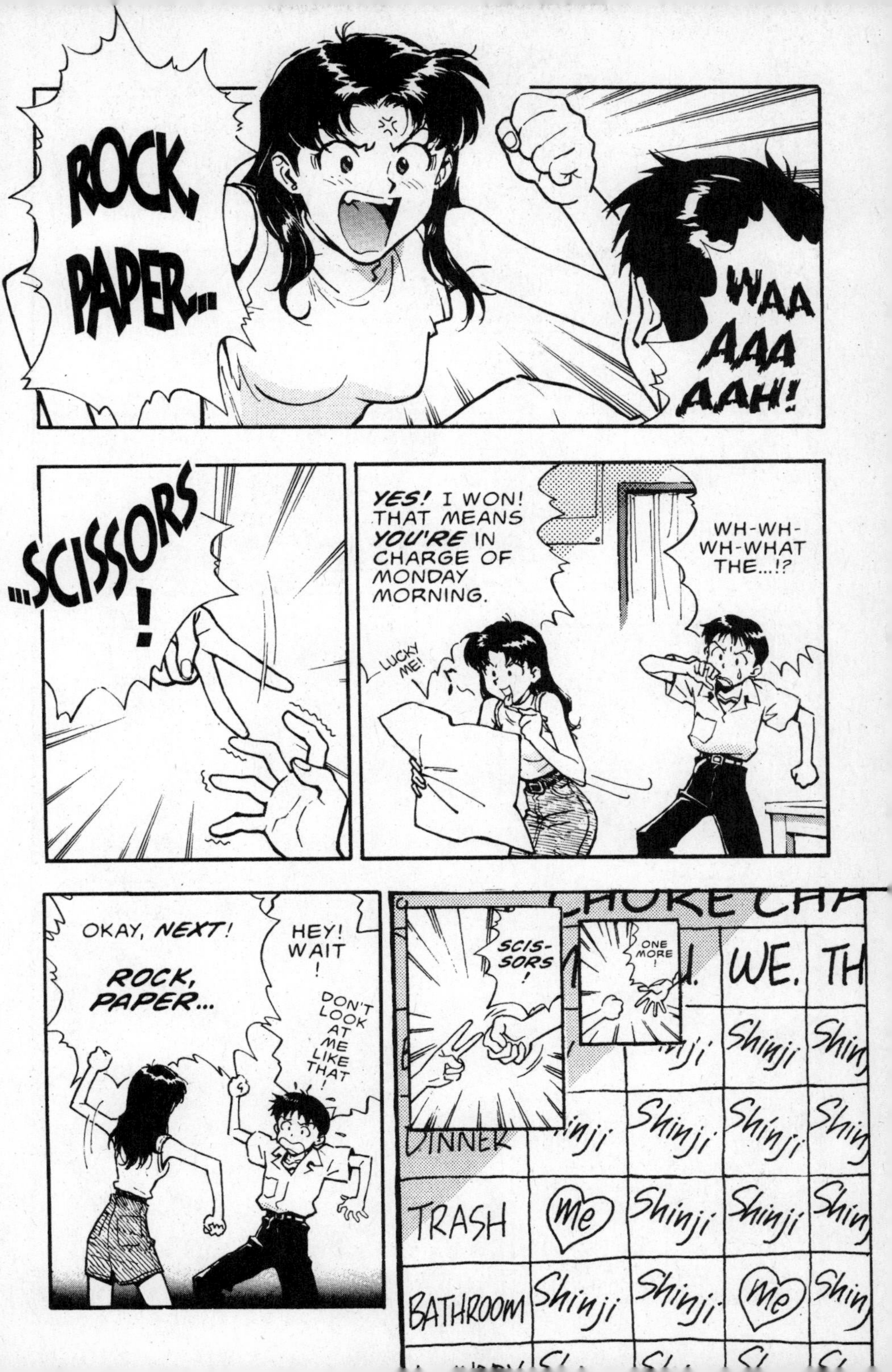

ROCK, PAPER...
WAAAAAAAH!
...SCISSORS!
YES! I WON! THAT MEANS YOU'RE IN CHARGE OF MONDAY MORNING.
LUCKY ME!
WH-WH-WH-WHAT THE...!?
OKAY, NEXT!
ROCK, PAPER...
HEY! WAIT!
DON'T LOOK AT ME LIKE THAT!
SCIS-SORS!
ONE MORE!
WE.
DINNER
TRASH
BATHROOM
Me
Shinji

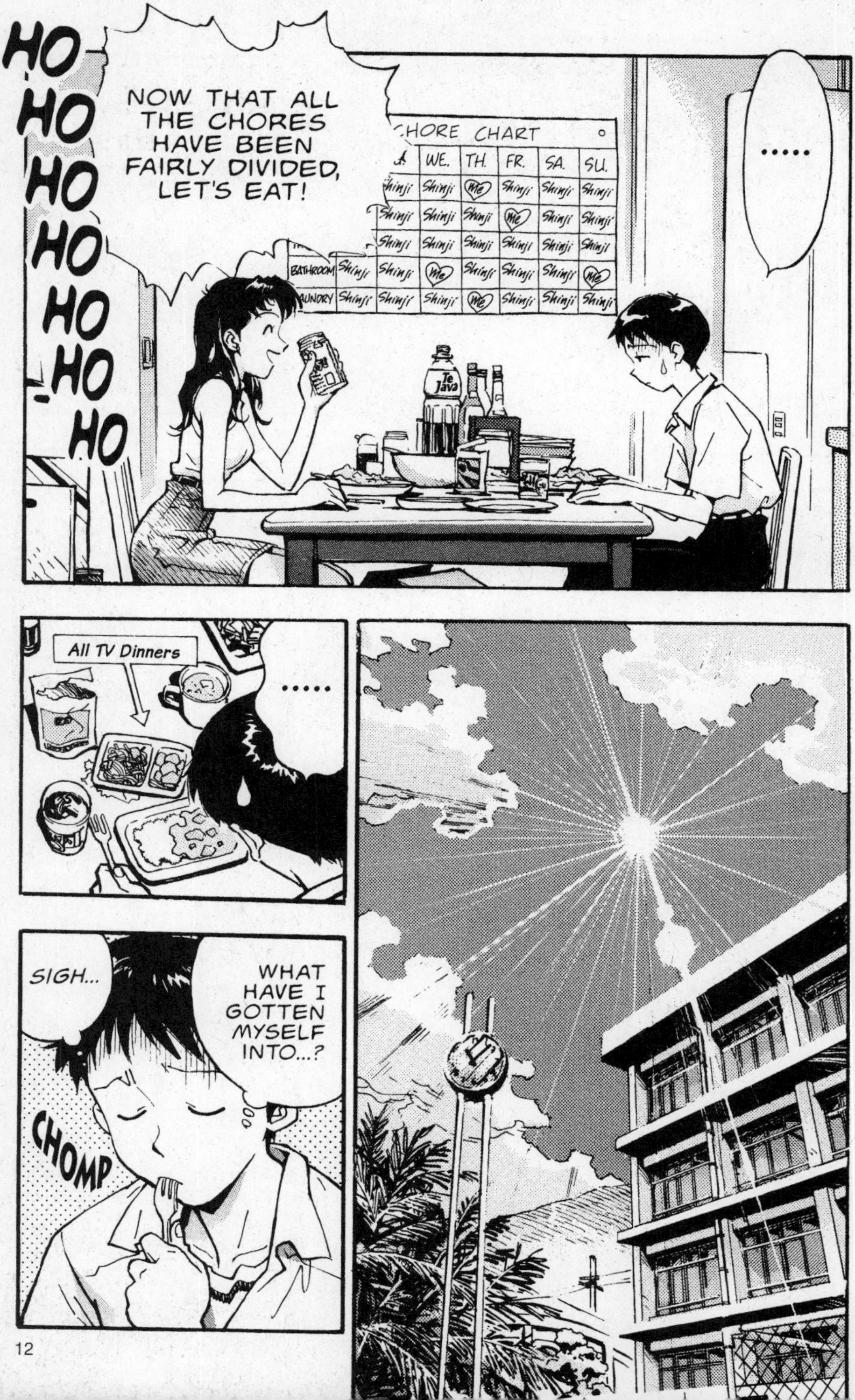
HO HO HO HO HO HO HO
NOW THAT ALL THE CHORES HAVE BEEN FAIRLY DIVIDED, LET'S EAT!
CHORE CHART
WE. TH. FR. SA. SU.
BATHROOM
.....
All TV Dinners
.....
SIGH...
WHAT HAVE I GOTTEN MYSELF INTO...?
CHOMP

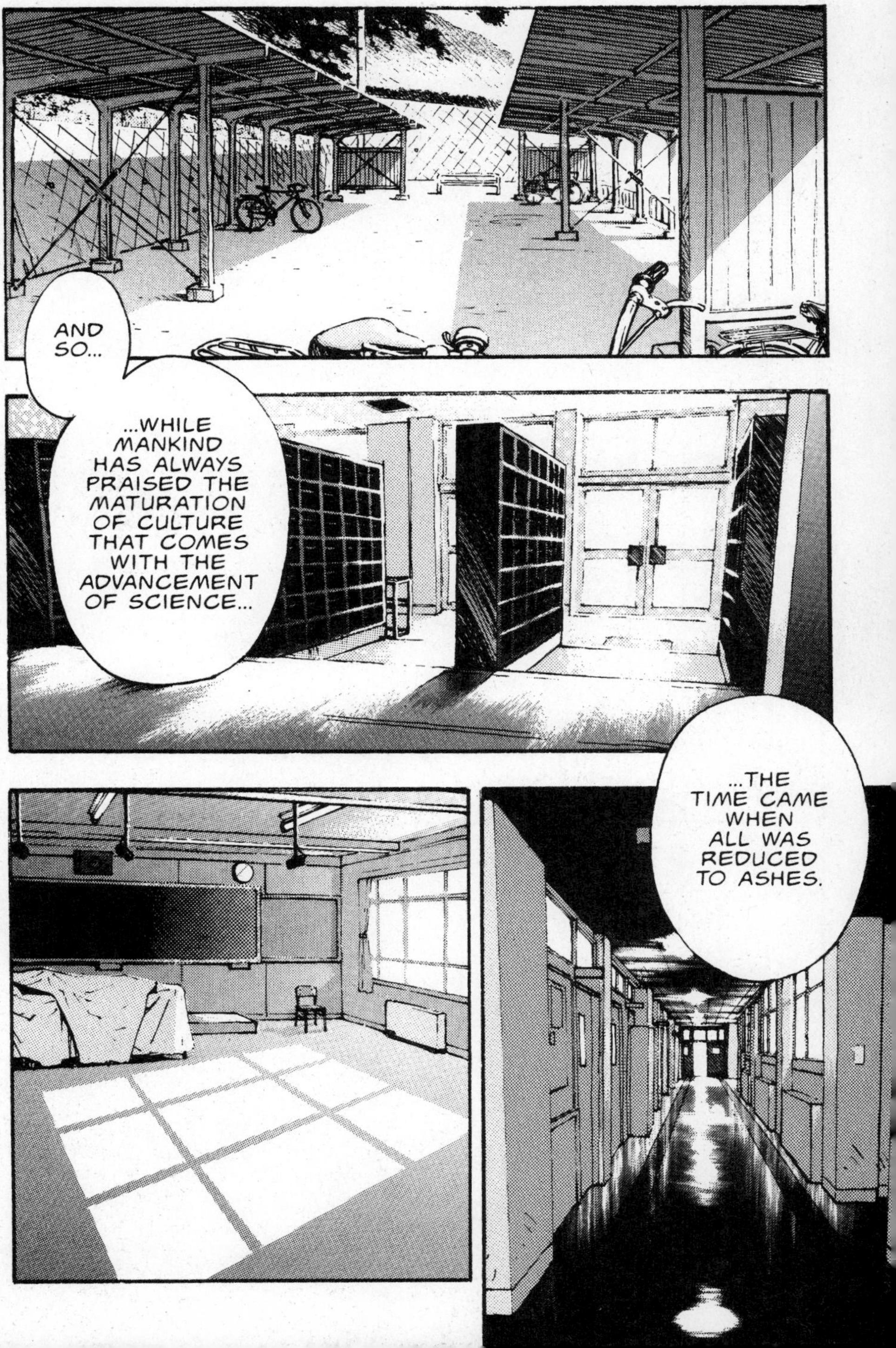
AND SO...
...WHILE MANKIND HAS ALWAYS PRAISED THE MATURATION OF CULTURE THAT COMES WITH THE ADVANCEMENT OF SCIENCE...
...THE TIME CAME WHEN ALL WAS REDUCED TO ASHES.

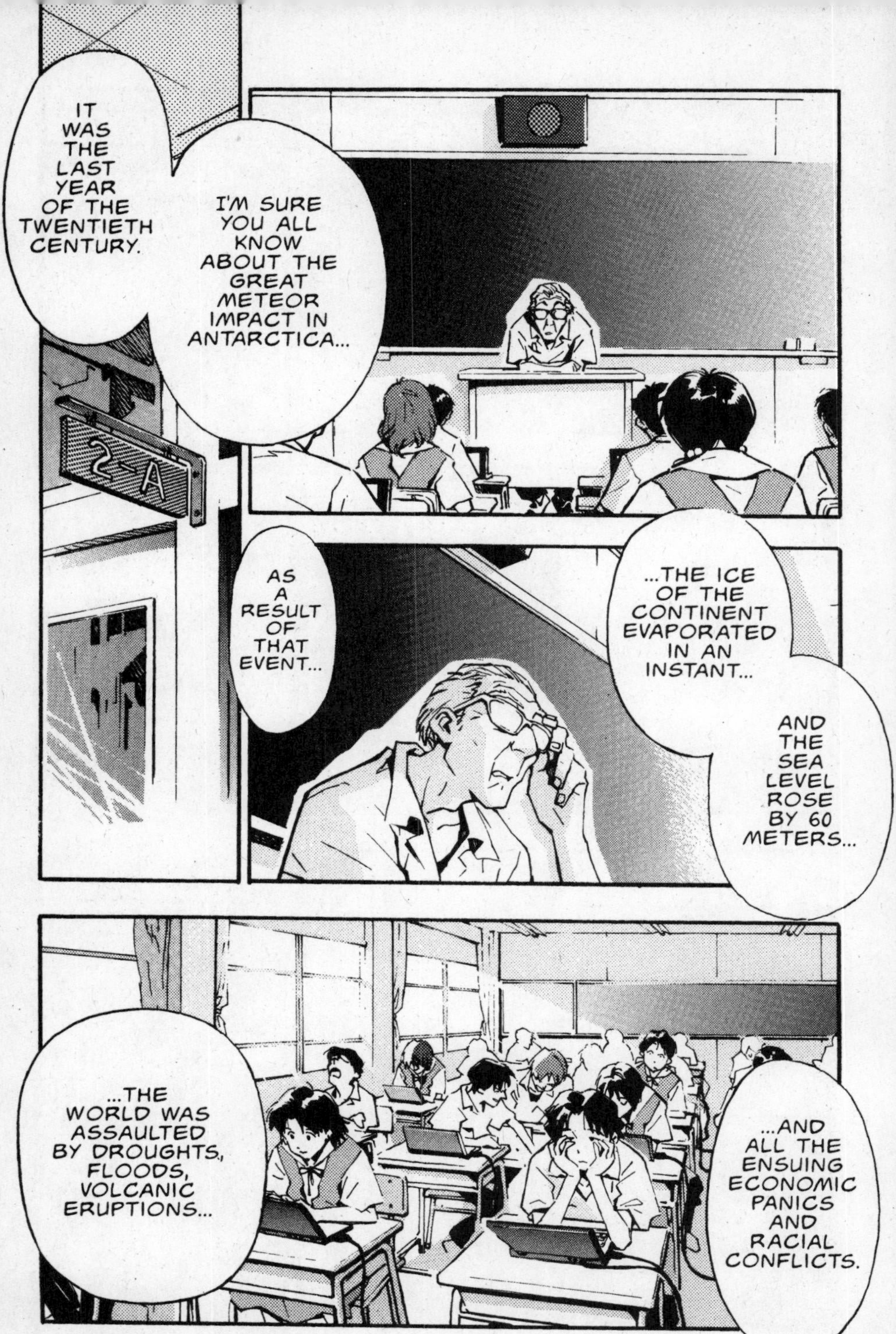
IT WAS THE LAST YEAR OF THE TWENTIETH CENTURY.
I'M SURE YOU ALL KNOW ABOUT THE GREAT METEOR IMPACT IN ANTARCTICA...
2-A
AS A RESULT OF THAT EVENT...
...THE ICE OF THE CONTINENT EVAPORATED IN AN INSTANT...
AND THE SEA LEVEL ROSE BY 60 METERS...
...THE WORLD WAS ASSAULTED BY DROUGHTS, FLOODS, VOLCANIC ERUPTIONS...
...AND ALL THE ENSUING ECONOMIC PANICS AND RACIAL CONFLICTS.

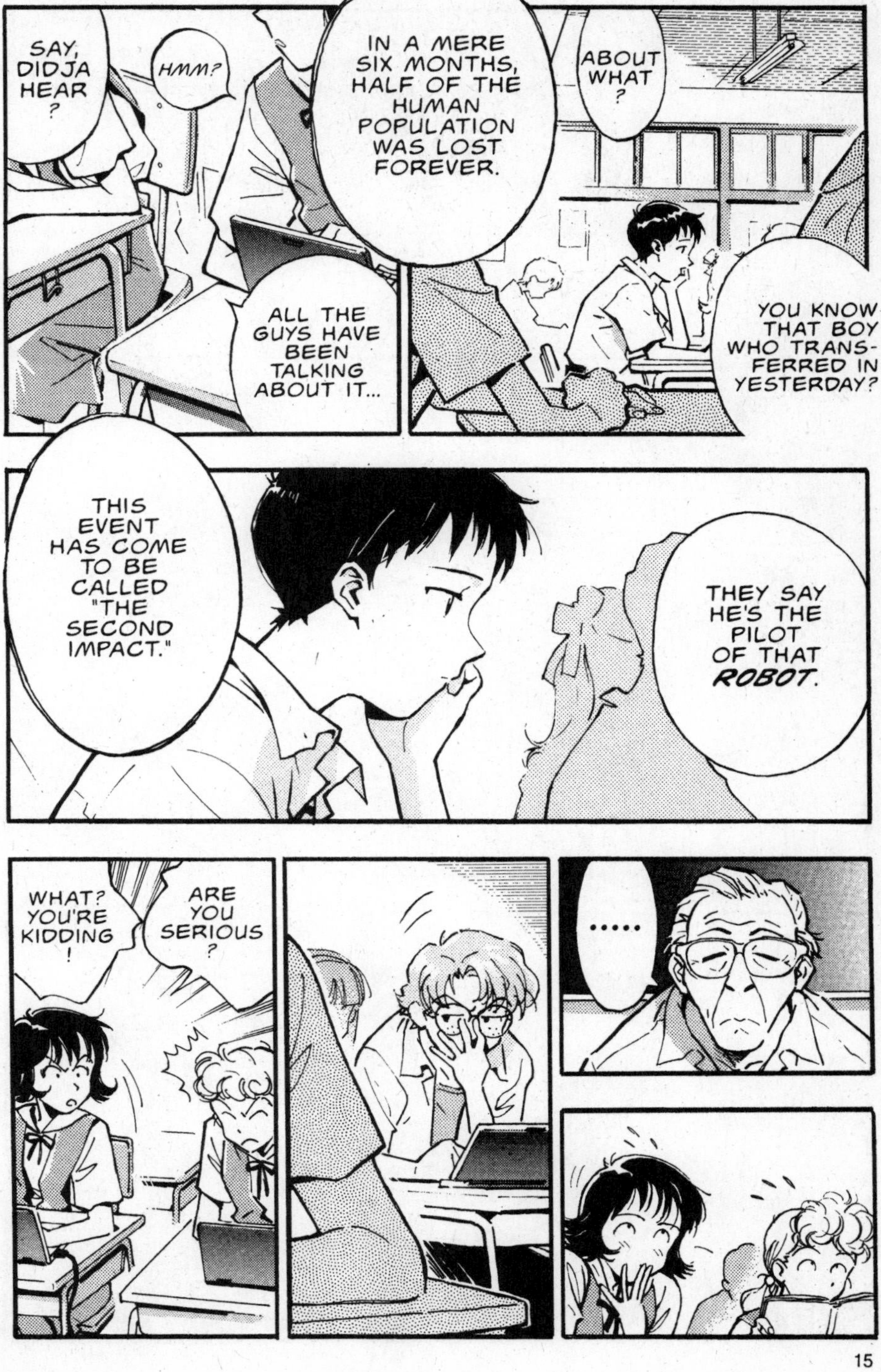
SAY, DIDJA HEAR?
HMM?
IN A MERE SIX MONTHS, HALF OF THE HUMAN POPULATION WAS LOST FOREVER.
ALL THE GUYS HAVE BEEN TALKING ABOUT IT...
ABOUT WHAT?
YOU KNOW THAT BOY WHO TRANS-FERRED IN YESTERDAY?
THIS EVENT HAS COME TO BE CALLED "THE SECOND IMPACT."
THEY SAY HE'S THE PILOT OF THAT *ROBOT*.
WHAT? YOU'RE KIDDING!
ARE YOU SERIOUS?
.....

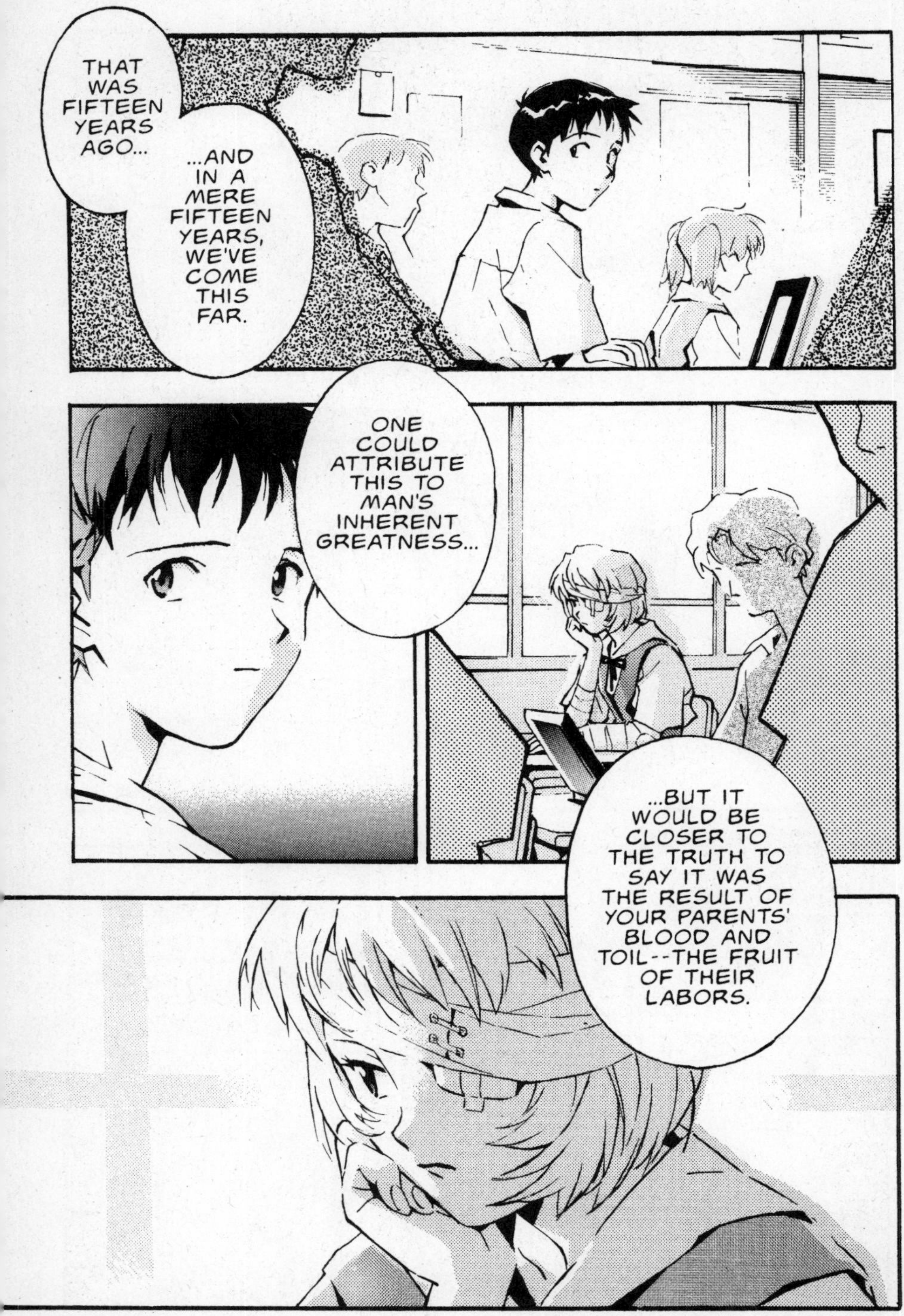
THAT WAS FIFTEEN YEARS AGO...
...AND IN A MERE FIFTEEN YEARS, WE'VE COME THIS FAR.
ONE COULD ATTRIBUTE THIS TO MAN'S INHERENT GREATNESS...
...BUT IT WOULD BE CLOSER TO THE TRUTH TO SAY IT WAS THE RESULT OF YOUR PARENTS' BLOOD AND TOIL--THE FRUIT OF THEIR LABORS.

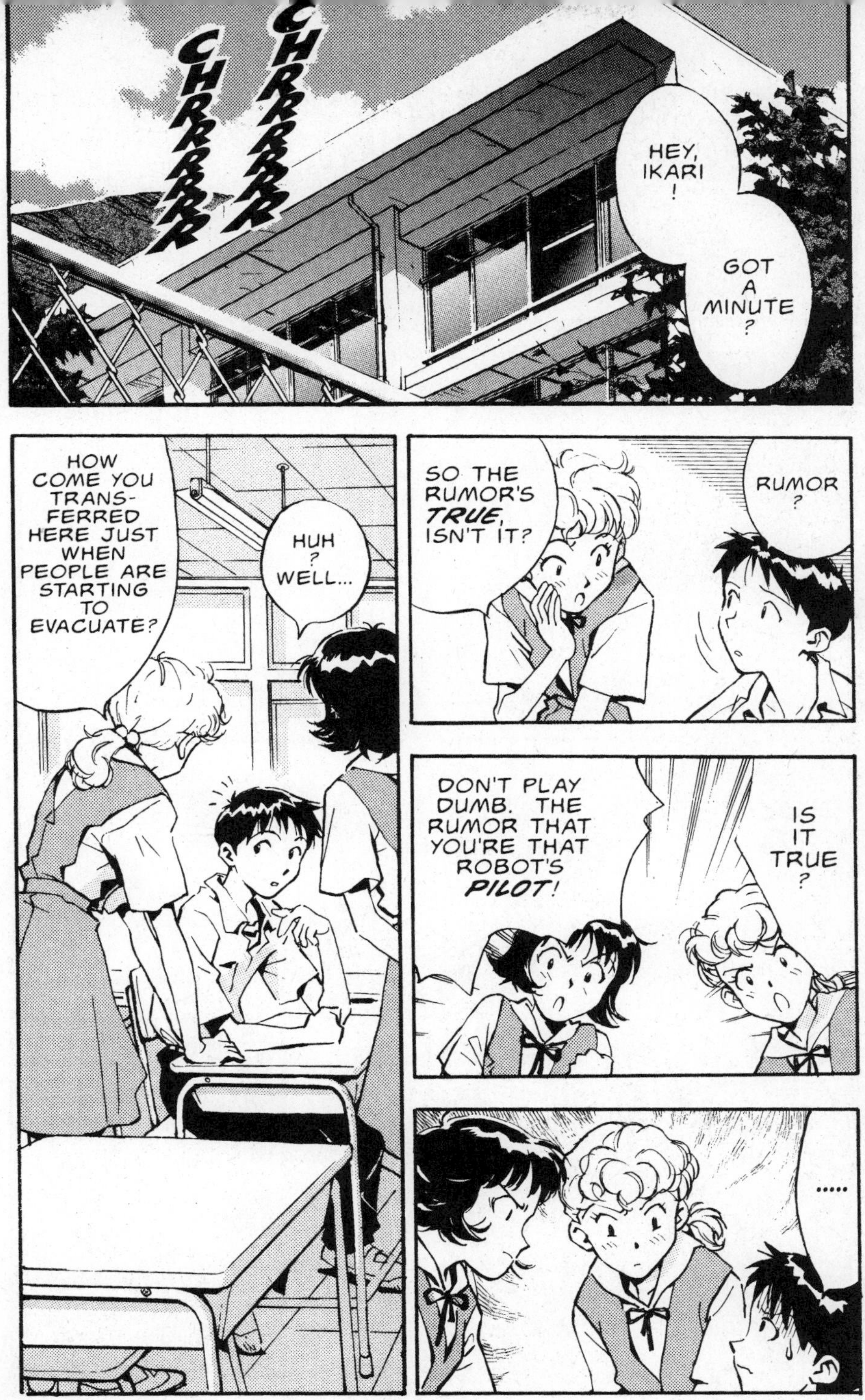
CHRRRRRR
CHRRRRRR
HEY, IKARI!
GOT A MINUTE?
HOW COME YOU TRANSFERRED HERE JUST WHEN PEOPLE ARE STARTING TO EVACUATE?
HUH? WELL...
SO THE RUMOR'S *TRUE*, ISN'T IT?
RUMOR?
DON'T PLAY DUMB. THE RUMOR THAT YOU'RE THAT ROBOT'S *PILOT*!
IS IT TRUE?
.....

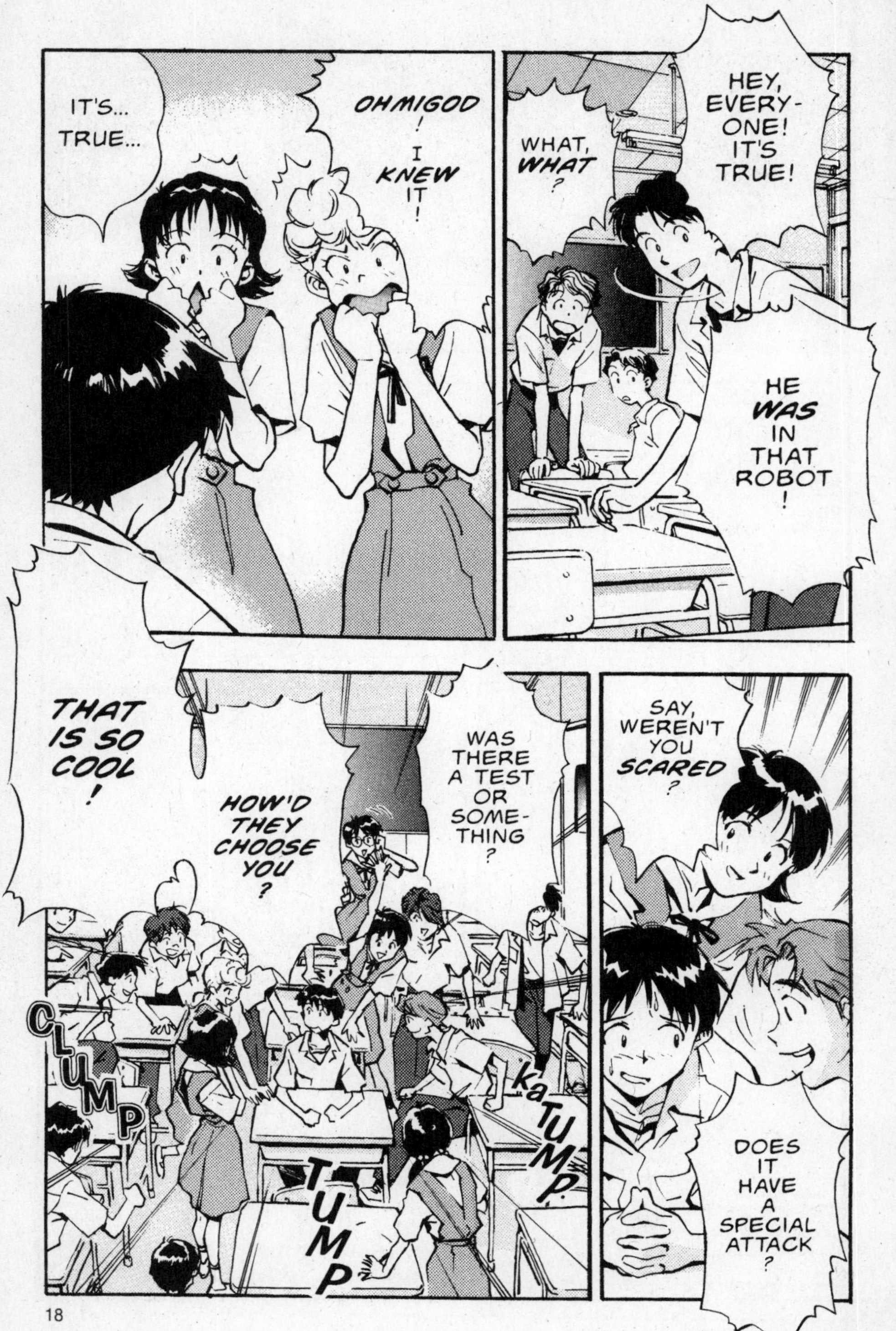
IT'S... TRUE...
OHMIGOD! I KNEW IT!
WHAT, WHAT?
HEY, EVERYONE! IT'S TRUE!
HE WAS IN THAT ROBOT!
THAT IS SO COOL!
HOW'D THEY CHOOSE YOU?
WAS THERE A TEST OR SOMETHING?
CLUMP
KaTUMP.
TUMP
SAY, WEREN'T YOU SCARED?
DOES IT HAVE A SPECIAL ATTACK?

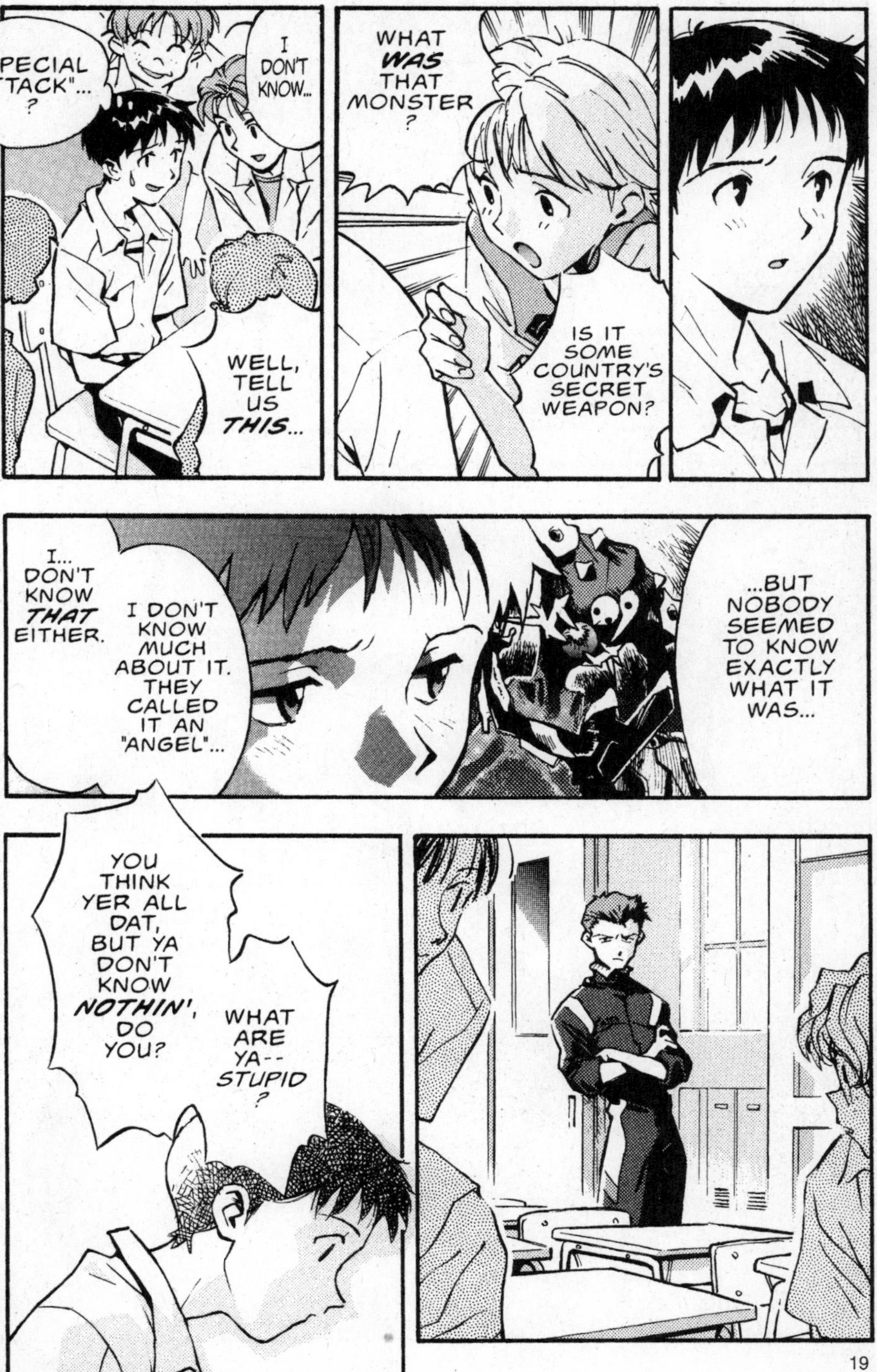
"SPECIAL ATTACK"...?
I DON'T KNOW...
WELL, TELL US *THIS*...
WHAT *WAS* THAT MONSTER?
IS IT SOME COUNTRY'S SECRET WEAPON?
I... DON'T KNOW *THAT* EITHER.
I DON'T KNOW MUCH ABOUT IT. THEY CALLED IT AN "ANGEL"...
...BUT NOBODY SEEMED TO KNOW EXACTLY WHAT IT WAS...
YOU THINK YER ALL DAT, BUT YA DON'T KNOW *NOTHIN'*, DO YOU?
WHAT ARE YA-- STUPID?

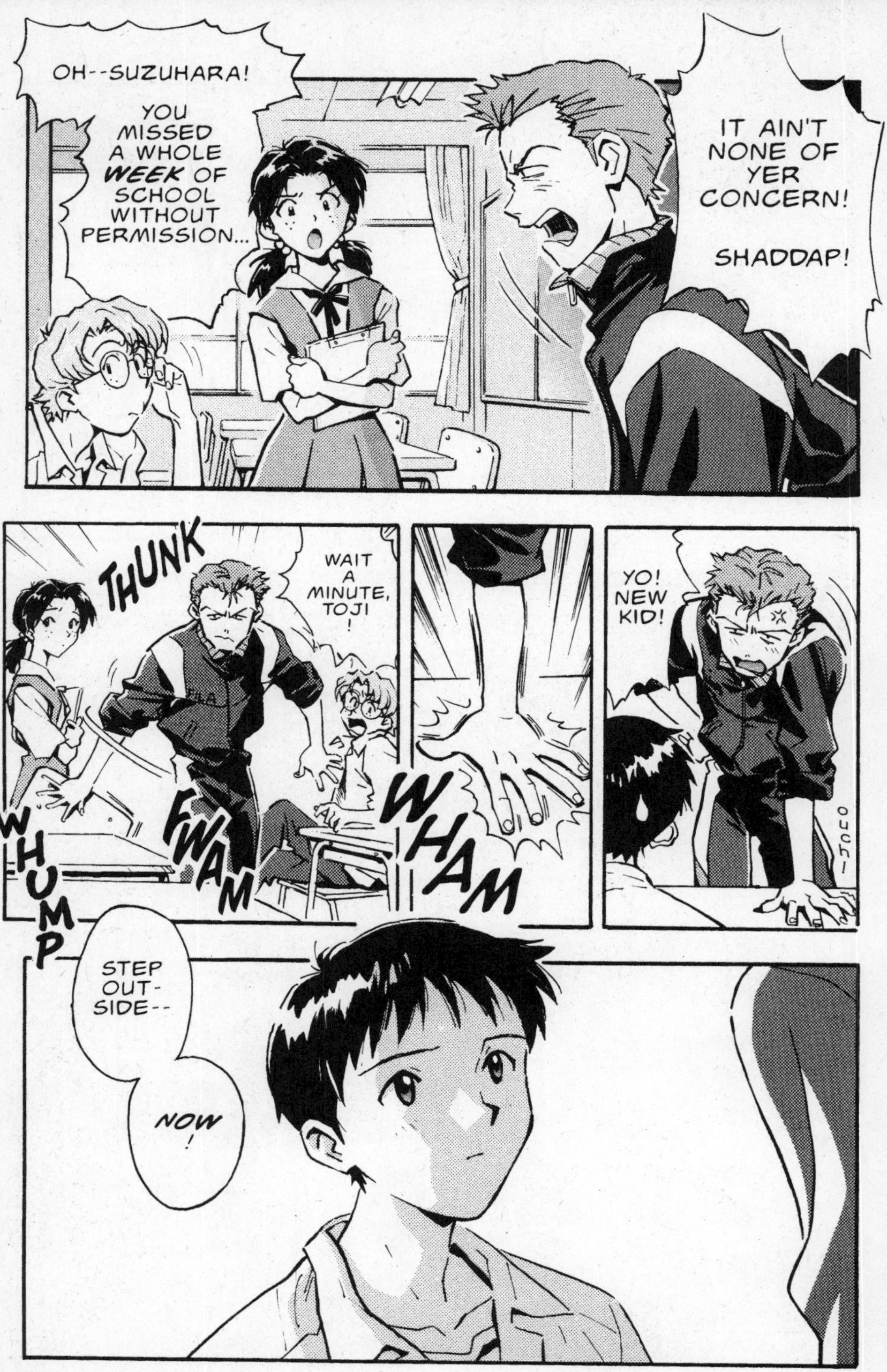

OH--SUZUHARA!
YOU MISSED A WHOLE WEEK OF SCHOOL WITHOUT PERMISSION...
IT AIN'T NONE OF YER CONCERN!
SHADDAP!
THUNK
WAIT A MINUTE, TOJI!
WHUMP
FWAM
WHAM
YO! NEW KID!
ouch!
STEP OUT-SIDE--
NOW!

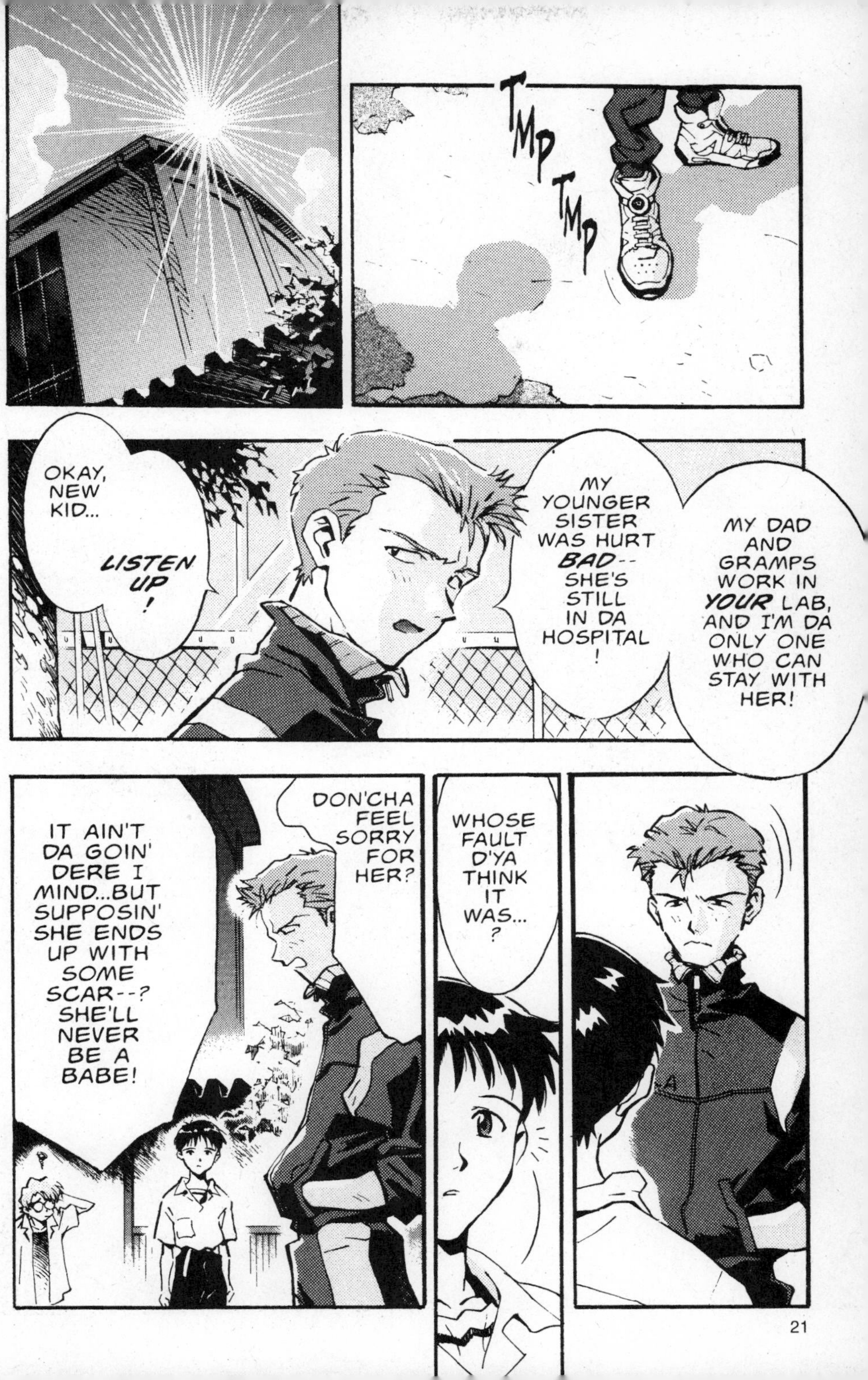
TMP TMP
OKAY, NEW KID... LISTEN UP!
MY YOUNGER SISTER WAS HURT BAD-- SHE'S STILL IN DA HOSPITAL!
MY DAD AND GRAMPS WORK IN YOUR LAB, AND I'M DA ONLY ONE WHO CAN STAY WITH HER!
IT AIN'T DA GOIN' DERE I MIND...BUT SUPPOSIN' SHE ENDS UP WITH SOME SCAR--? SHE'LL NEVER BE A BABE!
DON'CHA FEEL SORRY FOR HER?
WHOSE FAULT D'YA THINK IT WAS...?

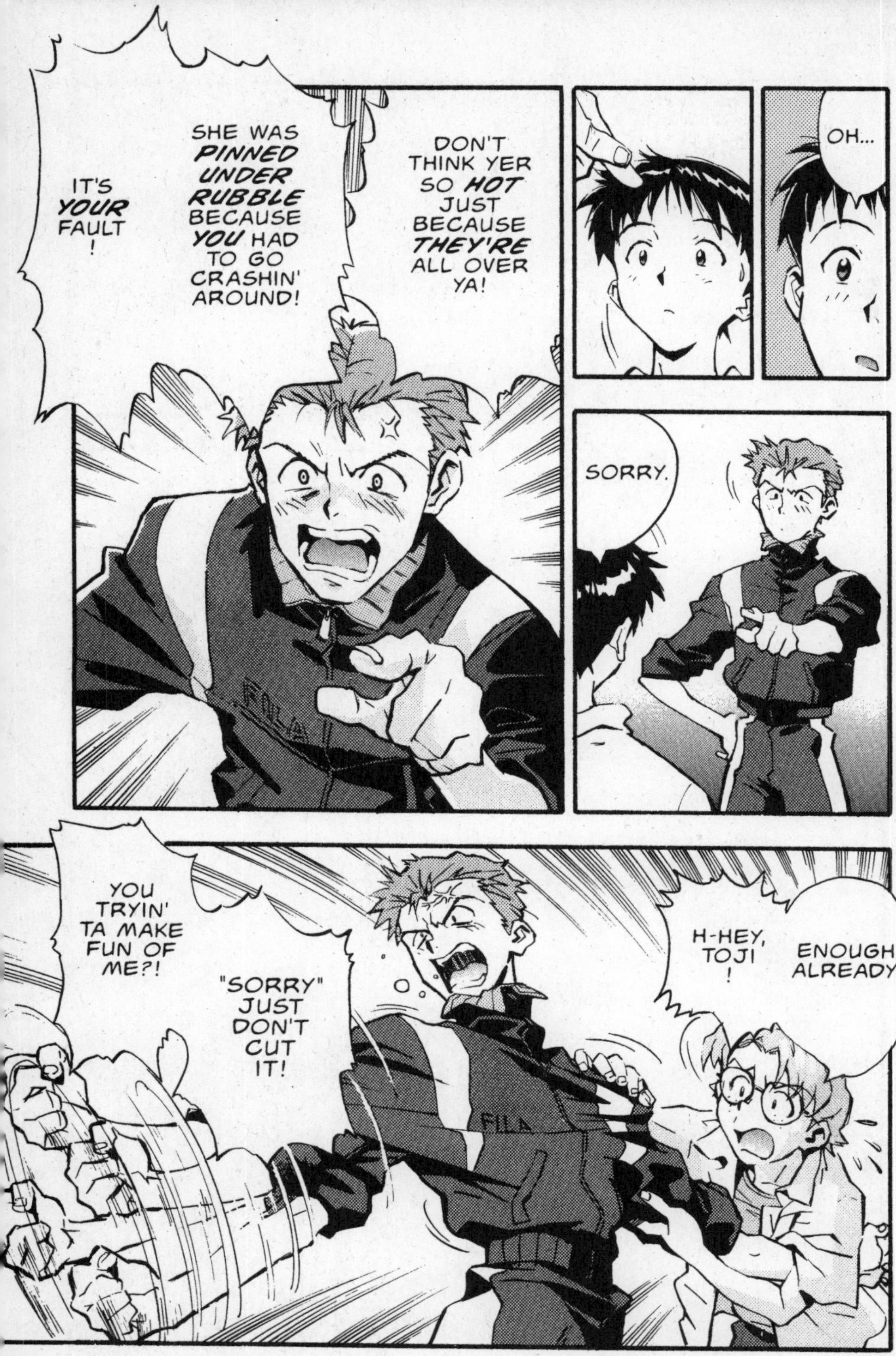

IT'S *YOUR* FAULT!
SHE WAS *PINNED UNDER RUBBLE* BECAUSE *YOU* HAD TO GO CRASHIN' AROUND!
DON'T THINK YER SO *HOT* JUST BECAUSE *THEY'RE* ALL OVER YA!
OH...
SORRY.
YOU TRYIN' TA MAKE FUN OF ME?!
"SORRY" JUST DON'T CUT IT!
H-HEY, TOJI!
ENOUGH ALREADY.

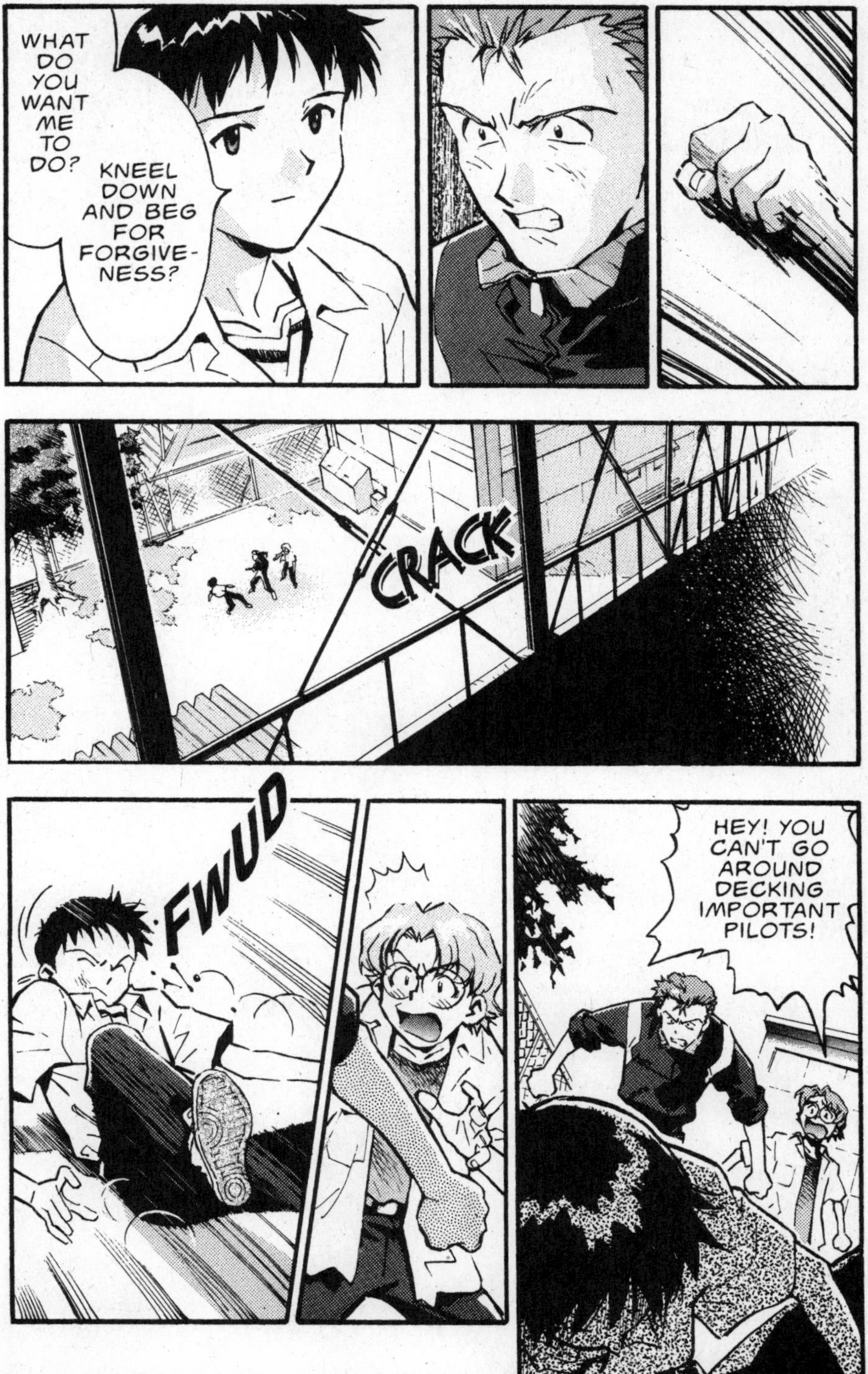
WHAT DO YOU WANT ME TO DO?
KNEEL DOWN AND BEG FOR FORGIVE-NESS?
CRACK
FWUD
HEY! YOU CAN'T GO AROUND DECKING IMPORTANT PILOTS!

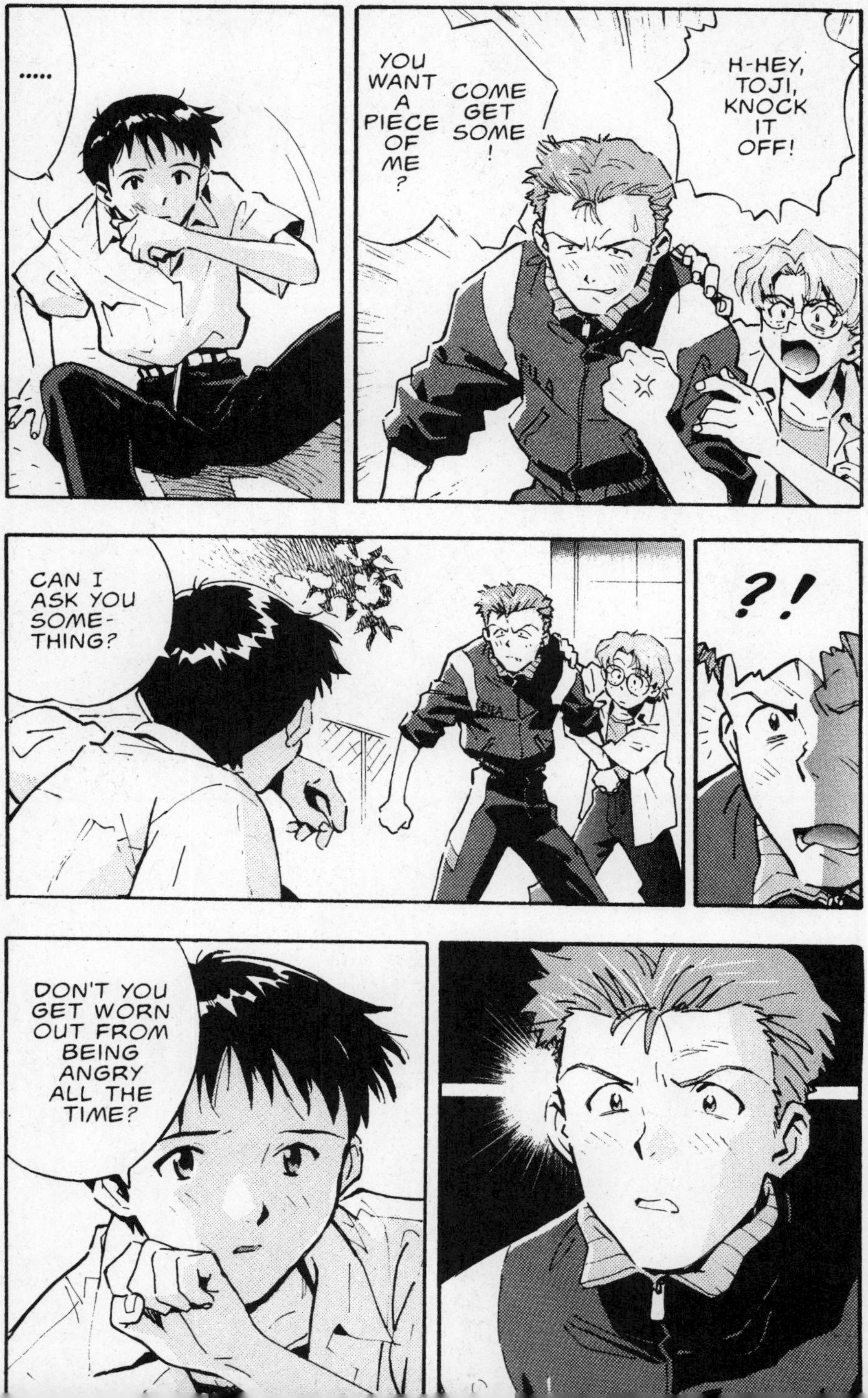
......
YOU WANT A PIECE OF ME?
COME GET SOME!
H-HEY, TOJI, KNOCK IT OFF!
CAN I ASK YOU SOME-THING?
?!
DON'T YOU GET WORN OUT FROM BEING ANGRY ALL THE TIME?

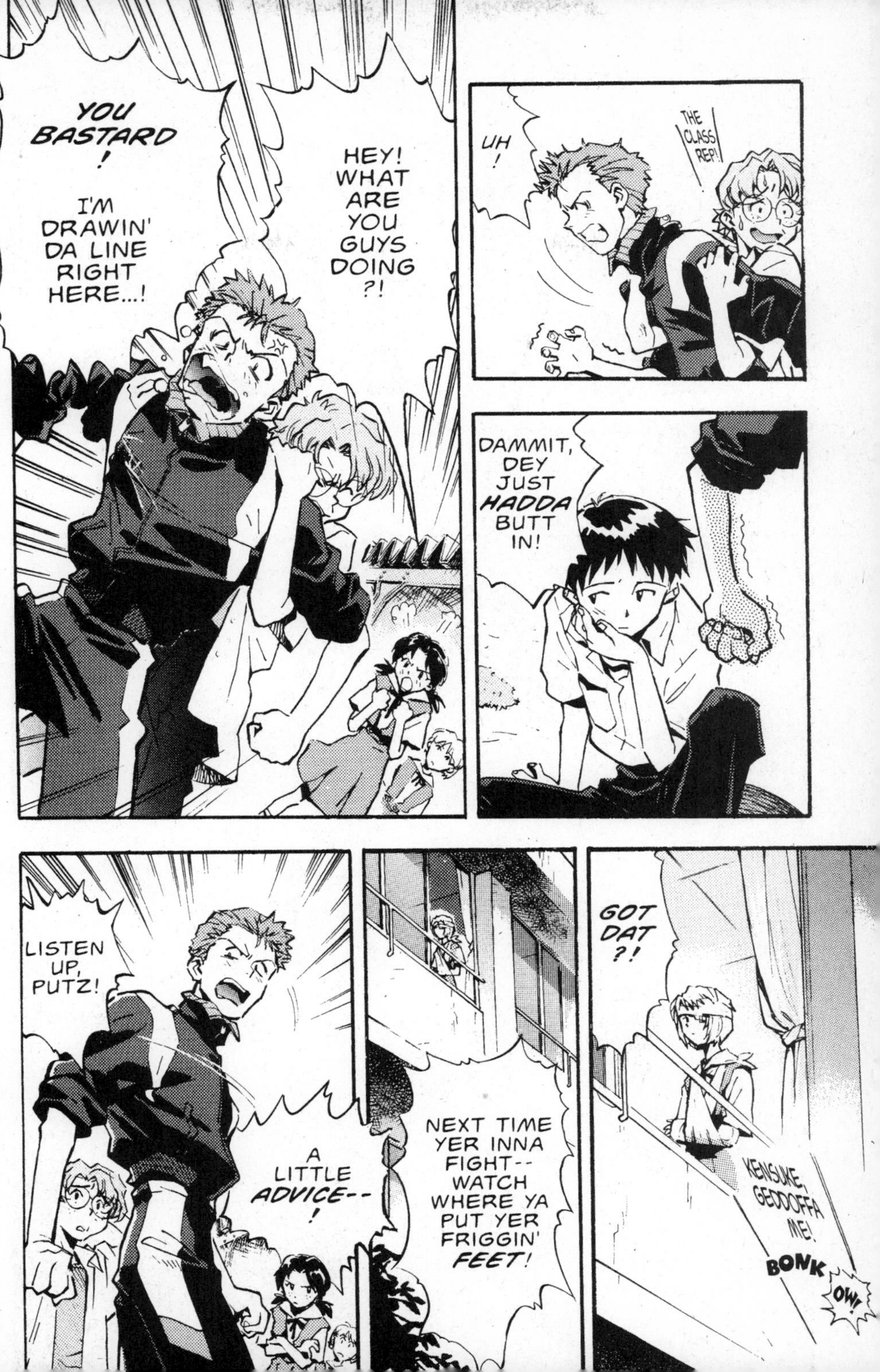
YOU BASTARD!
I'M DRAWIN' DA LINE RIGHT HERE...!
HEY! WHAT ARE YOU GUYS DOING?!
UH!
THE CLASS REP!
DAMMIT, DEY JUST HADDA BUTT IN!
LISTEN UP, PUTZ!
A LITTLE ADVICE--!
NEXT TIME YER INNA FIGHT-- WATCH WHERE YA PUT YER FRIGGIN' FEET!
GOT DAT?!
KENSUKE, GEDDOFFA ME!
BONK
OW!

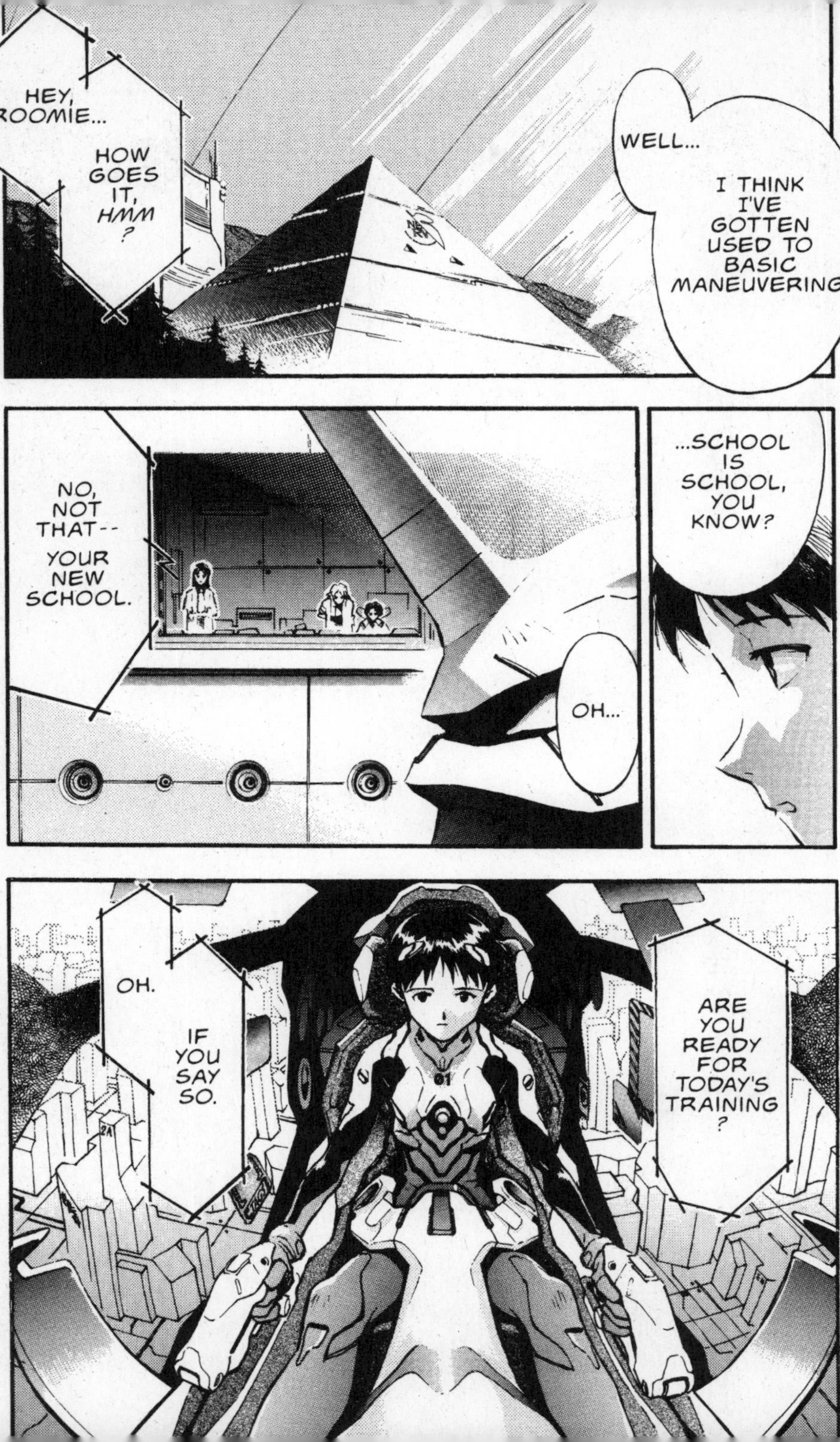
HEY, ROOMIE... HOW GOES IT, HMM?
WELL... I THINK I'VE GOTTEN USED TO BASIC MANEUVERING.
NO, NOT THAT-- YOUR NEW SCHOOL.
OH...
...SCHOOL IS SCHOOL, YOU KNOW?
OH. IF YOU SAY SO.
ARE YOU READY FOR TODAY'S TRAINING?

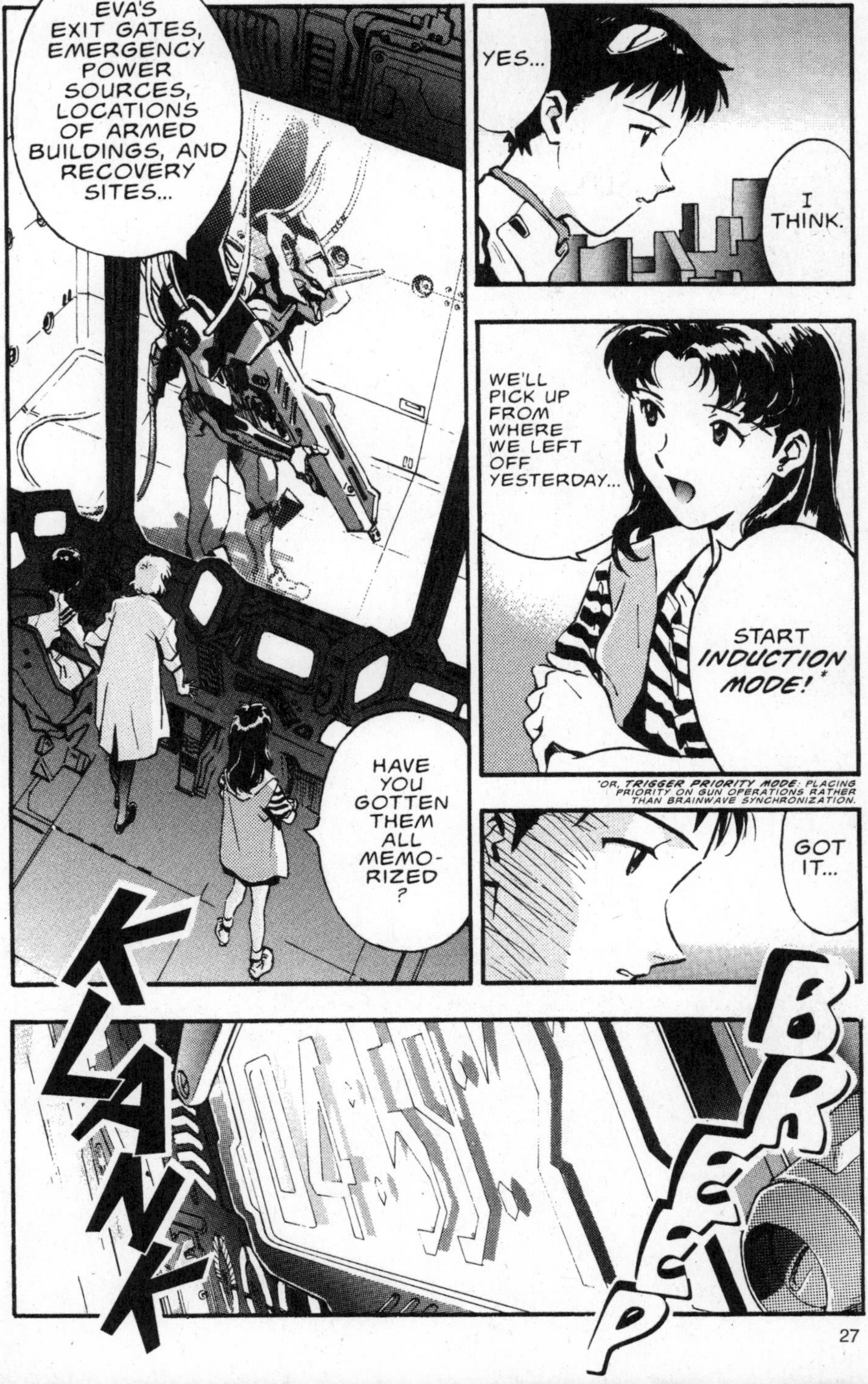
EVA'S EXIT GATES, EMERGENCY POWER SOURCES, LOCATIONS OF ARMED BUILDINGS, AND RECOVERY SITES...
HAVE YOU GOTTEN THEM ALL MEMORIZED?
YES...
I THINK.
WE'LL PICK UP FROM WHERE WE LEFT OFF YESTERDAY...
START *INDUCTION MODE!**
*OR, *TRIGGER PRIORITY MODE*: PLACING PRIORITY ON GUN OPERATIONS RATHER THAN BRAINWAVE SYNCHRONIZATION.
GOT IT...
KLANK
BREEEP

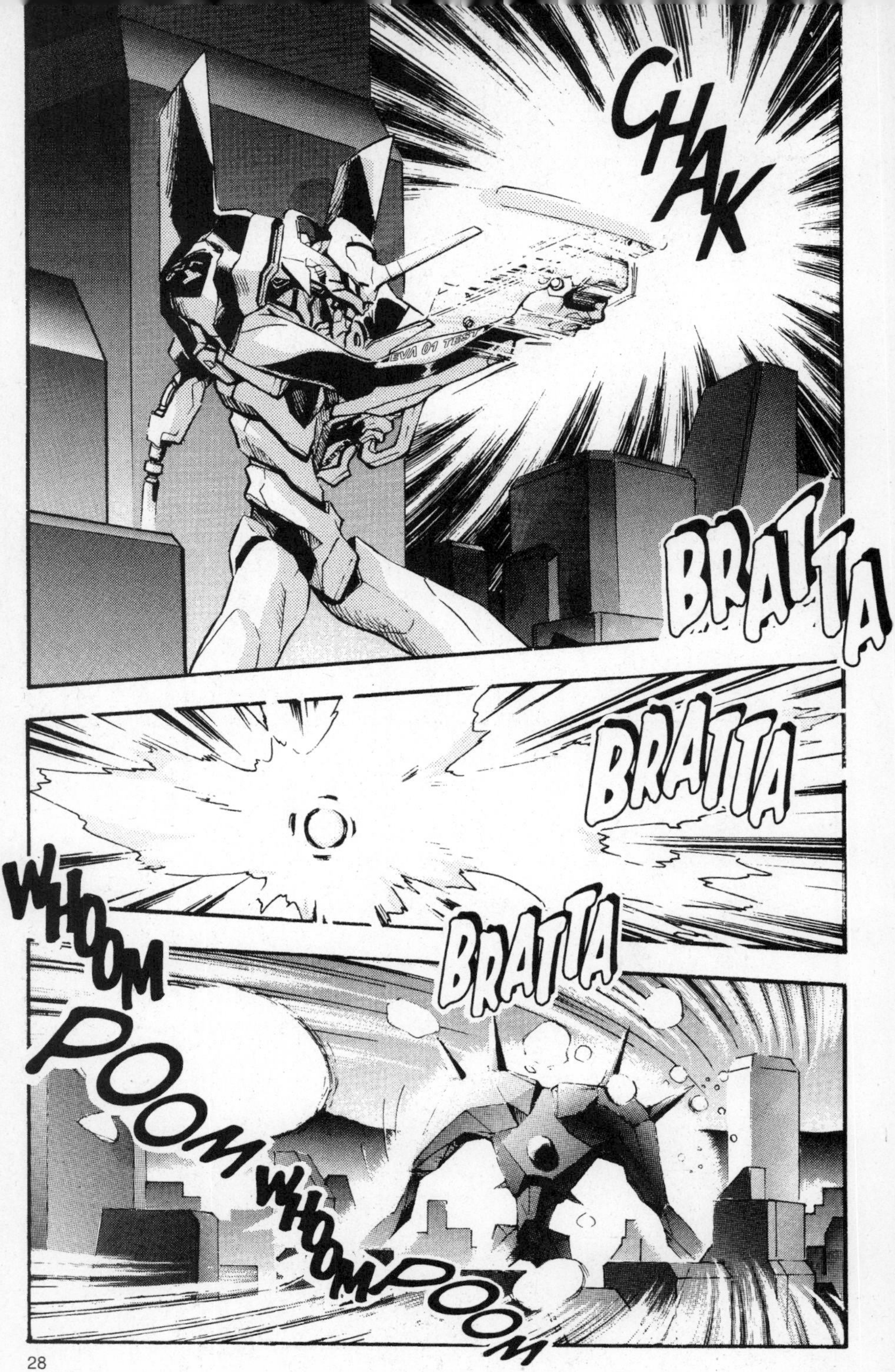
CHAK
EVA 01 TEST
BRATTA
BRATTA
WHOOM
POOM
BRATTA
WHOOM
POOM

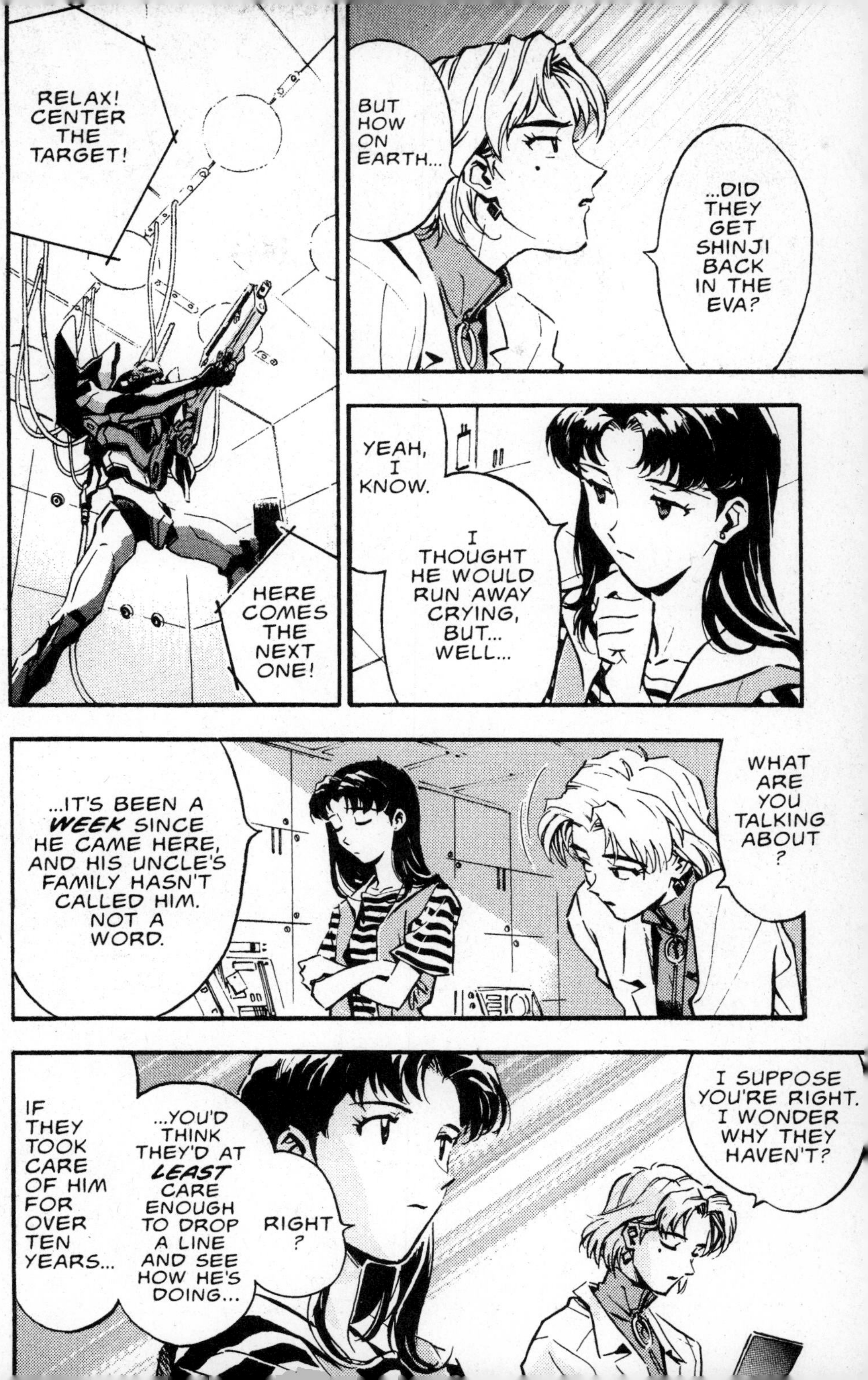
RELAX! CENTER THE TARGET!
HERE COMES THE NEXT ONE!
BUT HOW ON EARTH...
...DID THEY GET SHINJI BACK IN THE EVA?
YEAH, I KNOW.
I THOUGHT HE WOULD RUN AWAY CRYING, BUT... WELL...
...IT'S BEEN A WEEK SINCE HE CAME HERE, AND HIS UNCLE'S FAMILY HASN'T CALLED HIM. NOT A WORD.
WHAT ARE YOU TALKING ABOUT?
IF THEY TOOK CARE OF HIM FOR OVER TEN YEARS...
...YOU'D THINK THEY'D AT LEAST CARE ENOUGH TO DROP A LINE AND SEE HOW HE'S DOING...
RIGHT?
I SUPPOSE YOU'RE RIGHT. I WONDER WHY THEY HAVEN'T?

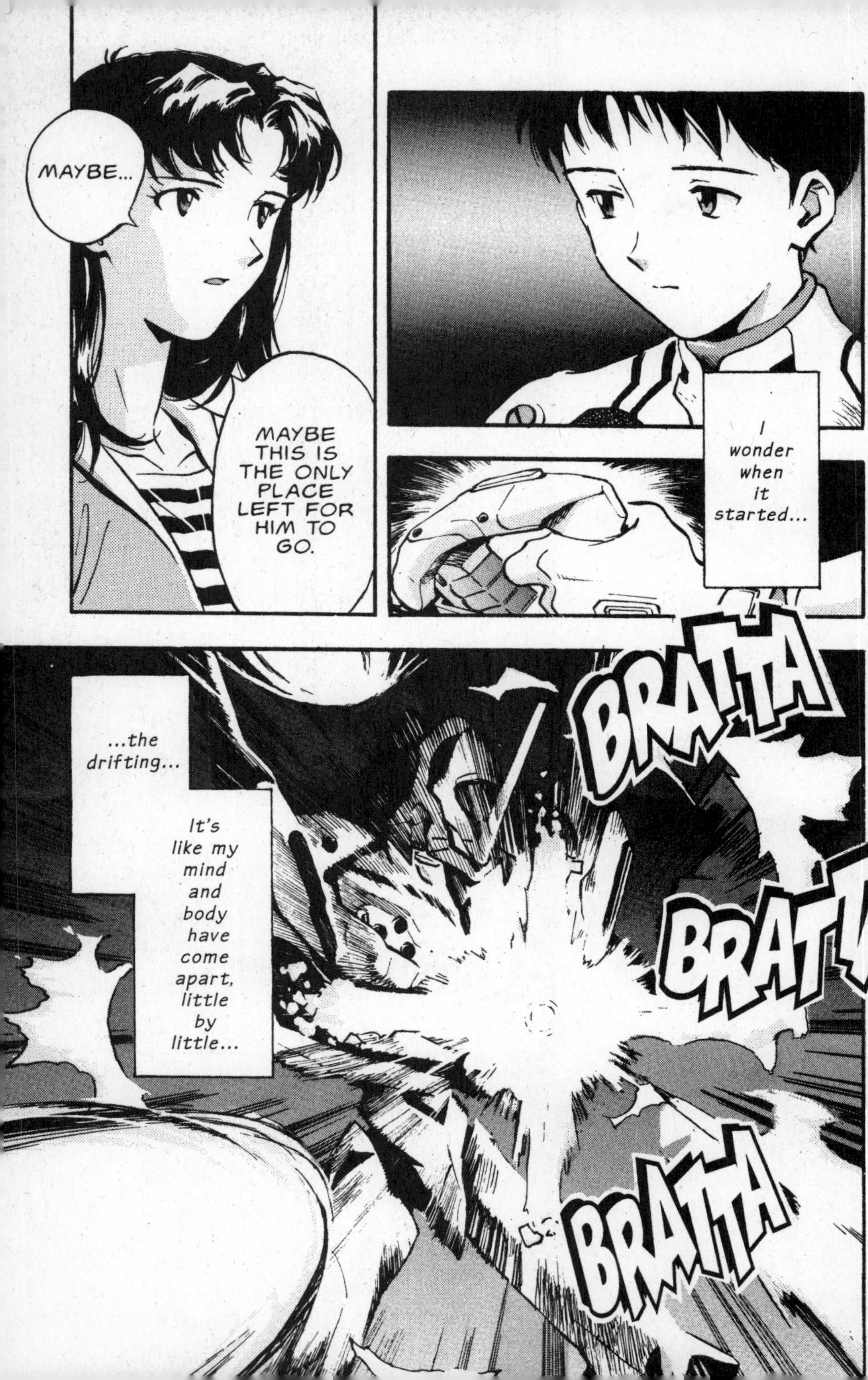
MAYBE...
MAYBE THIS IS THE ONLY PLACE LEFT FOR HIM TO GO.
I wonder when it started...
...the drifting...
It's like my mind and body have come apart, little by little...
BRATTA
BRATTA
BRATTA

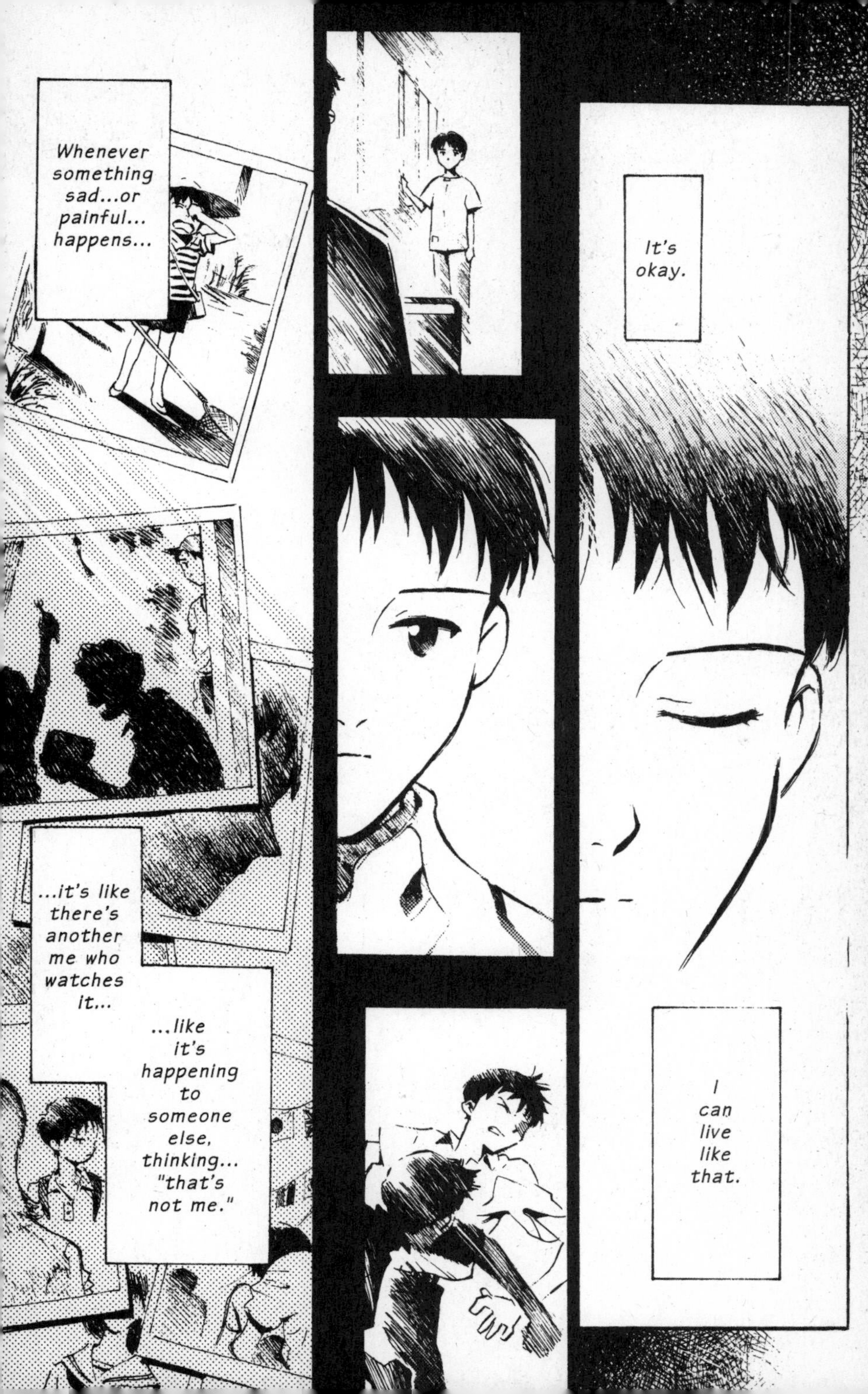
Whenever something sad...or painful... happens...
...it's like there's another me who watches it...
...like it's happening to someone else, thinking... "that's not me."
It's okay.
I can live like that.

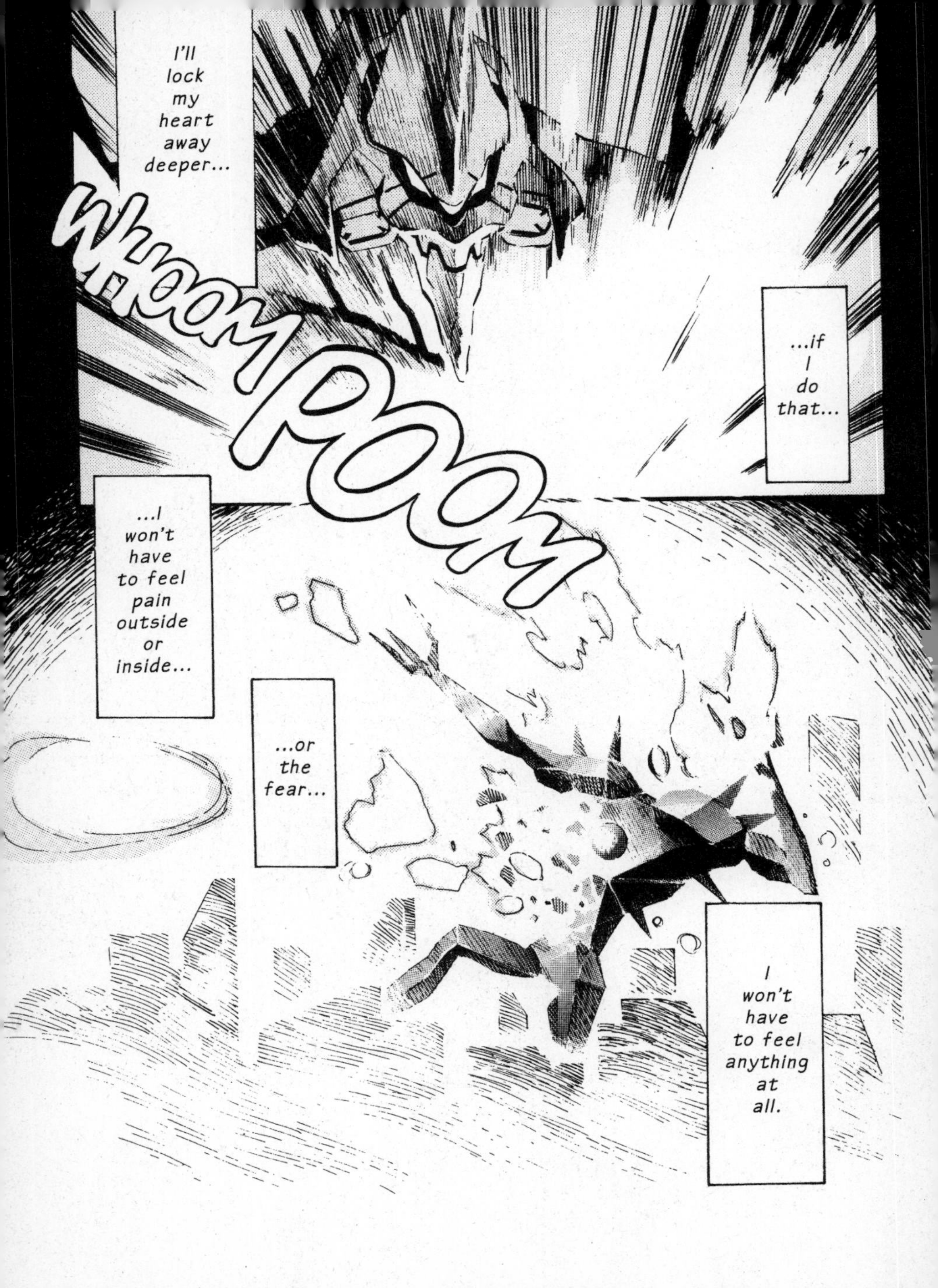
I'll lock my heart away deeper...
WHOOM
...if I do that...
POOM
...I won't have to feel pain outside or inside...
...or the fear...
I won't have to feel anything at all.

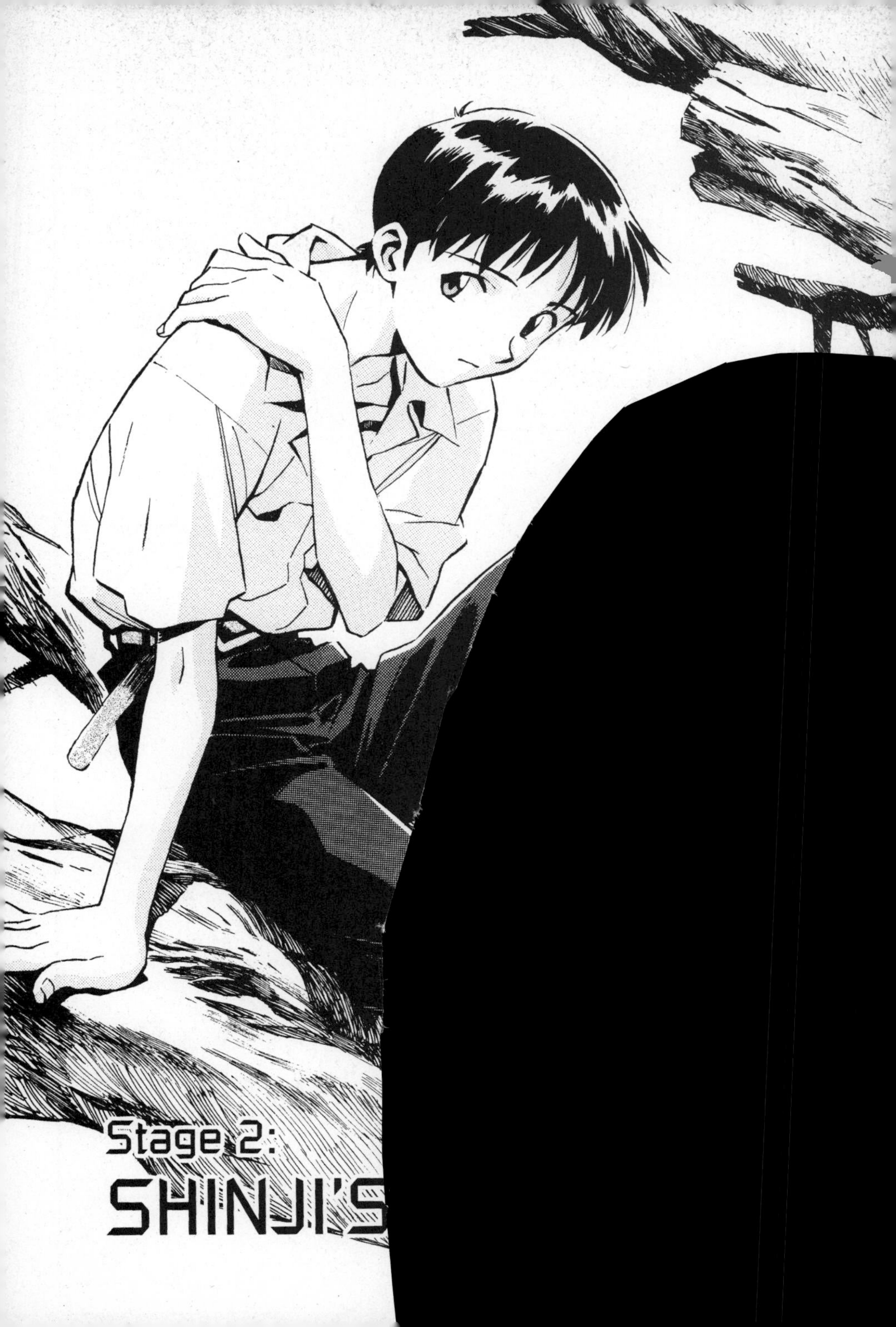
Stage 2:
SHINJI'S [redacted]

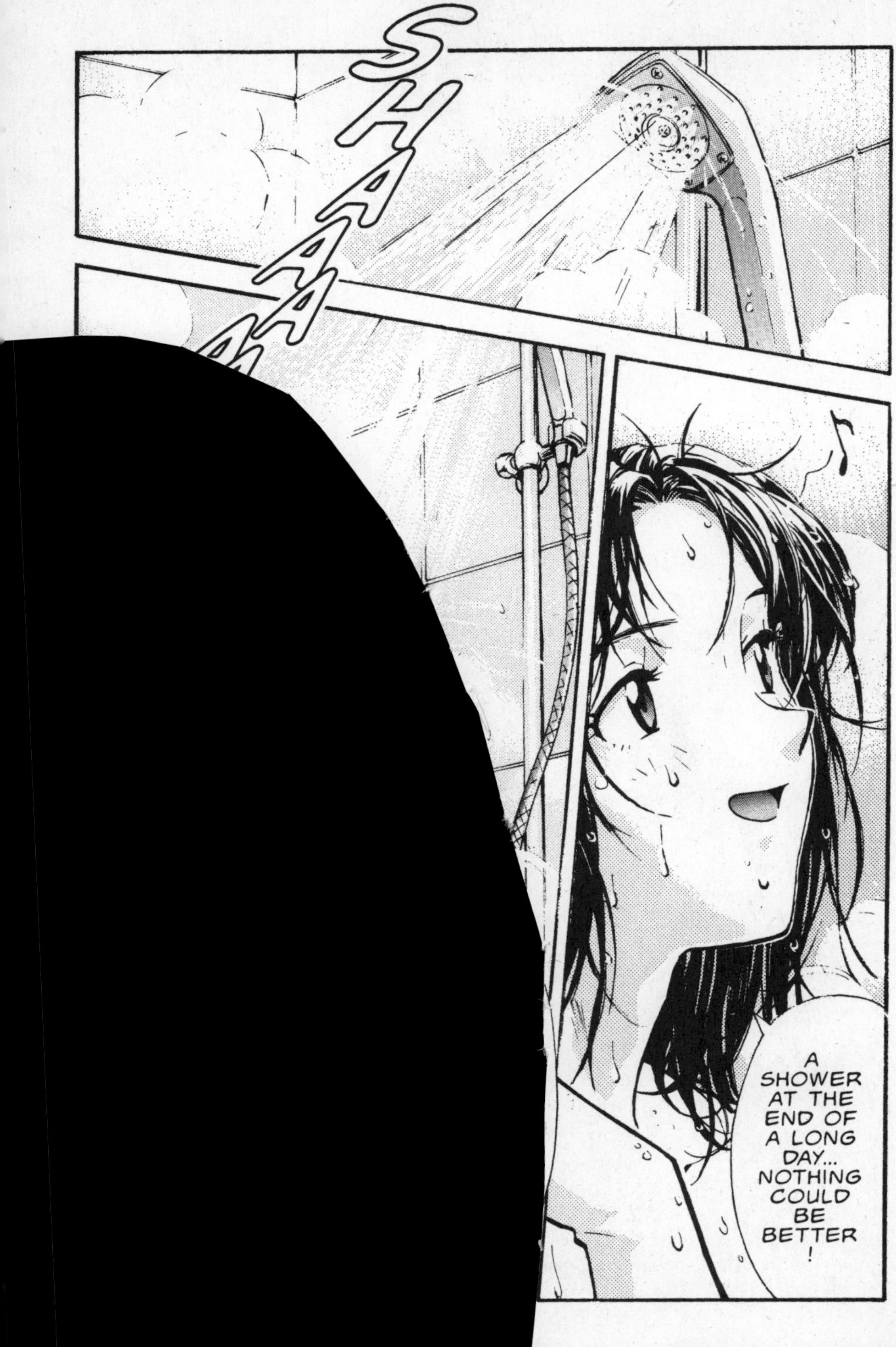
SHAAA [redacted]
A SHOWER AT THE END OF A LONG DAY... NOTHING COULD BE BETTER!

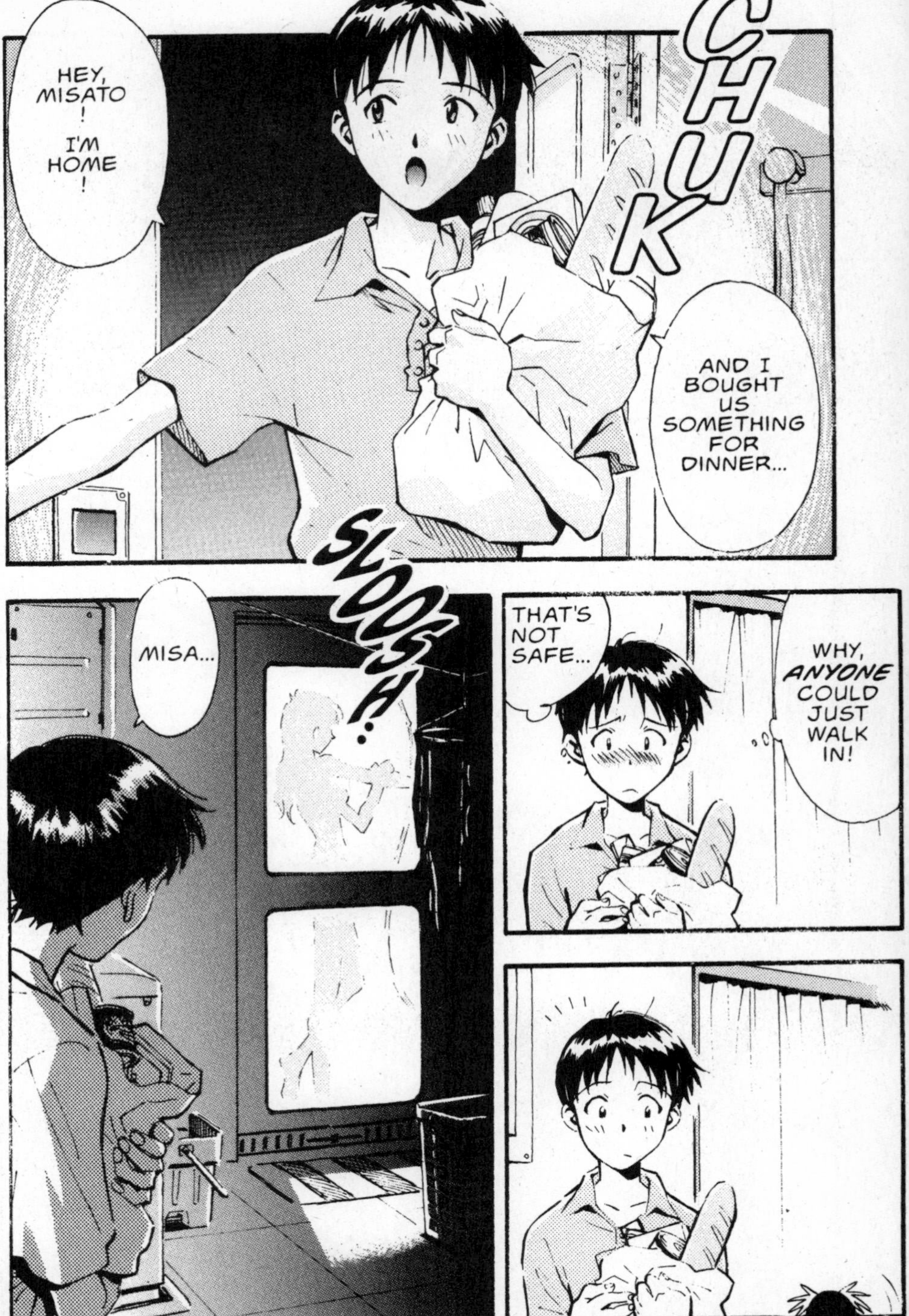
HEY, MISATO! I'M HOME!
CHUK
AND I BOUGHT US SOMETHING FOR DINNER...
MISA...
SLOOSH!
THAT'S NOT SAFE...
WHY, *ANYONE* COULD JUST WALK IN!

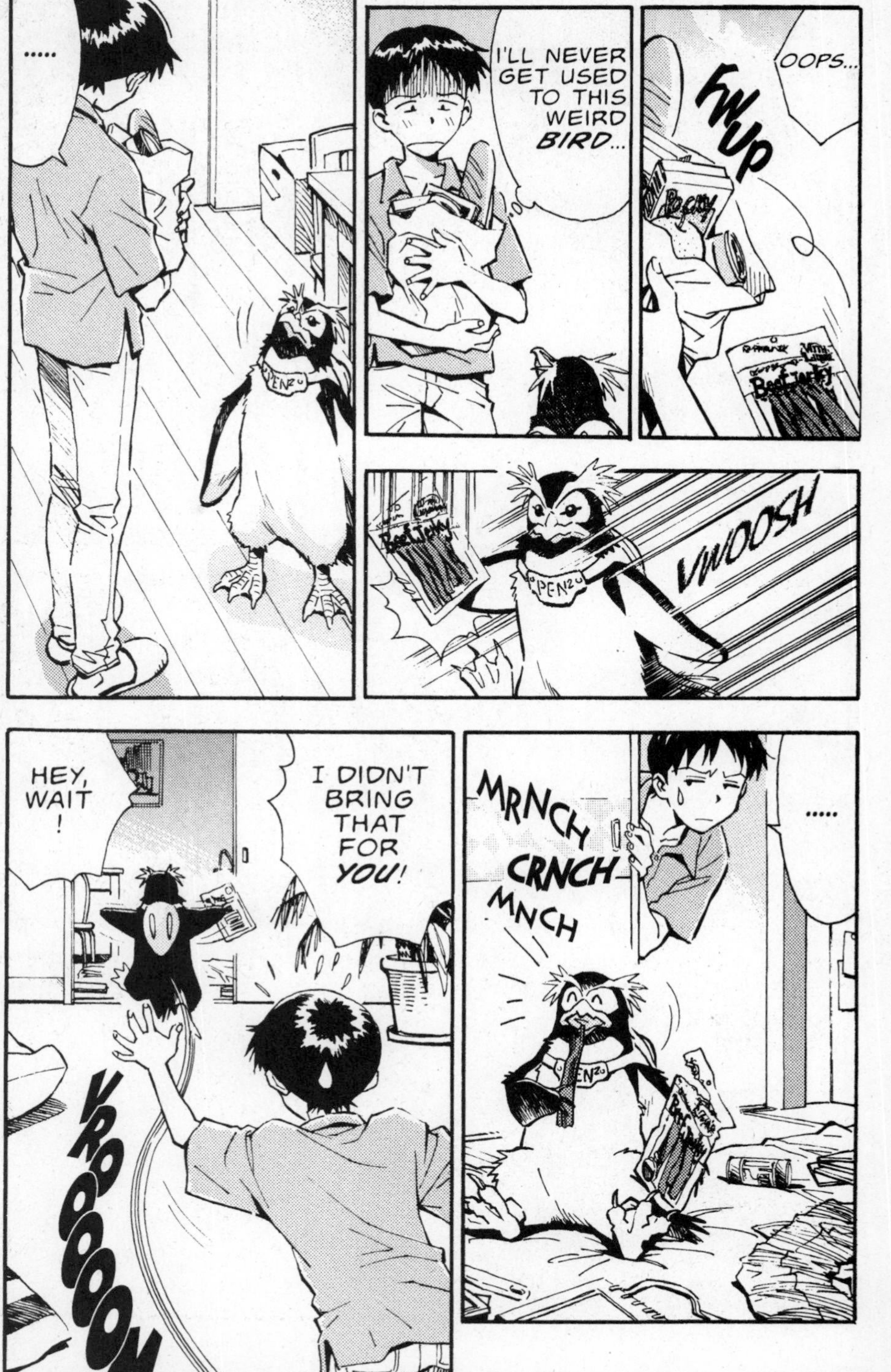
.....
I'LL NEVER GET USED TO THIS WEIRD *BIRD*...
FWUP
OOPS...
VWOOSH
HEY, WAIT!
I DIDN'T BRING THAT FOR *YOU*!
VROOOOOOM
MRNCH
CRNCH
MNCH
.....

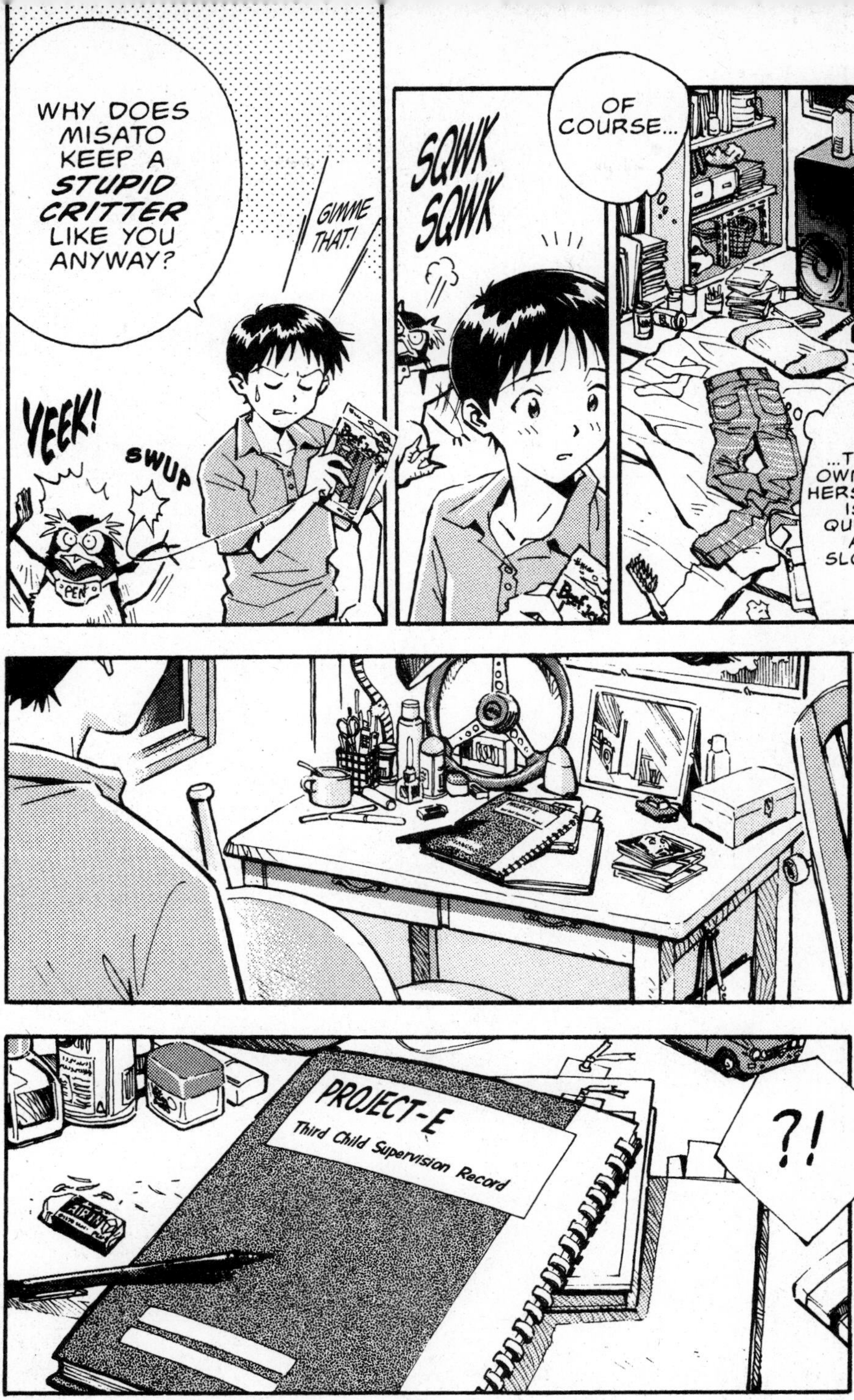
WHY DOES MISATO KEEP A STUPID CRITTER LIKE YOU ANYWAY?
GIMME THAT!
YEEK!
SWUP
SQWK SQWK
OF COURSE...
...THE OWNER HERSELF IS QUITE A SLOB.
PROJECT-E
Third Child Supervision Record
?!

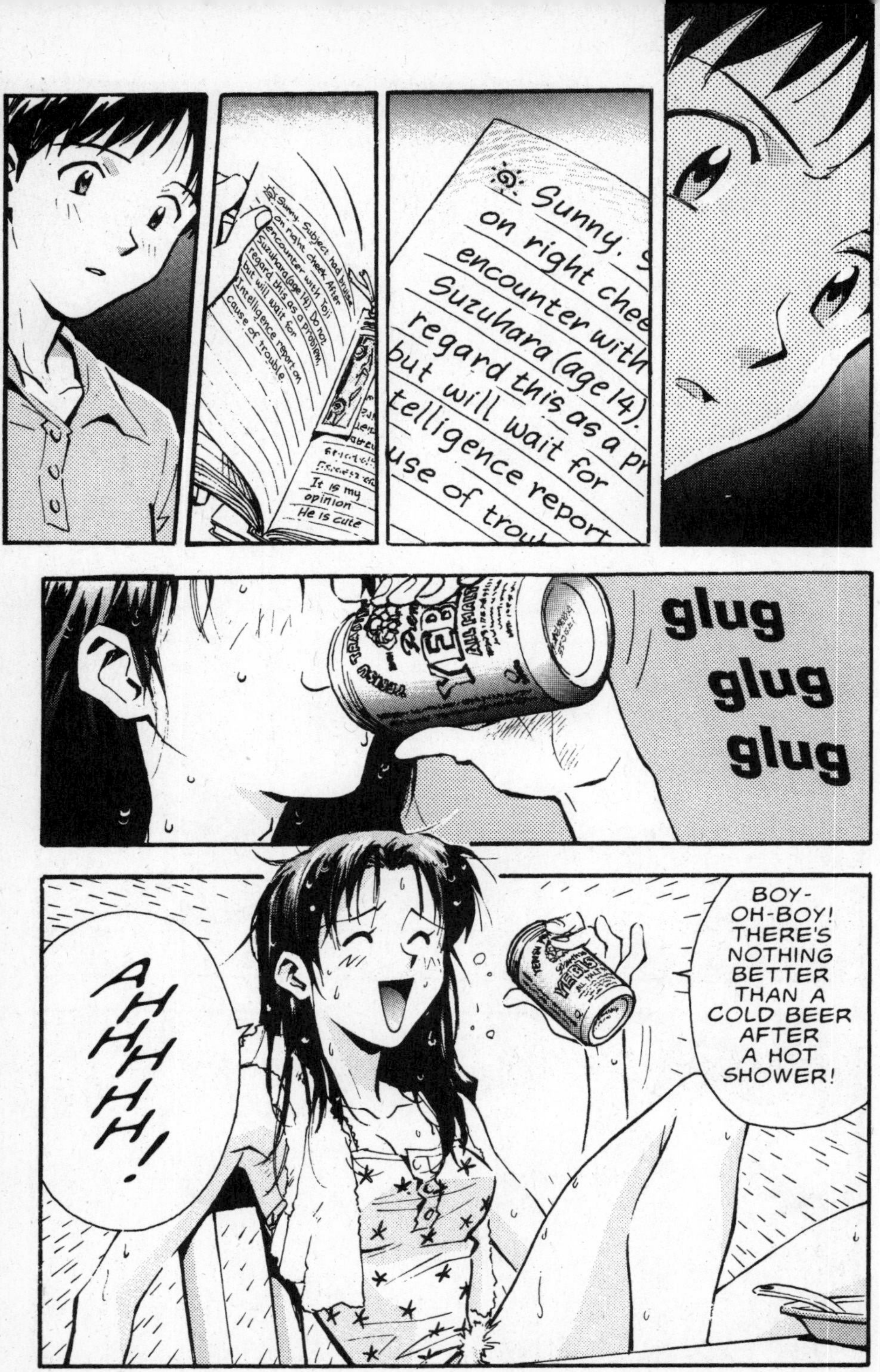

Sunny. Subject had bruise on right cheek. After encounter with Toji Suzuhara (age 14). Do not regard this as a problem, but will wait for intelligence report on cause of trouble.
It is my opinion
He is cute
Sunny. S
on right chee
encounter with
Suzuhara (age 14).
regard this as a pr
but will wait for
telligence report
use of trou
glug glug glug
AHHHH!
BOY-OH-BOY! THERE'S NOTHING BETTER THAN A COLD BEER AFTER A HOT SHOWER!

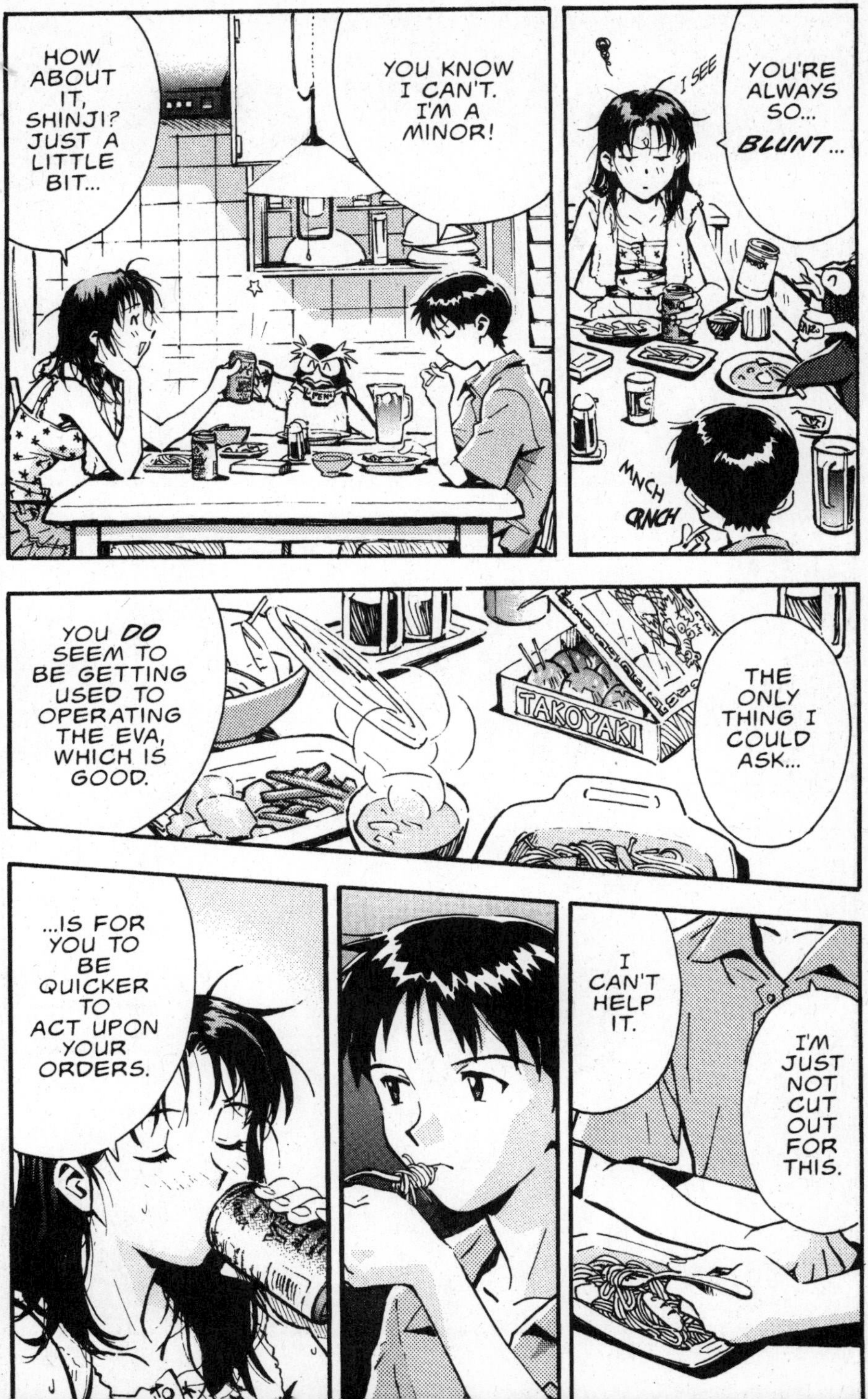
HOW ABOUT IT, SHINJI? JUST A LITTLE BIT...
YOU KNOW I CAN'T. I'M A MINOR!
I SEE
YOU'RE ALWAYS SO... BLUNT...
MNCH
CRNCH
YOU DO SEEM TO BE GETTING USED TO OPERATING THE EVA, WHICH IS GOOD.
TAKOYAKI
THE ONLY THING I COULD ASK...
...IS FOR YOU TO BE QUICKER TO ACT UPON YOUR ORDERS.
I CAN'T HELP IT.
I'M JUST NOT CUT OUT FOR THIS.

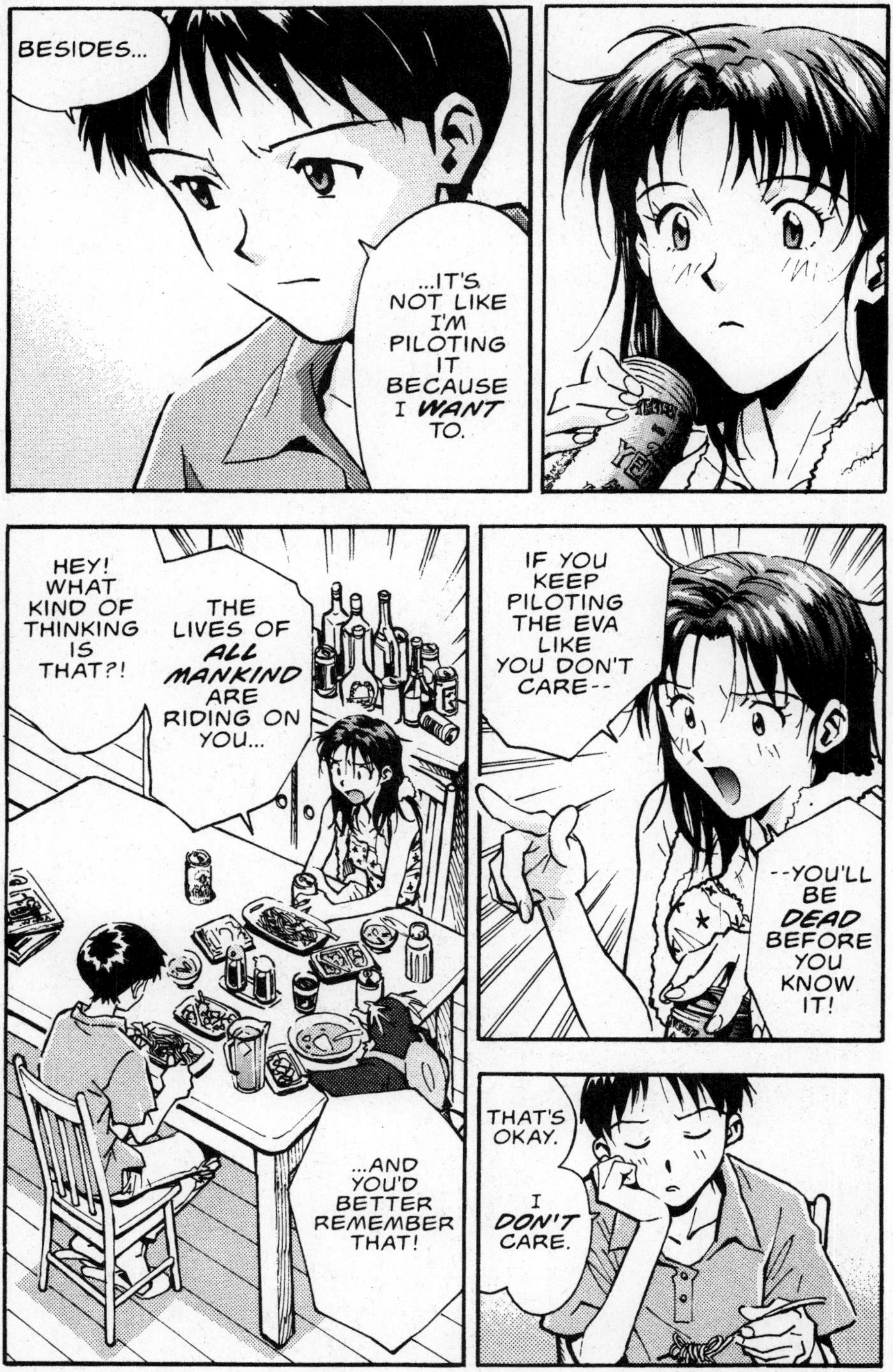
BESIDES...
...IT'S NOT LIKE I'M PILOTING IT BECAUSE I *WANT* TO.
HEY! WHAT KIND OF THINKING IS THAT?!
THE LIVES OF *ALL MANKIND* ARE RIDING ON YOU...
...AND YOU'D BETTER REMEMBER THAT!
IF YOU KEEP PILOTING THE EVA LIKE YOU DON'T CARE--
--YOU'LL BE *DEAD* BEFORE YOU KNOW IT!
THAT'S OKAY.
I *DON'T* CARE.

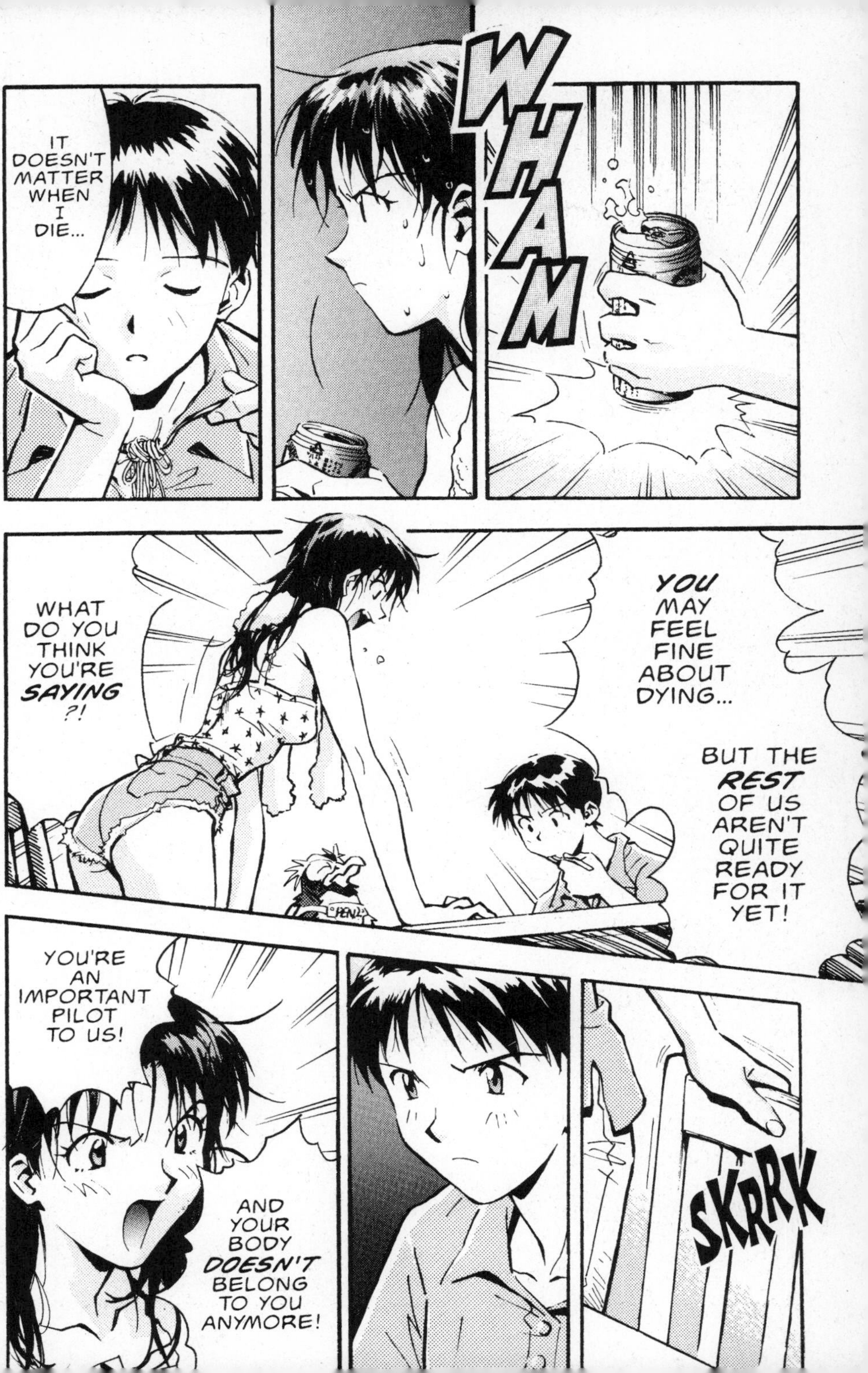
IT DOESN'T MATTER WHEN I DIE...
WHAM
WHAT DO YOU THINK YOU'RE SAYING ?!
YOU MAY FEEL FINE ABOUT DYING...
BUT THE REST OF US AREN'T QUITE READY FOR IT YET!
YOU'RE AN IMPORTANT PILOT TO US!
AND YOUR BODY DOESN'T BELONG TO YOU ANYMORE!
SKRRK

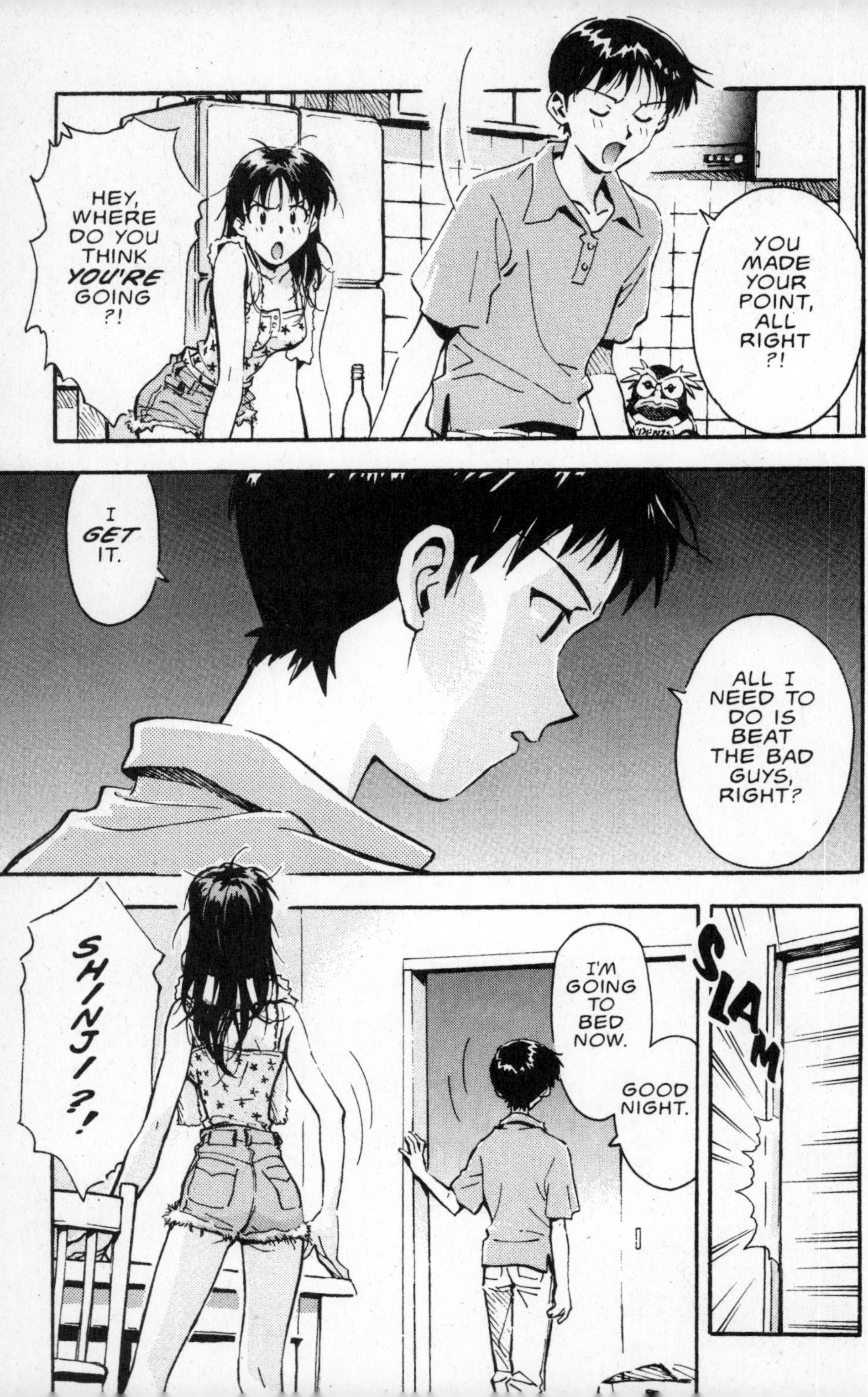
HEY, WHERE DO YOU THINK *YOU'RE* GOING ?!
YOU MADE YOUR POINT, ALL RIGHT ?!
I *GET* IT.
ALL I NEED TO DO IS BEAT THE BAD GUYS, RIGHT?
SHINJI ?!
I'M GOING TO BED NOW.
GOOD NIGHT.
SLAM

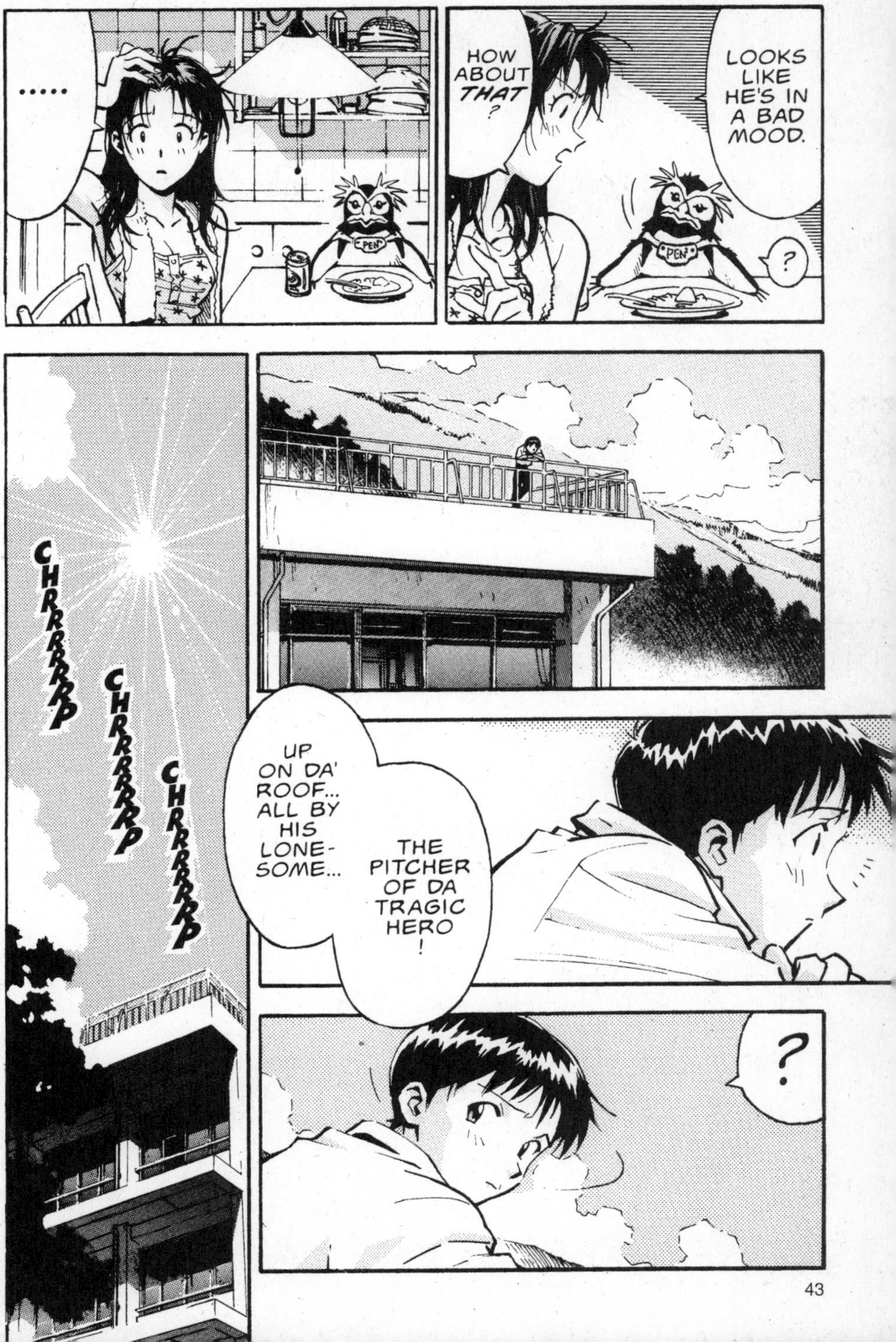
.....
HOW ABOUT *THAT* ?
LOOKS LIKE HE'S IN A BAD MOOD.
?
CHRRRRRP
CHRRRRRP
CHRRRRRRP
UP ON DA' ROOF... ALL BY HIS LONE-SOME...
THE PITCHER OF DA TRAGIC HERO !
?

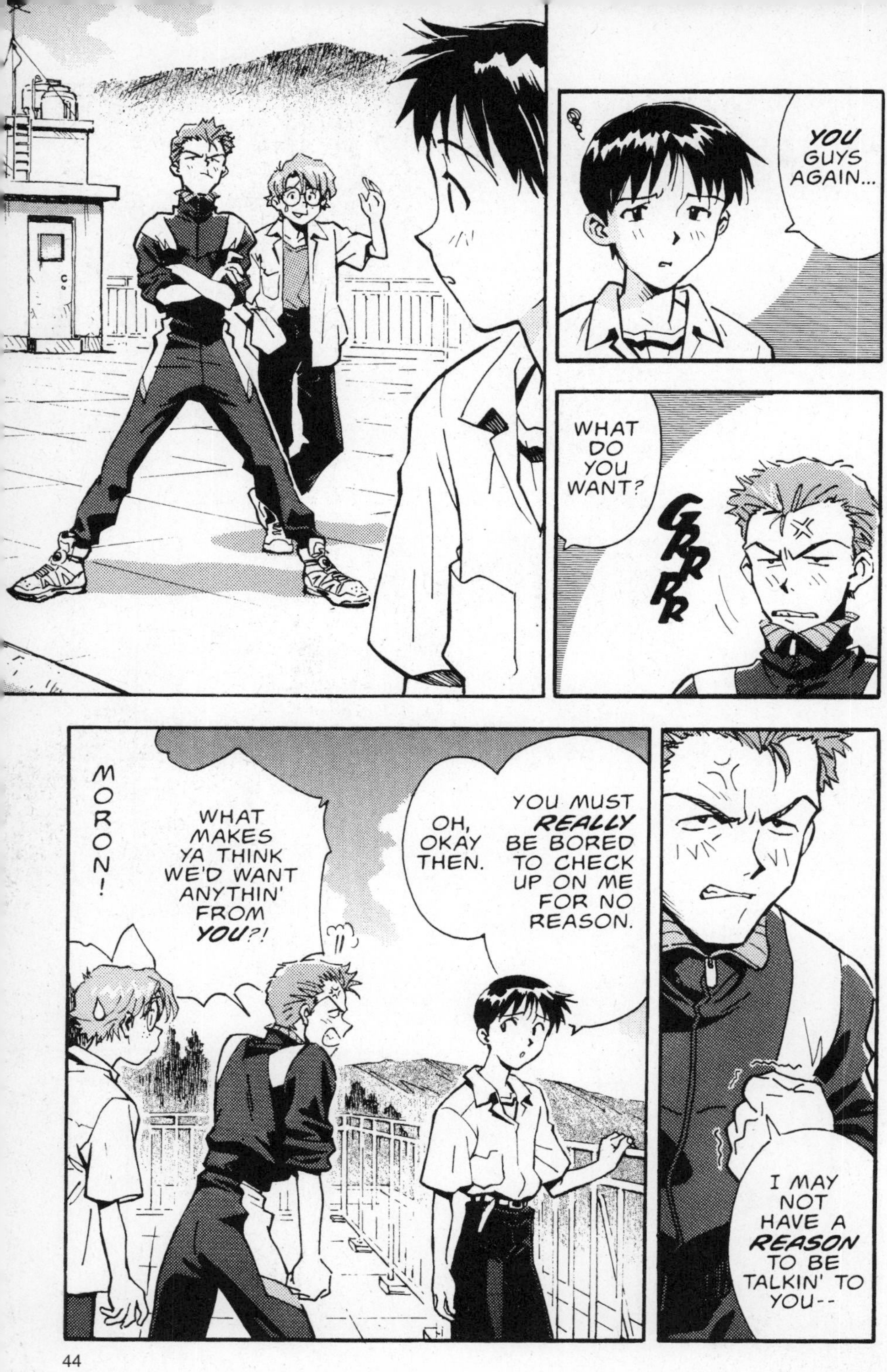
YOU GUYS AGAIN...
WHAT DO YOU WANT?
GRRRR
MORON!
WHAT MAKES YA THINK WE'D WANT ANYTHIN' FROM YOU?!
OH, OKAY THEN.
YOU MUST REALLY BE BORED TO CHECK UP ON ME FOR NO REASON.
I MAY NOT HAVE A REASON TO BE TALKIN' TO YOU--

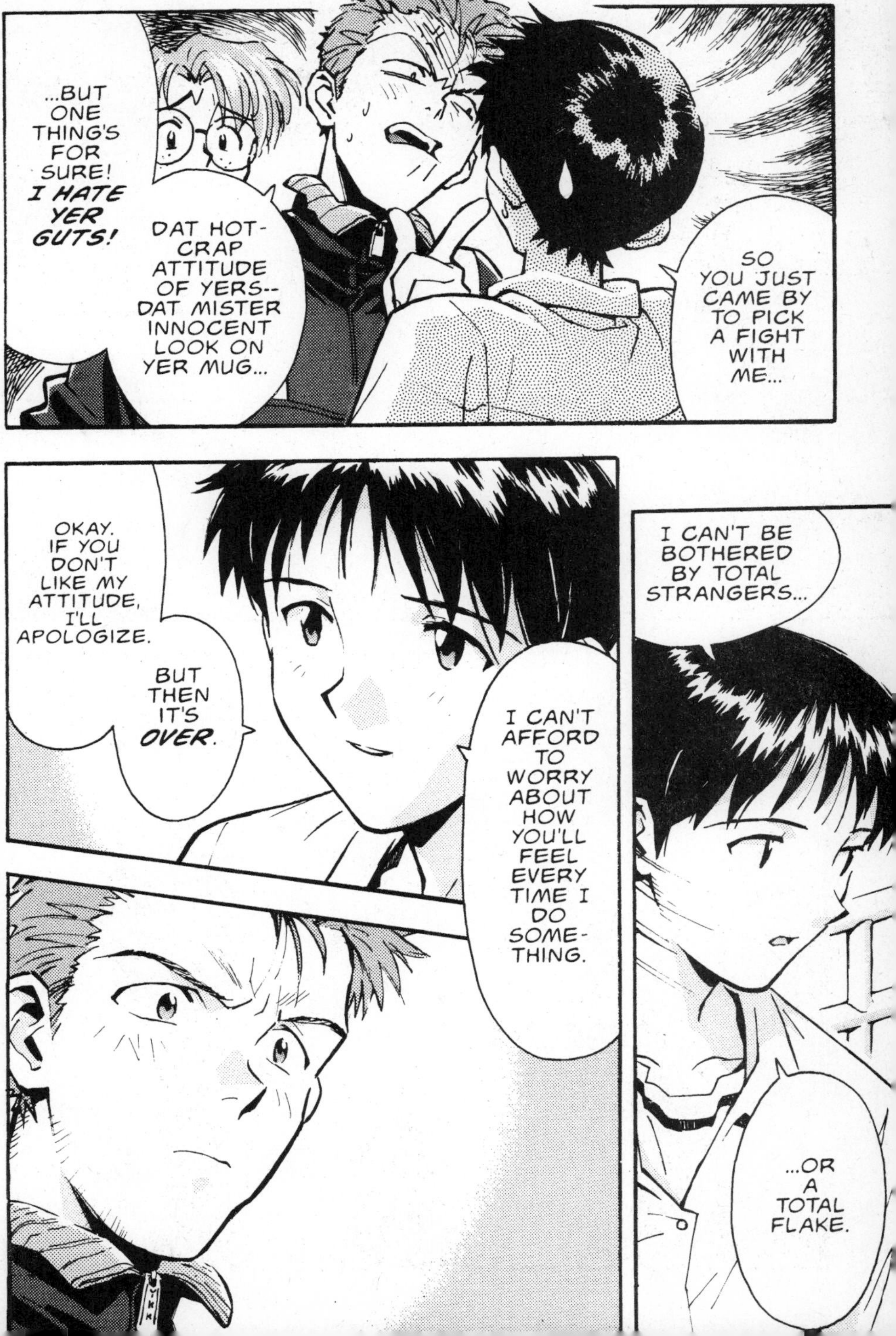
...BUT ONE THING'S FOR SURE! *I HATE YER GUTS!*
DAT HOT-CRAP ATTITUDE OF YERS-- DAT MISTER INNOCENT LOOK ON YER MUG...
SO YOU JUST CAME BY TO PICK A FIGHT WITH ME...
OKAY. IF YOU DON'T LIKE MY ATTITUDE, I'LL APOLOGIZE.
BUT THEN IT'S *OVER*.
I CAN'T AFFORD TO WORRY ABOUT HOW YOU'LL FEEL EVERY TIME I DO SOME-THING.
I CAN'T BE BOTHERED BY TOTAL STRANGERS...
...OR A TOTAL FLAKE.

HEY!

YOU CAN'T WALK AWAY!

YOU WANT TO PUNCH ME AGAIN...?

THAT'S FINE WITH ME...

...BUT THIS TIME, *DON'T HOLD BACK*!

DO IT LIKE YOU'RE TRYING TO BREAK AN ARM OR TWO.

IF YOU WANT, YOU CAN EVEN PUSH ME OFF THIS ROOF.

FINE!

REMEMBER, YA ASKED FOR IT!

DON'T GO CRYIN' TA NOBODY AFTERWARDS!

HOW COME THIS ALWAYS HAPPENS?

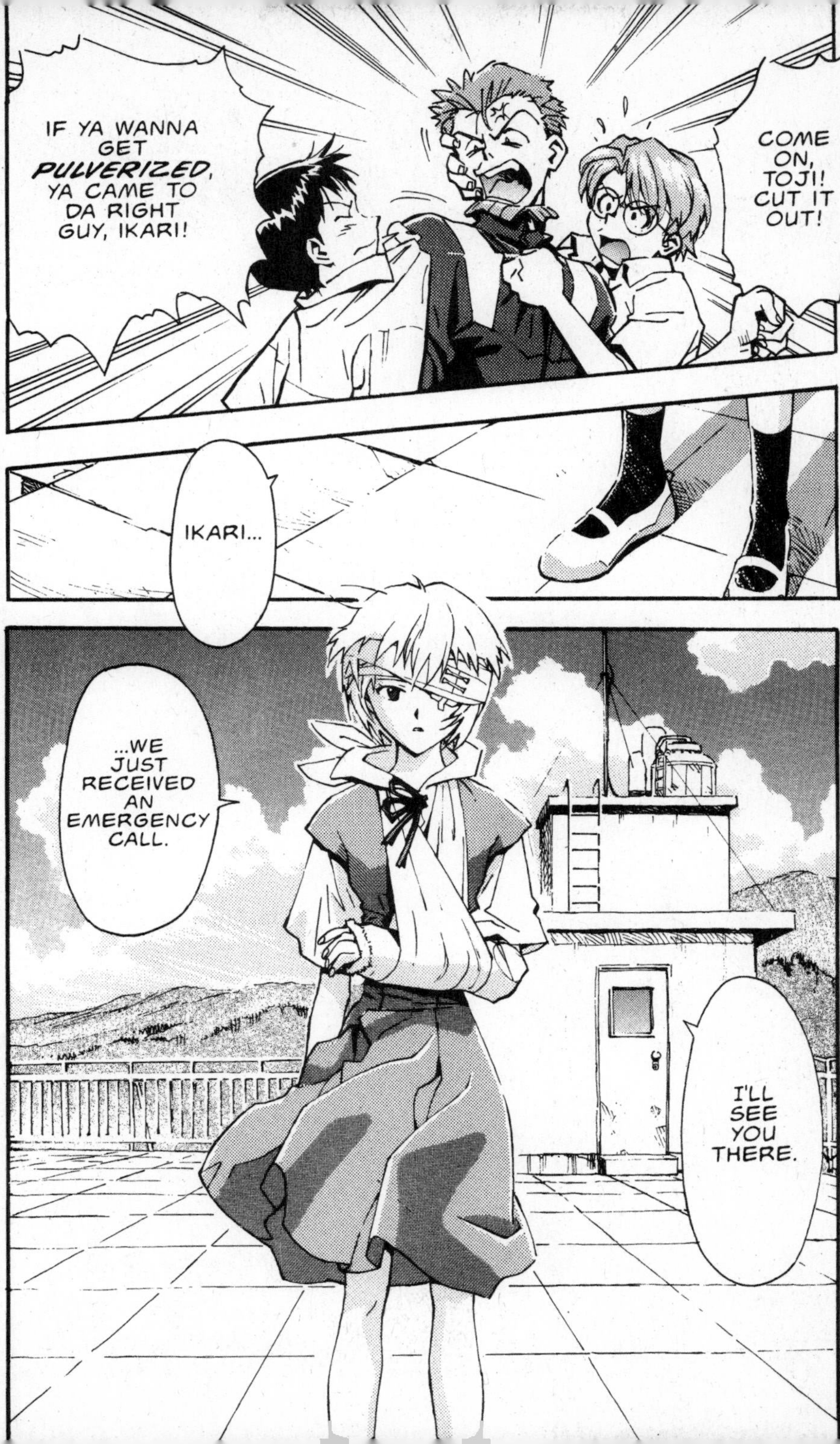
IF YA WANNA GET **PULVERIZED**, YA CAME TO DA RIGHT GUY, IKARI!
COME ON, TOJI! CUT IT OUT!
IKARI...
...WE JUST RECEIVED AN EMERGENCY CALL.
I'LL SEE YOU THERE.

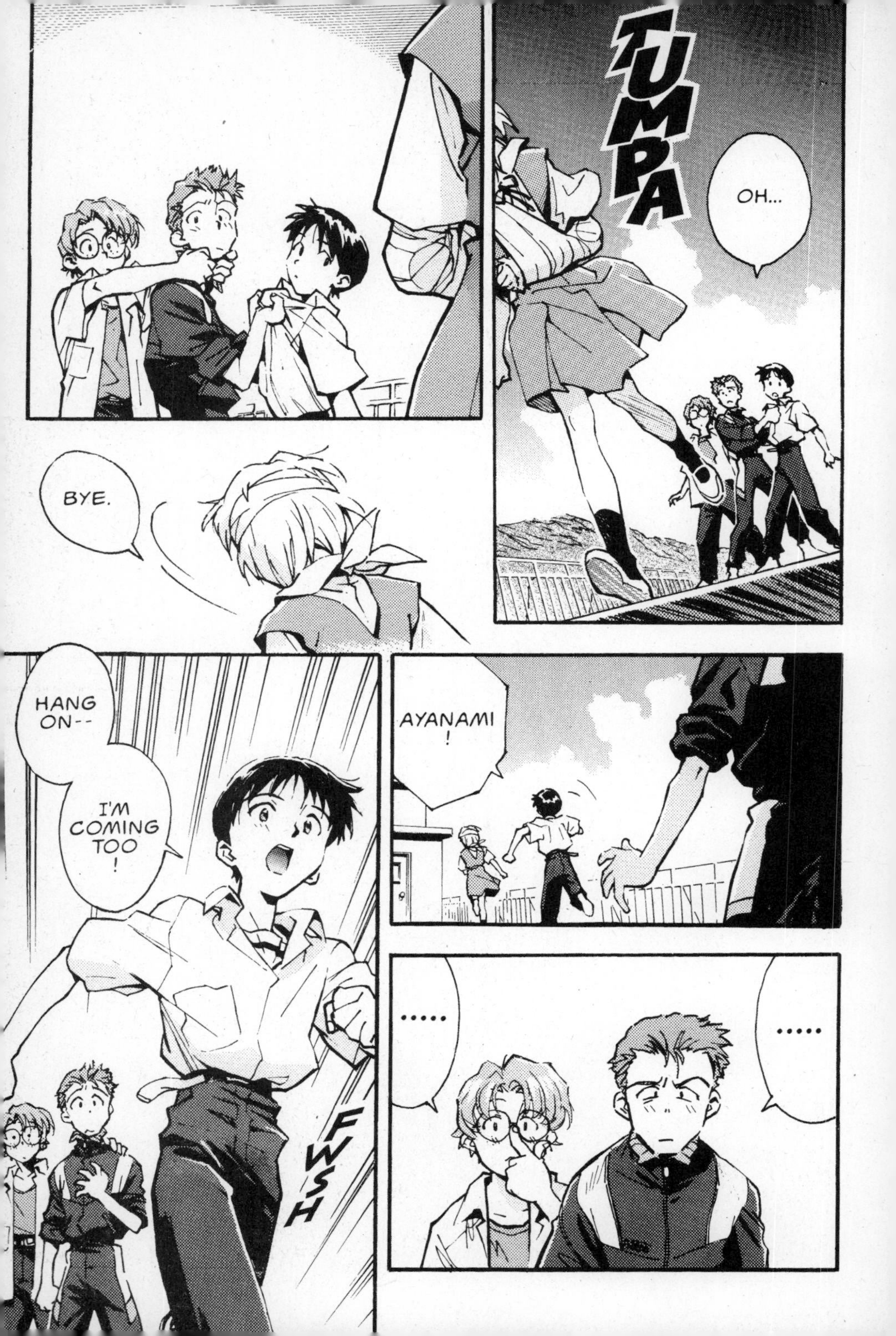
TUMPA
OH...
BYE.
HANG ON--
I'M COMING TOO!
AYANAMI!
.....
.....
FWSH

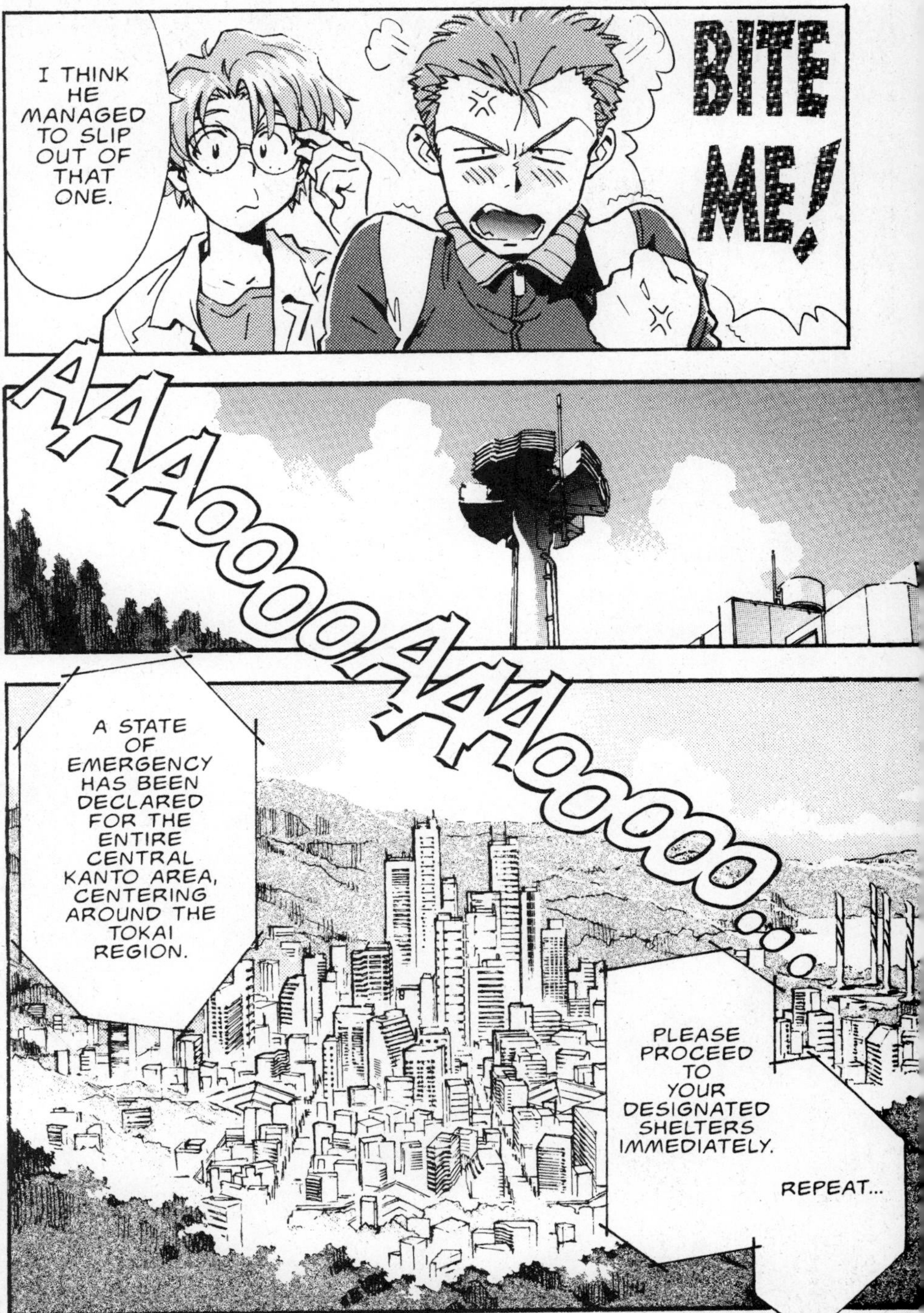
I THINK HE MANAGED TO SLIP OUT OF THAT ONE.
BITE ME!
AAAOOOOAAAOOOOO...
A STATE OF EMERGENCY HAS BEEN DECLARED FOR THE ENTIRE CENTRAL KANTO AREA, CENTERING AROUND THE TOKAI REGION.
PLEASE PROCEED TO YOUR DESIGNATED SHELTERS IMMEDIATELY.
REPEAT...

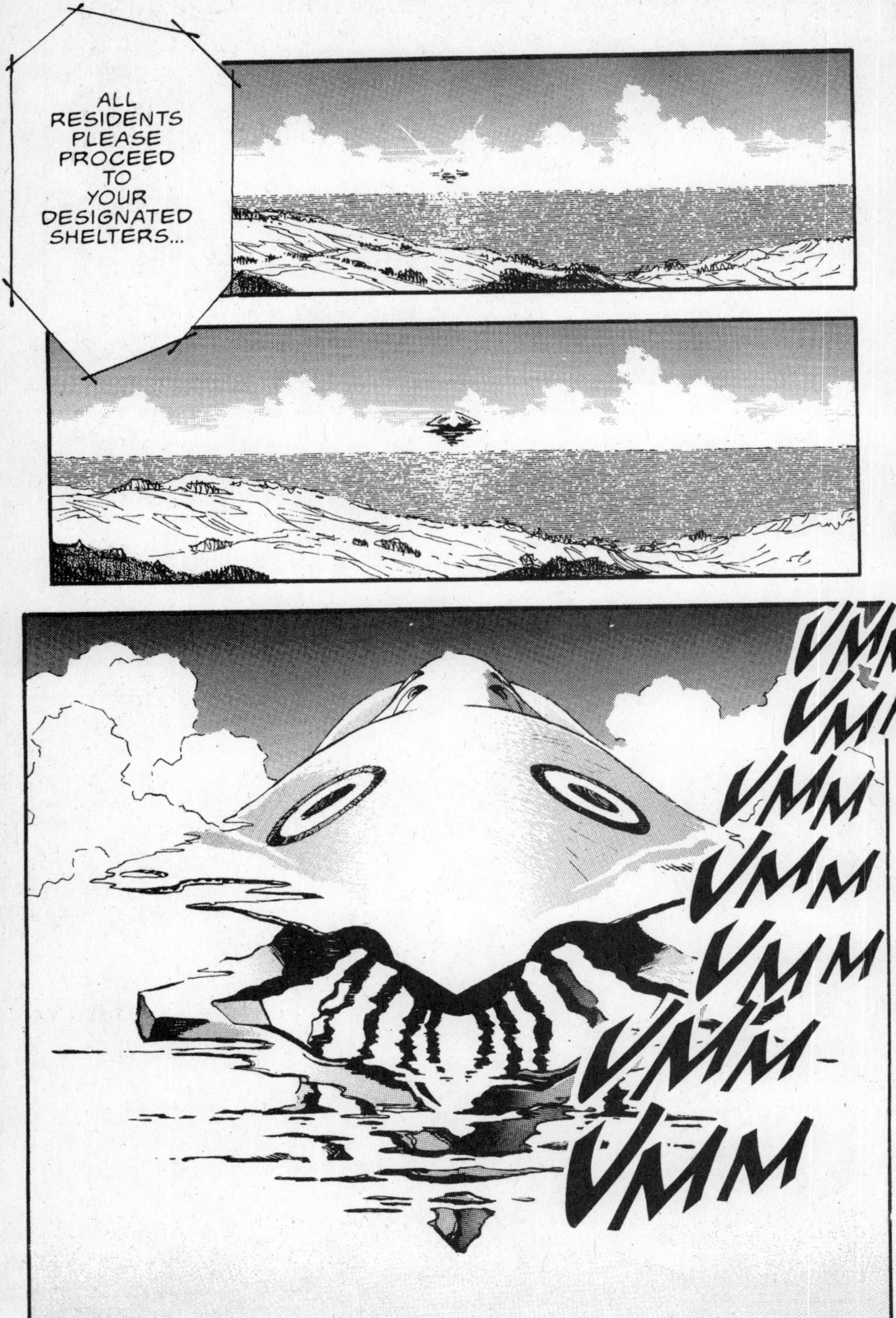
ALL RESIDENTS PLEASE PROCEED TO YOUR DESIGNATED SHELTERS...
VMMMVMMMVMMMVMMMVMMMVMMMVMM

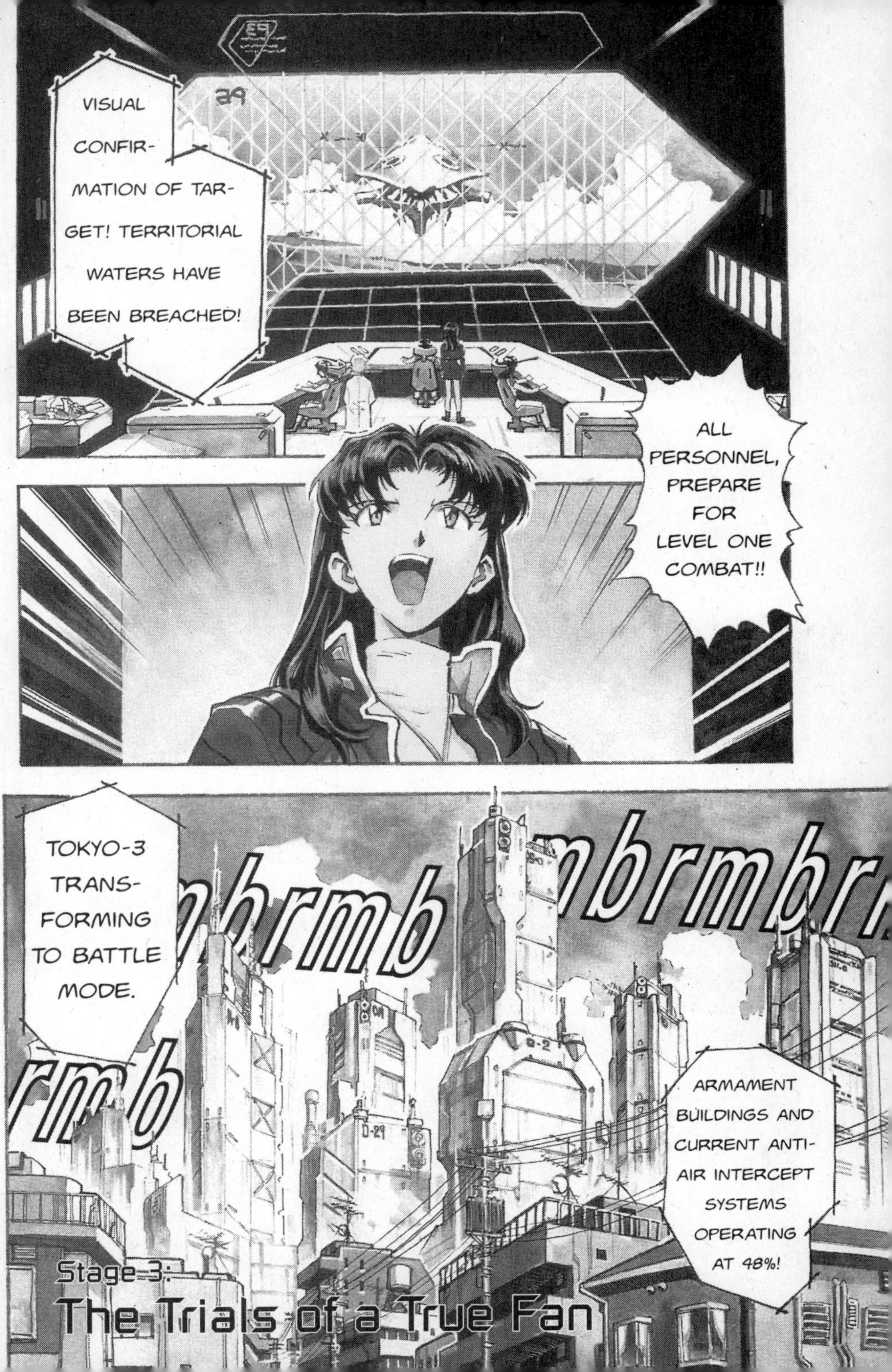
VISUAL CONFIR-MATION OF TAR-GET! TERRITORIAL WATERS HAVE BEEN BREACHED!
ALL PERSONNEL, PREPARE FOR LEVEL ONE COMBAT!!
TOKYO-3 TRANS-FORMING TO BATTLE MODE.
mbrmb
mbrmbr
rmb
ARMAMENT BUILDINGS AND CURRENT ANTI-AIR INTERCEPT SYSTEMS OPERATING AT 48%!
Stage 3:
The Trials of a True Fan

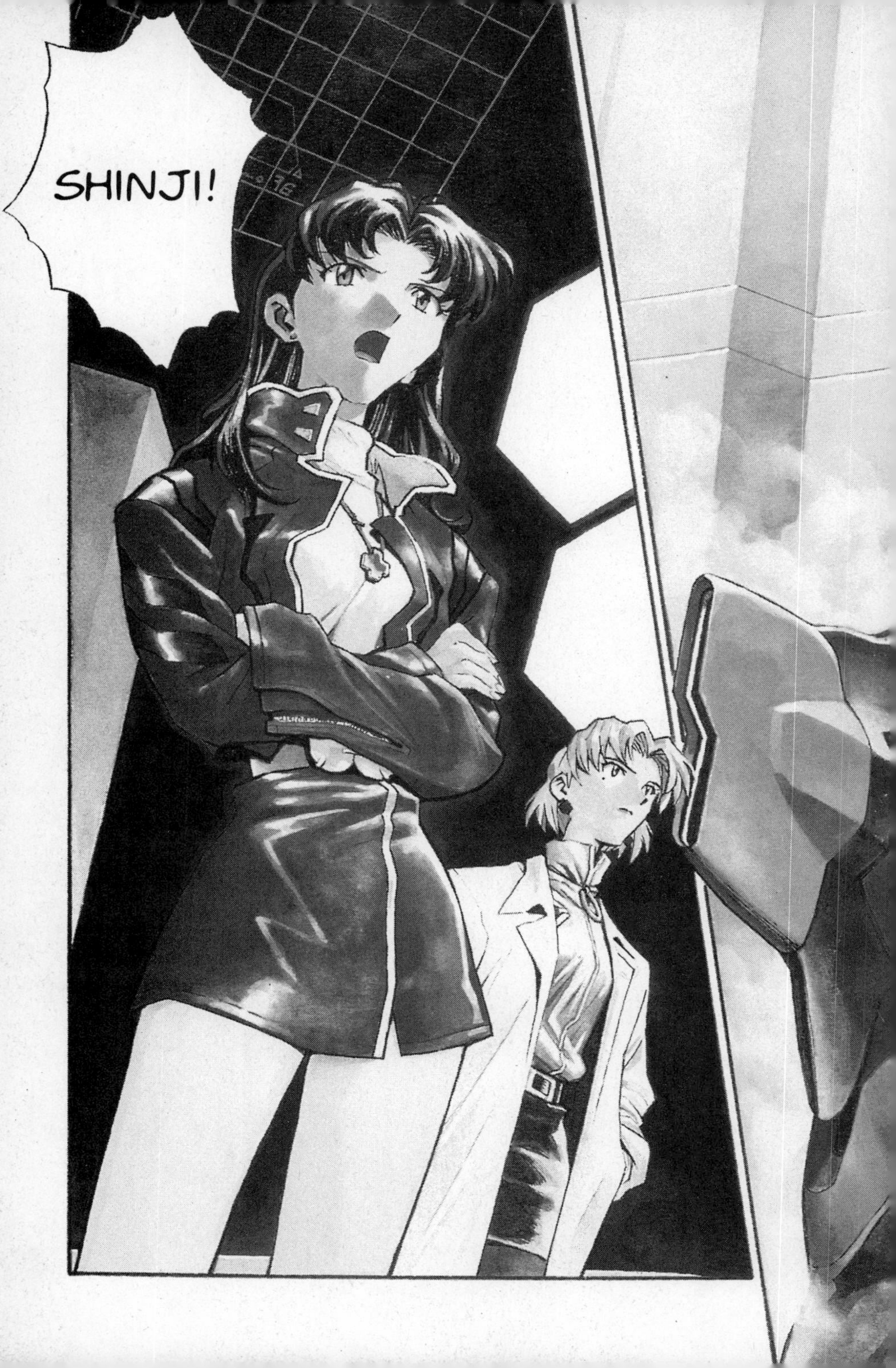
SHINJI!

Stage 3:
The Trials of a True Fan

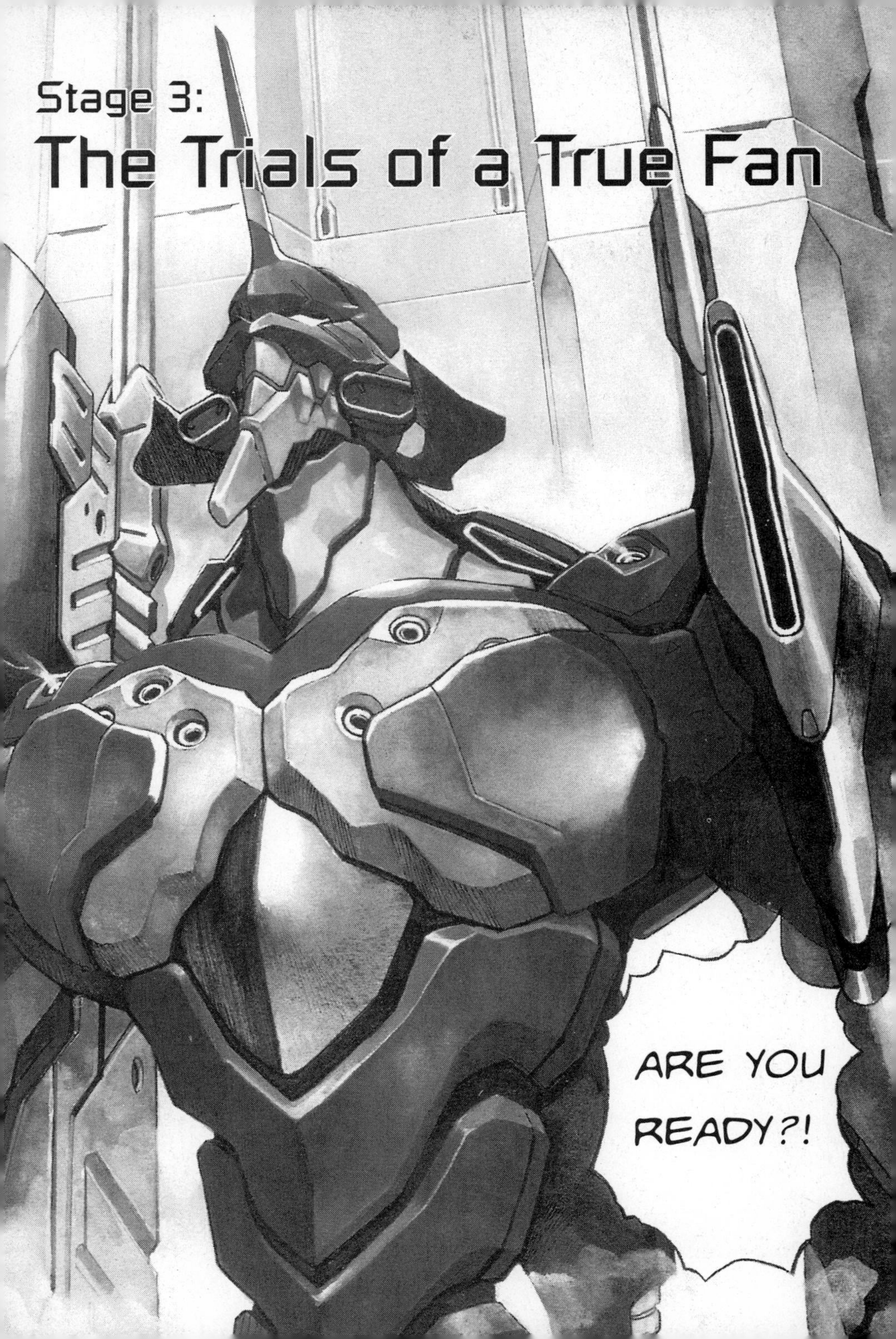
ARE YOU READY?!

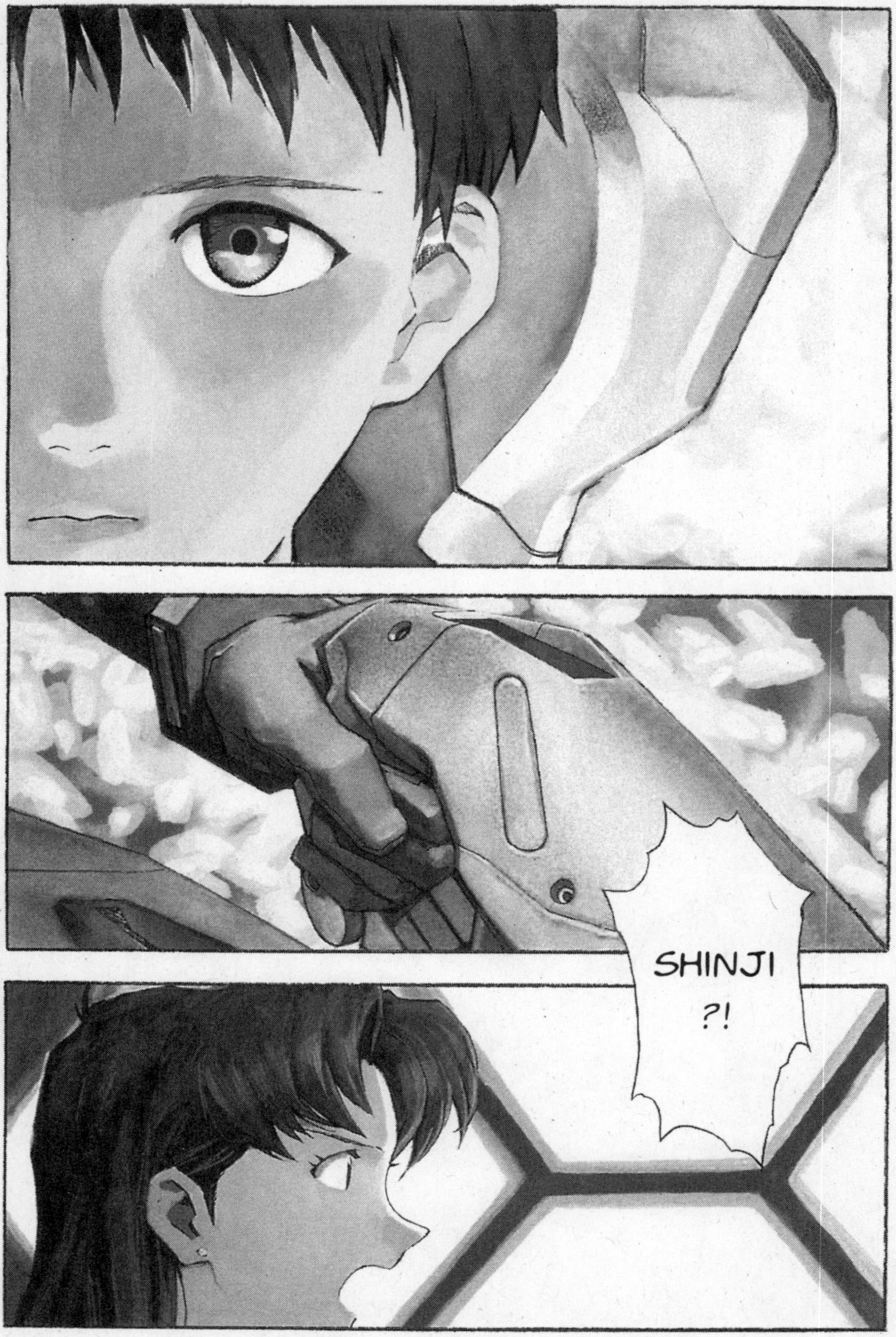
SHINJI ?!

DO YOU *HEAR* ME, SHINJI ?!

YOU DON'T HAVE TO YELL, MISATO.

IT'S NOT LIKE I'M *DEAF* OR ANYTHING.

SO THE FOURTH ANGEL ATTACKS WHILE THE COMMANDER'S AWAY...

THAT LITTLE...

STILL IN A *ROTTEN* MOOD I SEE.

?

THIS IS SOONER THAN WE EXPECTED.

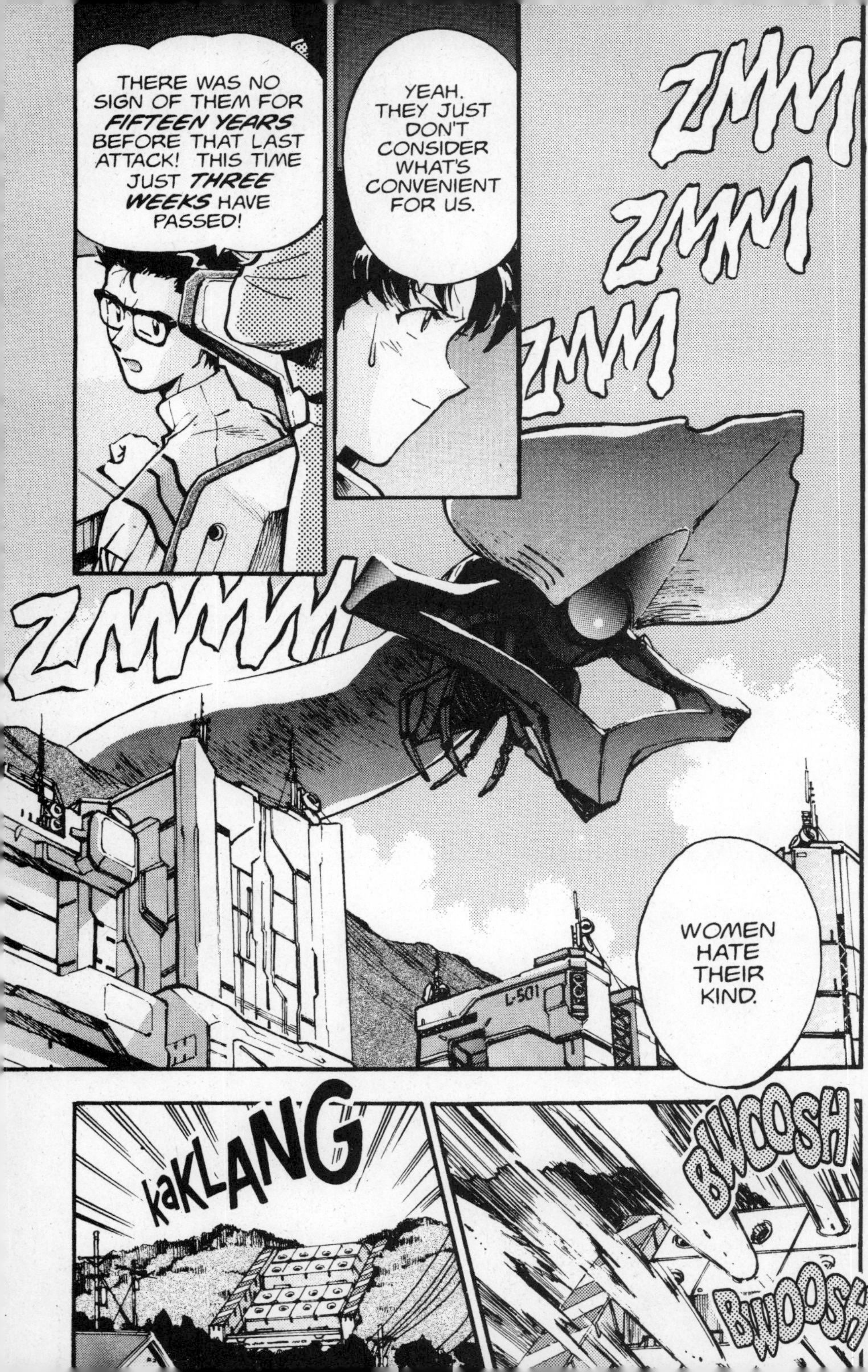
THERE WAS NO SIGN OF THEM FOR *FIFTEEN YEARS* BEFORE THAT LAST ATTACK! THIS TIME JUST *THREE WEEKS* HAVE PASSED!
YEAH. THEY JUST DON'T CONSIDER WHAT'S CONVENIENT FOR US.
ZMMM
ZMMM
ZMMM
ZMMMM
L-501
WOMEN HATE THEIR KIND.
kaKLANG
BWOOSH
BWOOSH

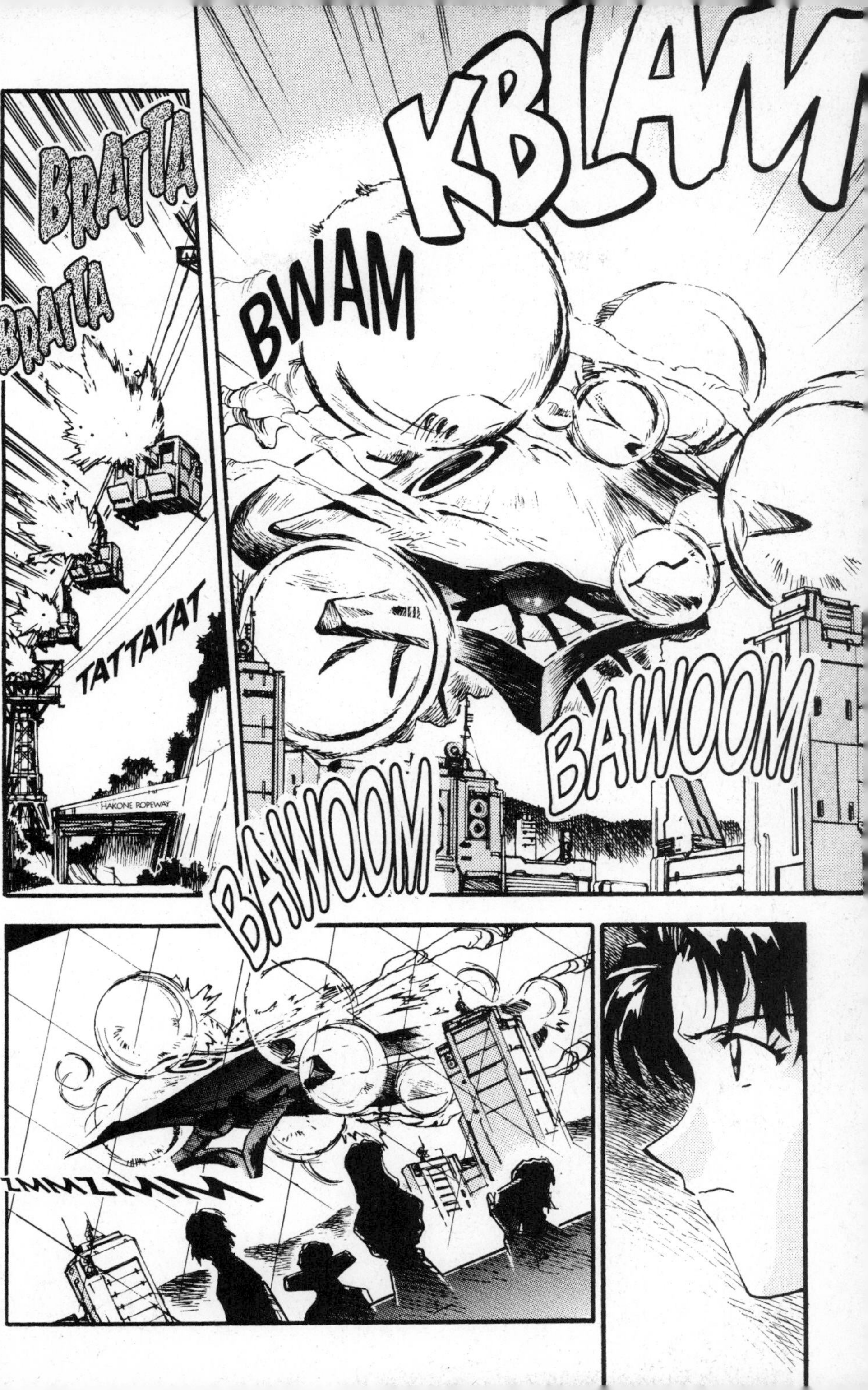
BRATTA
BRATTA
TATTATAT
HAKONE ROPEWAY
KBLAM
BWAM
BAWOOM
BAWOOM

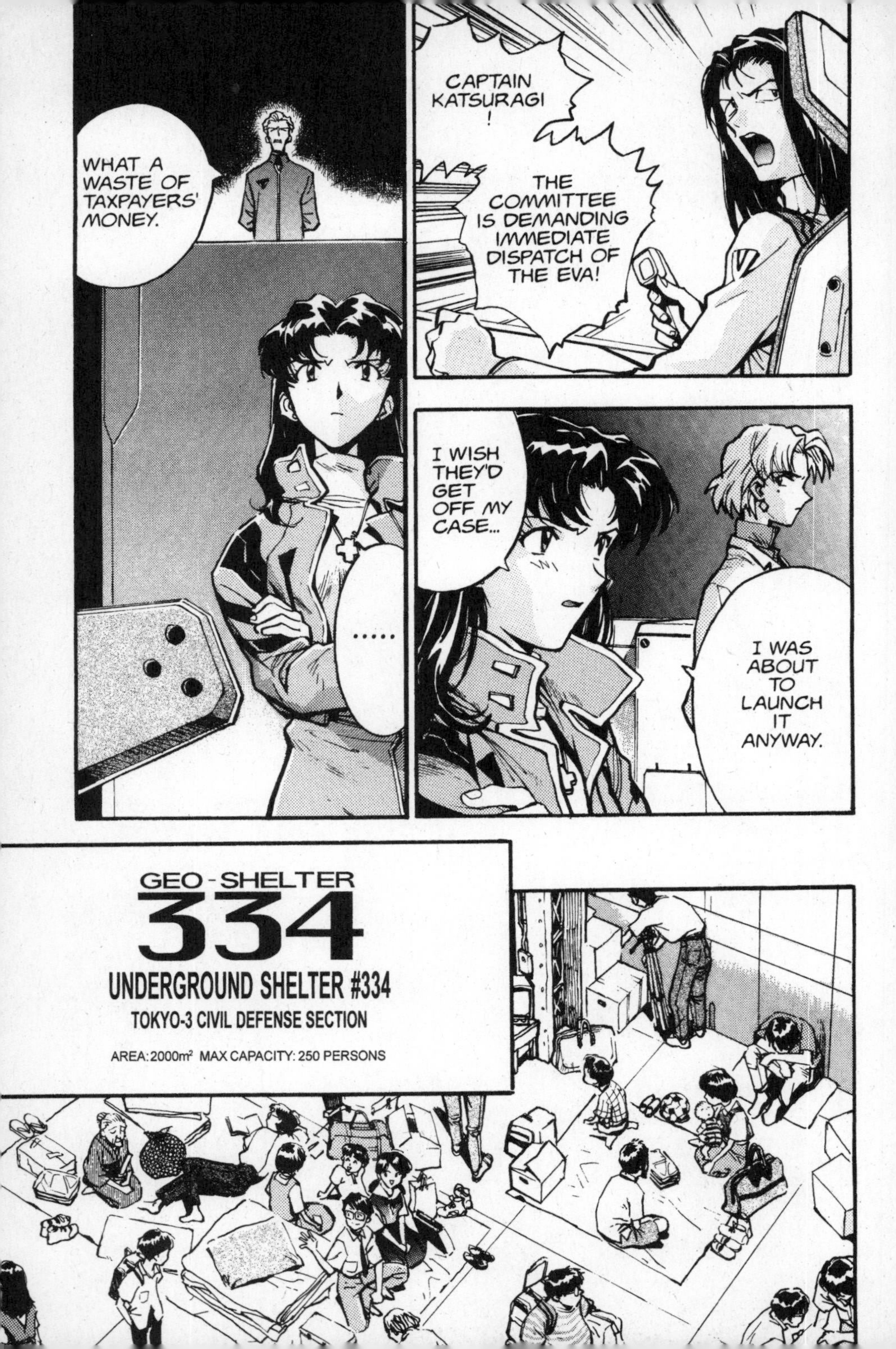
WHAT A WASTE OF TAXPAYERS' MONEY.
.....
CAPTAIN KATSURAGI!
THE COMMITTEE IS DEMANDING IMMEDIATE DISPATCH OF THE EVA!
I WISH THEY'D GET OFF MY CASE...
I WAS ABOUT TO LAUNCH IT ANYWAY.
GEO-SHELTER
334
UNDERGROUND SHELTER #334
TOKYO-3 CIVIL DEFENSE SECTION
AREA: 2000m² MAX CAPACITY: 250 PERSONS

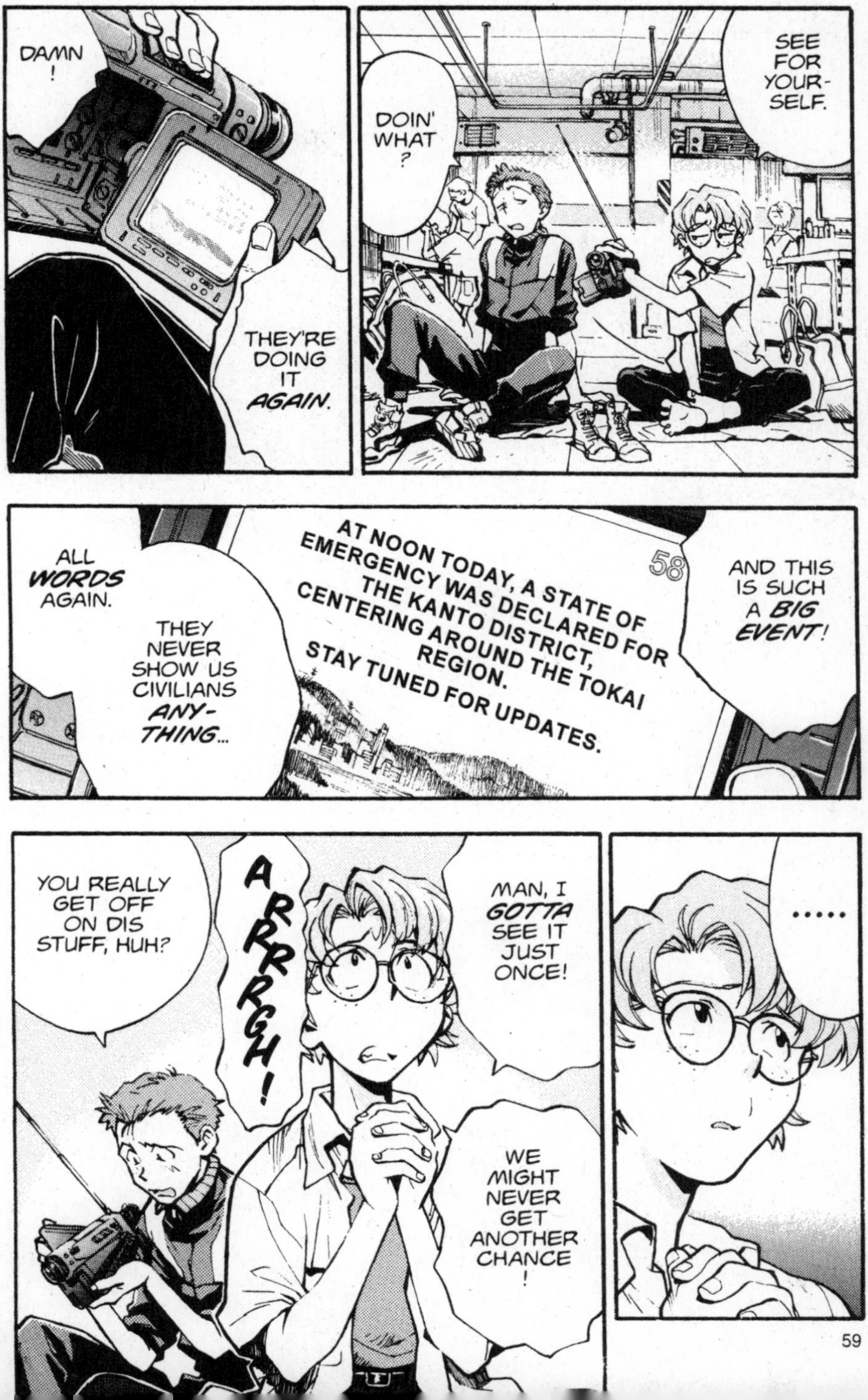
DAMN!
THEY'RE DOING IT AGAIN.
DOIN' WHAT?
SEE FOR YOUR-SELF.
ALL WORDS AGAIN.
THEY NEVER SHOW US CIVILIANS ANYTHING...
AT NOON TODAY, A STATE OF EMERGENCY WAS DECLARED FOR THE KANTO DISTRICT, CENTERING AROUND THE TOKAI REGION.
STAY TUNED FOR UPDATES.
58
AND THIS IS SUCH A BIG EVENT!
YOU REALLY GET OFF ON DIS STUFF, HUH?
ARRRRGH!
MAN, I GOTTA SEE IT JUST ONCE!
WE MIGHT NEVER GET ANOTHER CHANCE!
.....

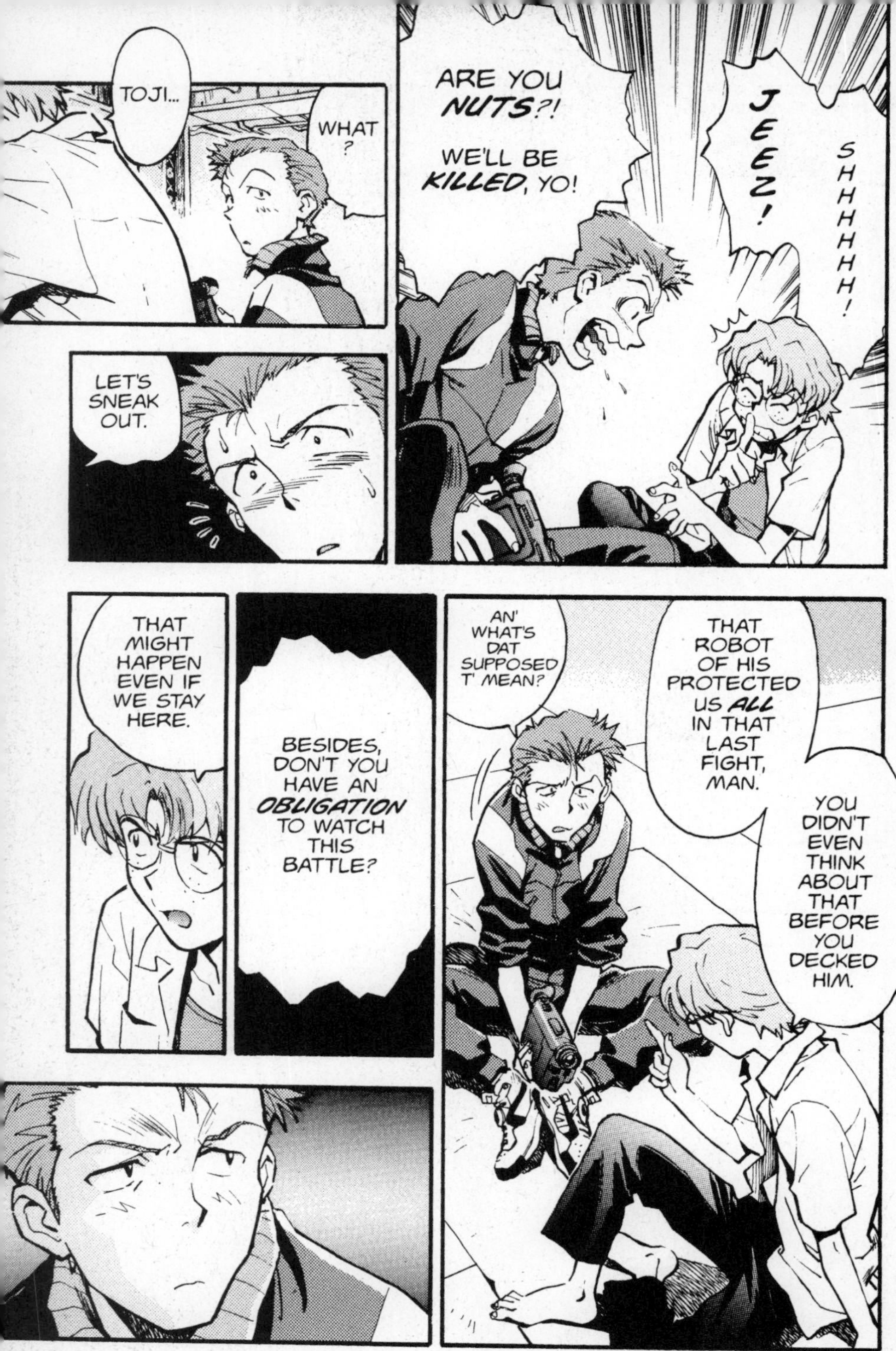
TOJI...
WHAT?
LET'S SNEAK OUT.
ARE YOU NUTS?!
WE'LL BE KILLED, YO!
JEEZ!
SHHHHHH!
THAT MIGHT HAPPEN EVEN IF WE STAY HERE.
BESIDES, DON'T YOU HAVE AN OBLIGATION TO WATCH THIS BATTLE?
AN' WHAT'S DAT SUPPOSED T' MEAN?
THAT ROBOT OF HIS PROTECTED US ALL IN THAT LAST FIGHT, MAN.
YOU DIDN'T EVEN THINK ABOUT THAT BEFORE YOU DECKED HIM.

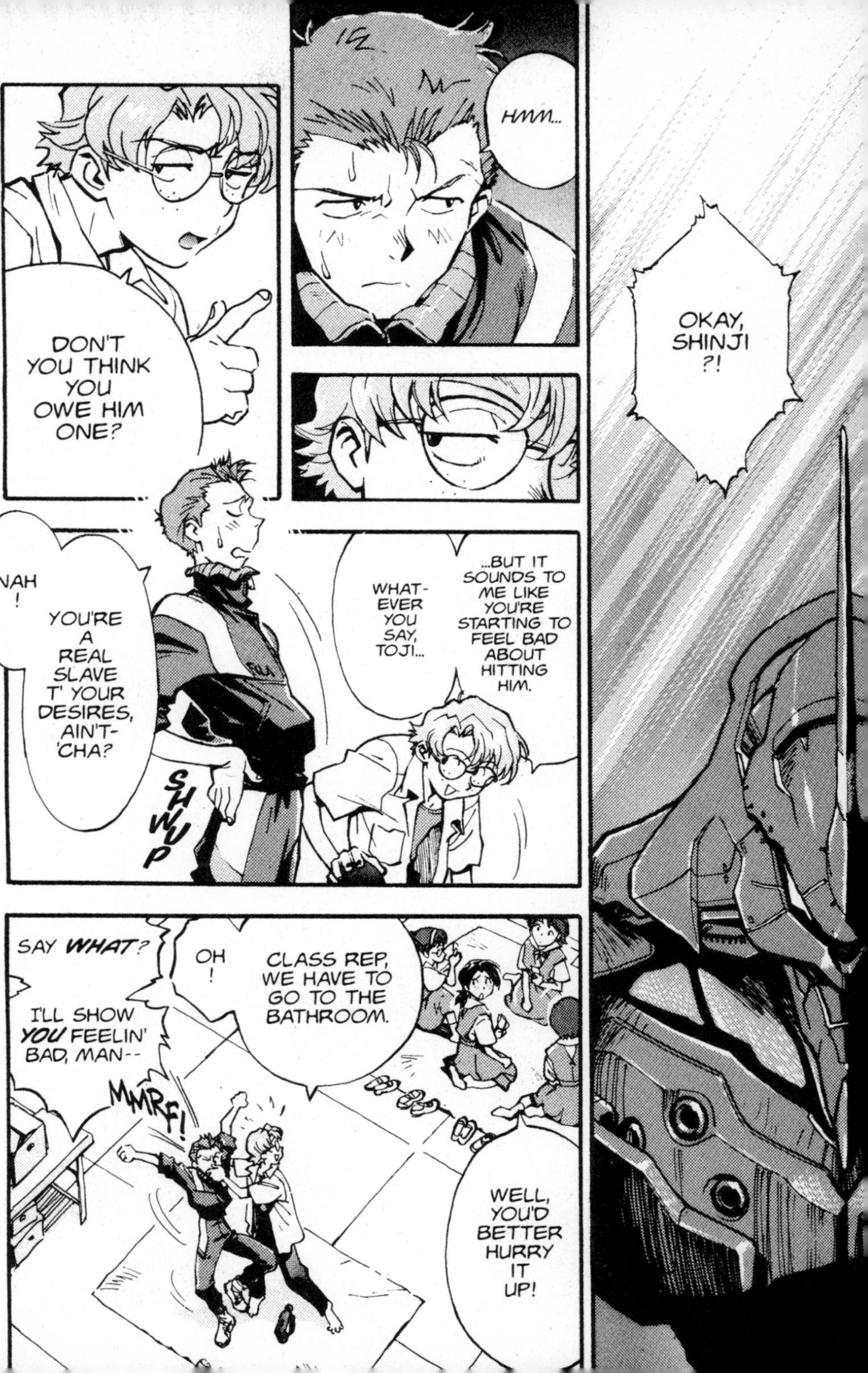
DON'T YOU THINK YOU OWE HIM ONE?
HMM...
NAH! YOU'RE A REAL SLAVE T' YOUR DESIRES, AIN'T-'CHA?
WHAT-EVER YOU SAY, TOJI...
...BUT IT SOUNDS TO ME LIKE YOU'RE STARTING TO FEEL BAD ABOUT HITTING HIM.
SHWUP
SAY WHAT?
I'LL SHOW YOU FEELIN' BAD, MAN--
MMRF!
OH!
CLASS REP, WE HAVE TO GO TO THE BATHROOM.
WELL, YOU'D BETTER HURRY IT UP!
OKAY, SHINJI?!

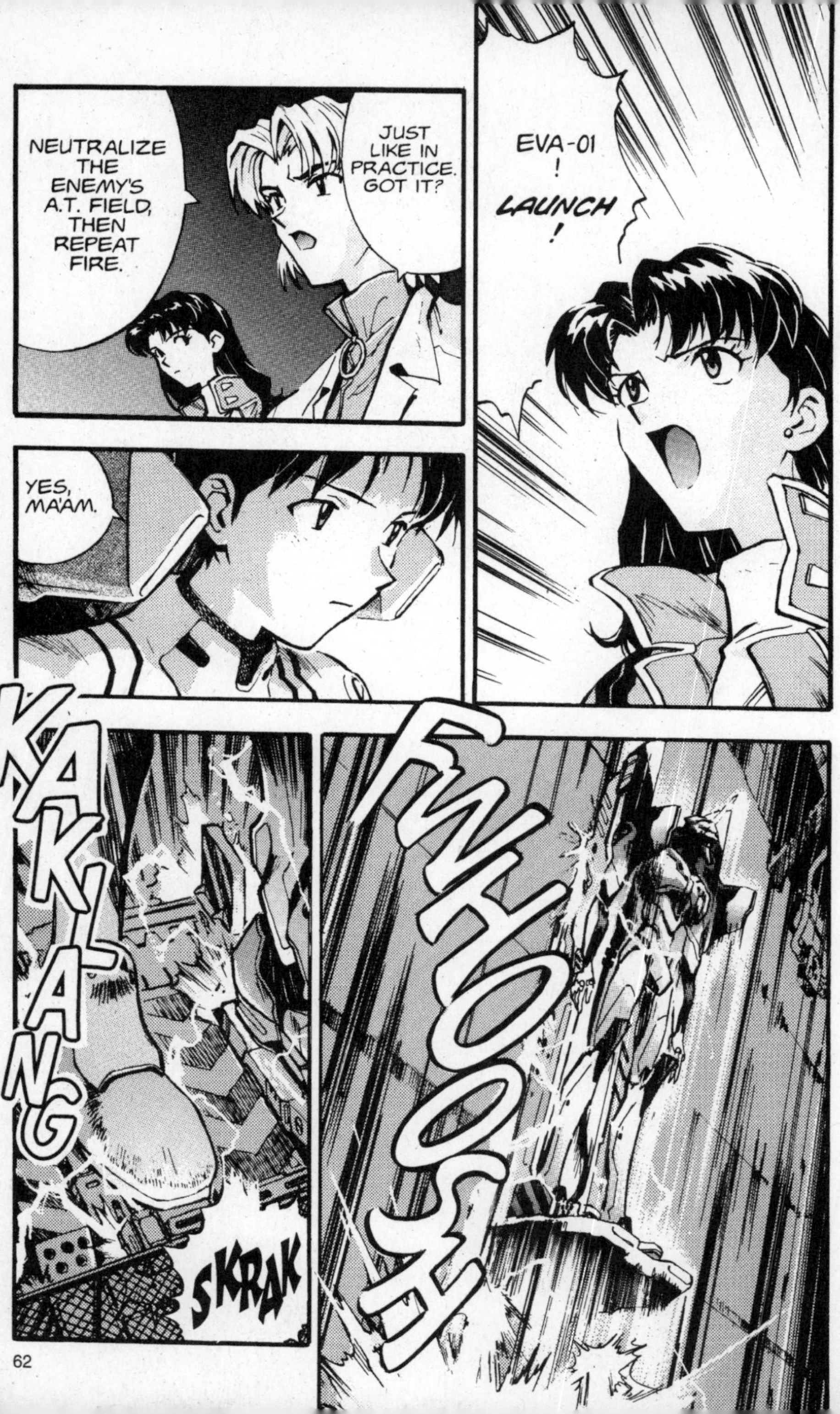
NEUTRALIZE THE ENEMY'S A.T. FIELD, THEN REPEAT FIRE.
JUST LIKE IN PRACTICE. GOT IT?
YES, MA'AM.
EVA-01 ! LAUNCH !
KAKLANG
SKRAK
FWHOOSH

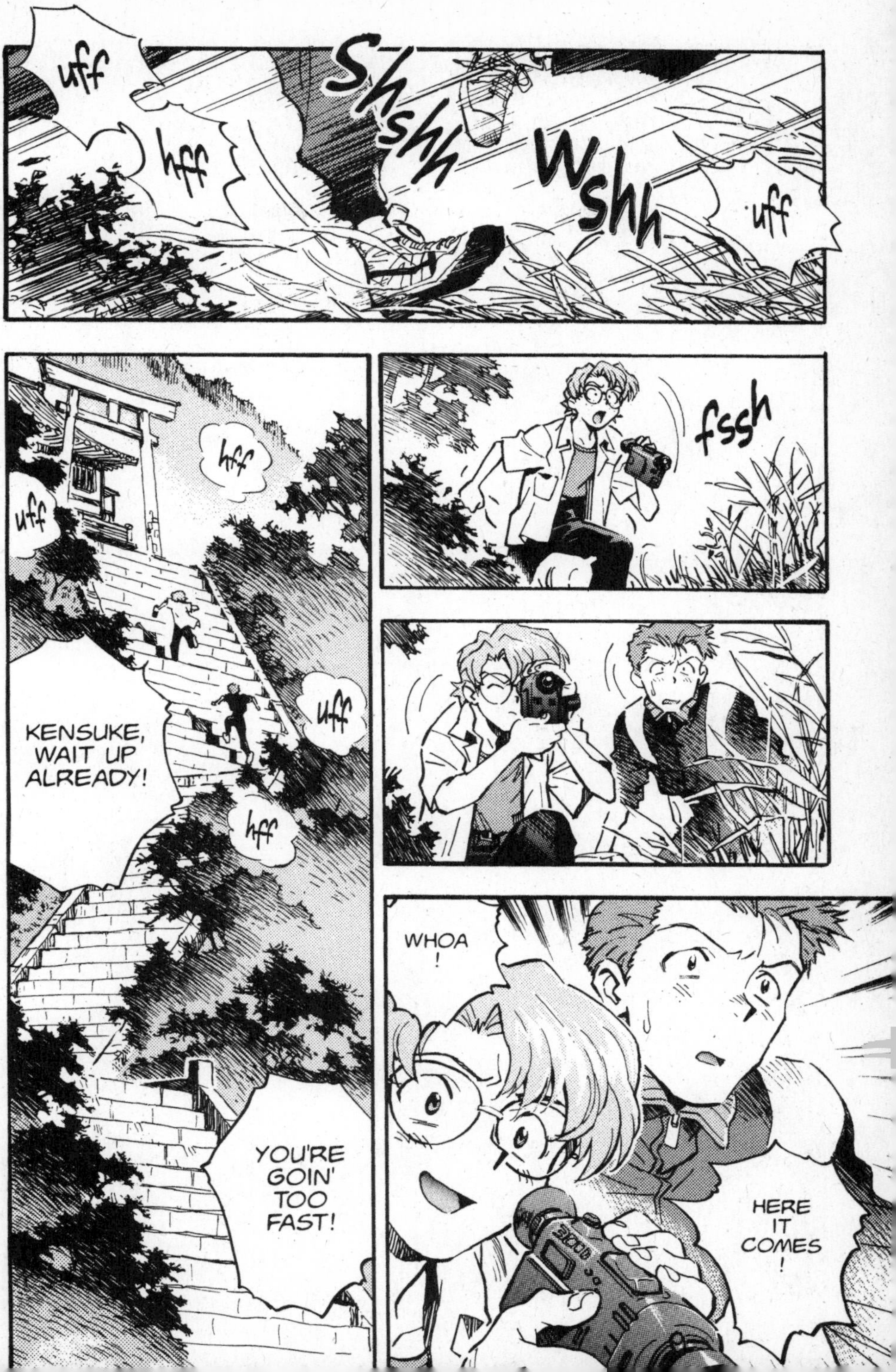
uff
hff
Shshh
Wshh
uff
hff
uff
uff
KENSUKE, WAIT UP ALREADY!
hff
YOU'RE GOIN' TOO FAST!
fssh
WHOA!
HERE IT COMES!

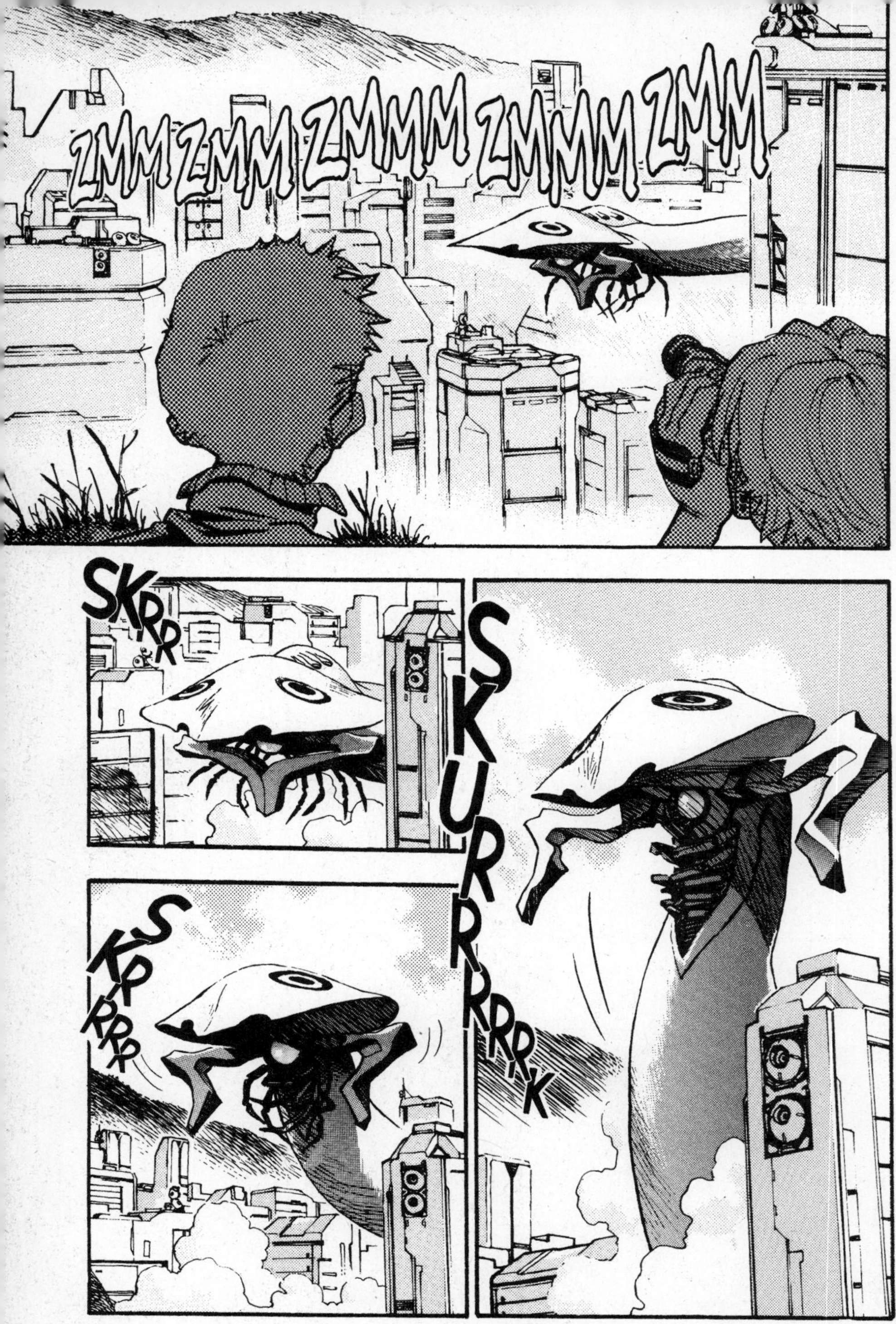
ZMM ZMM ZMMM ZMMM ZMM
SKRRR
SKRRRRR
SKURRRRRRK

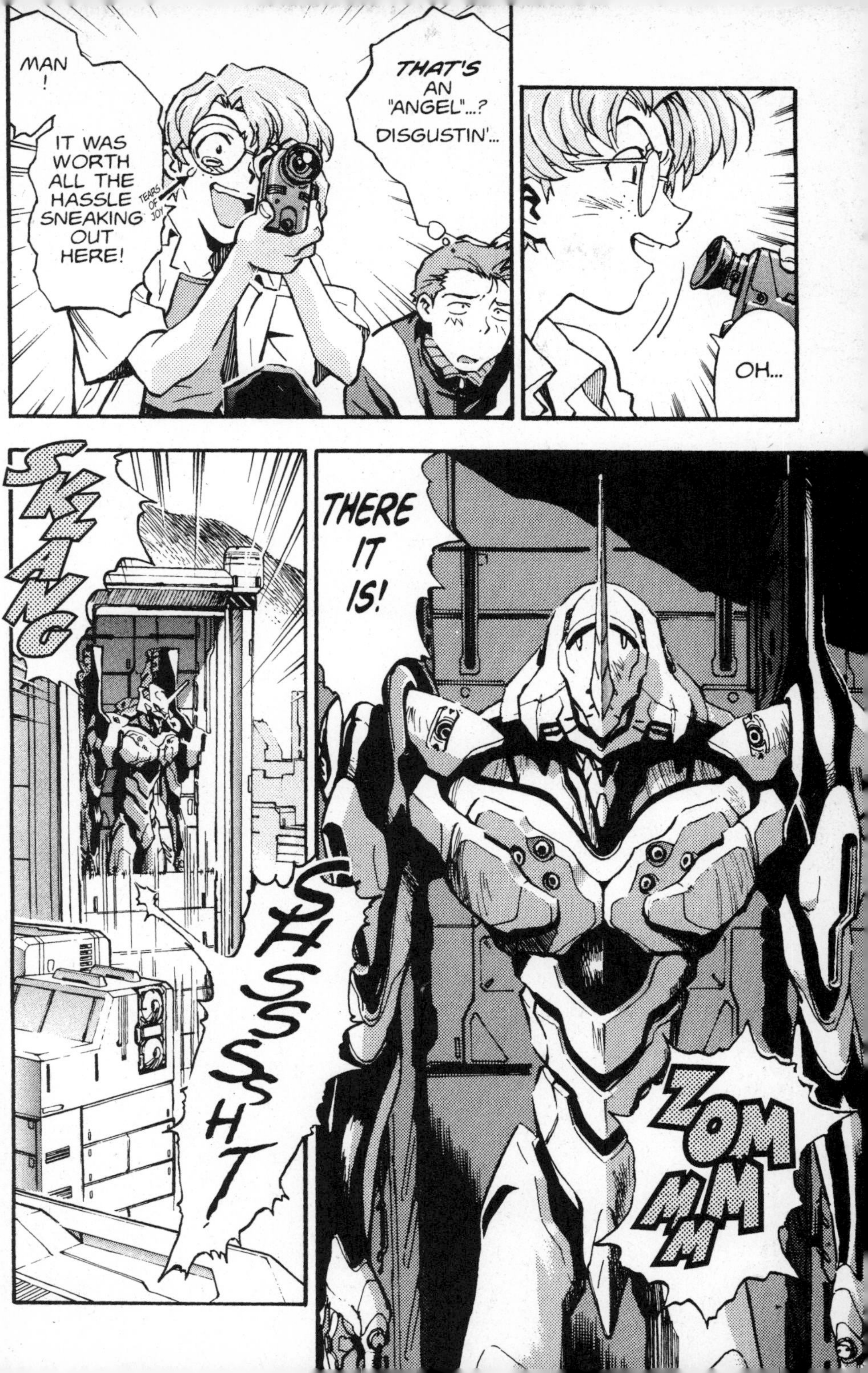
MAN!
IT WAS WORTH ALL THE HASSLE SNEAKING OUT HERE!
TEARS OF JOY
THAT'S AN "ANGEL"...? DISGUSTIN'...
OH...
SKKANG
SHSSSSHT!
THERE IT IS!
ZOMMMM

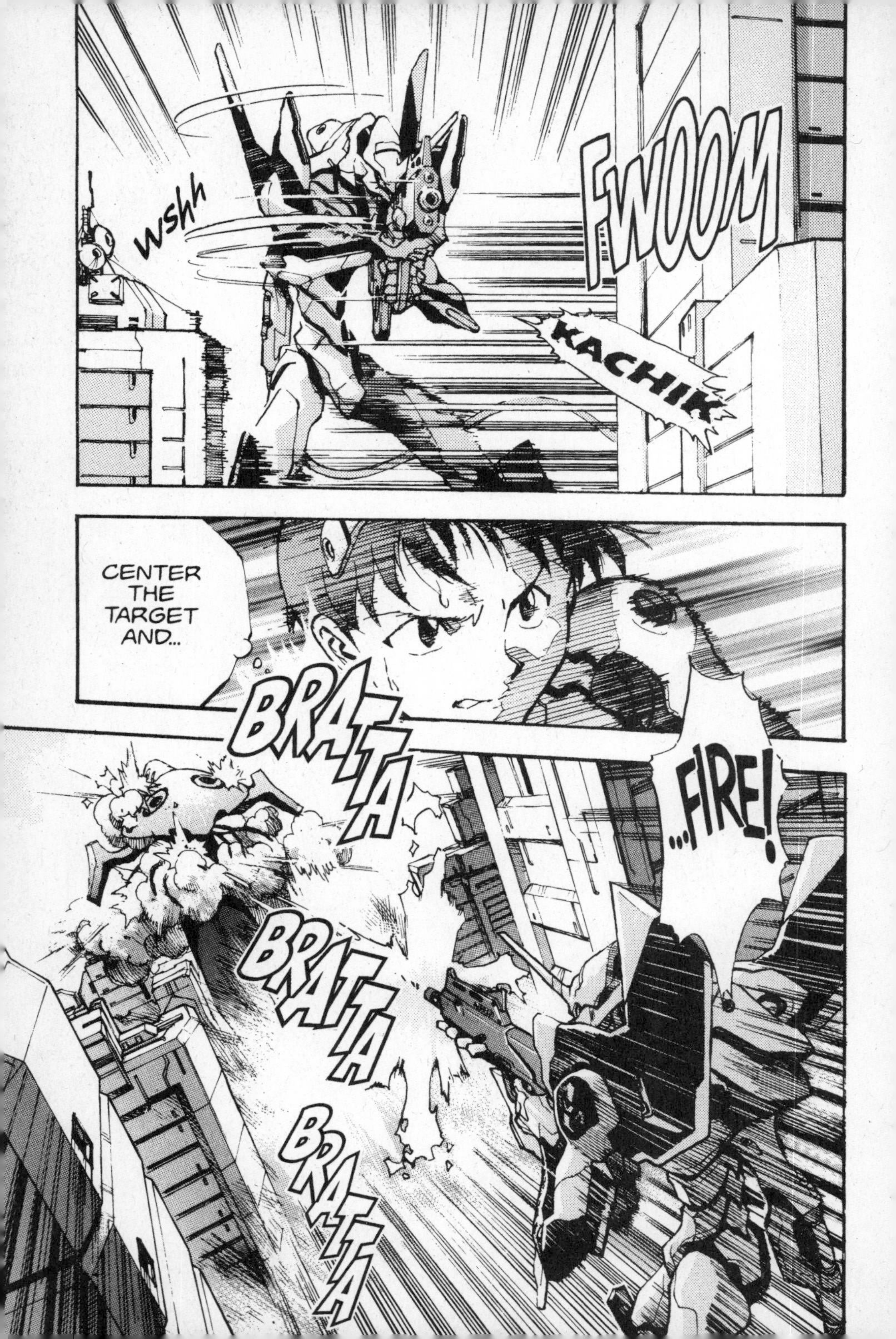
FWOOM
KACHIK
WSHH
CENTER THE TARGET AND...
...FIRE!
BRATTA
BRATTA
BRATTA

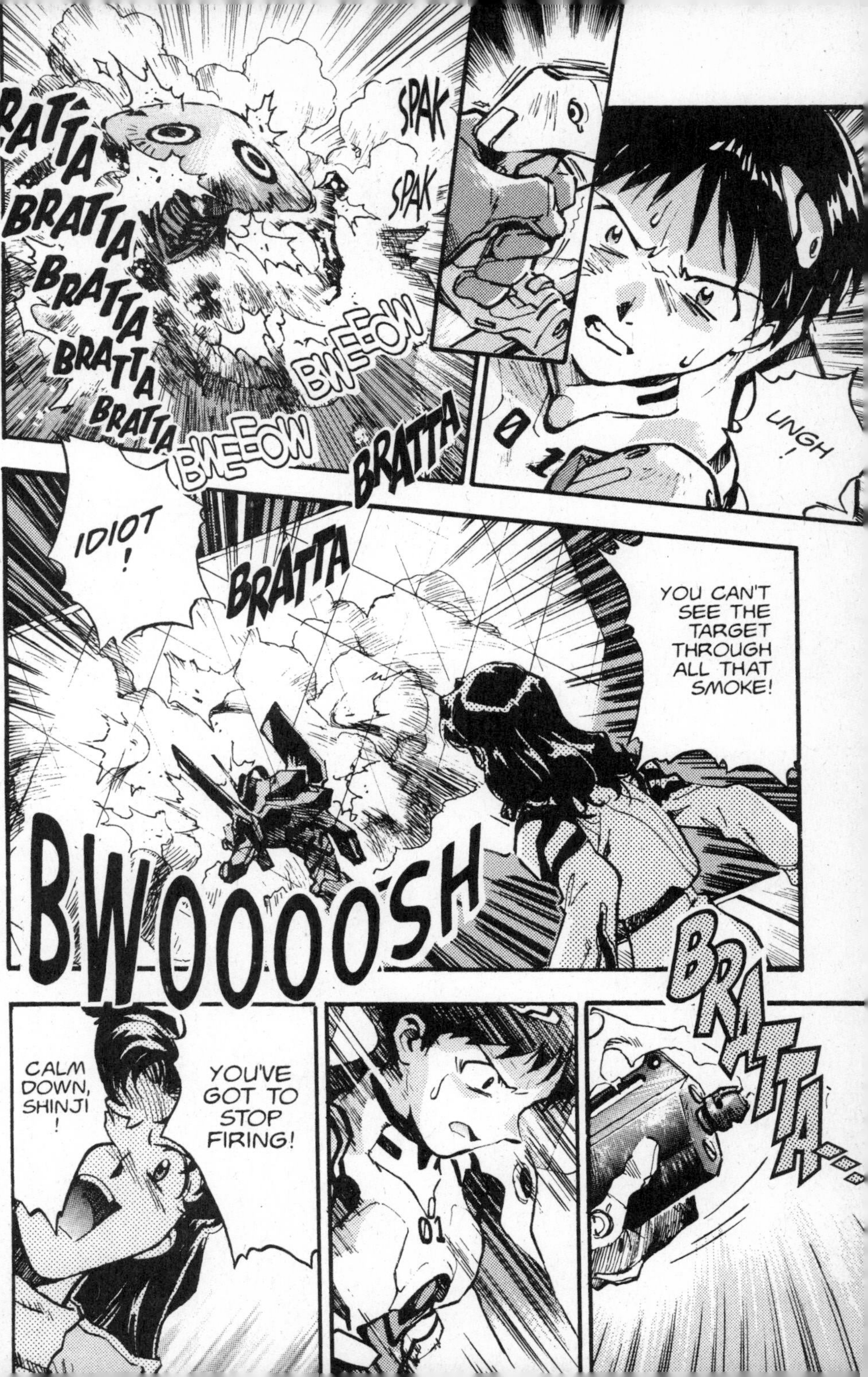
BRATTA BRATTA BRATTA BRATTA BRATTA BRATTA
SPAK SPAK
BWEEOW
BWEEOW
BRATTA
UNGH!
IDIOT!
BRATTA
YOU CAN'T SEE THE TARGET THROUGH ALL THAT SMOKE!
BWOOOOSH
BRATTA...
CALM DOWN, SHINJI!
YOU'VE GOT TO STOP FIRING!

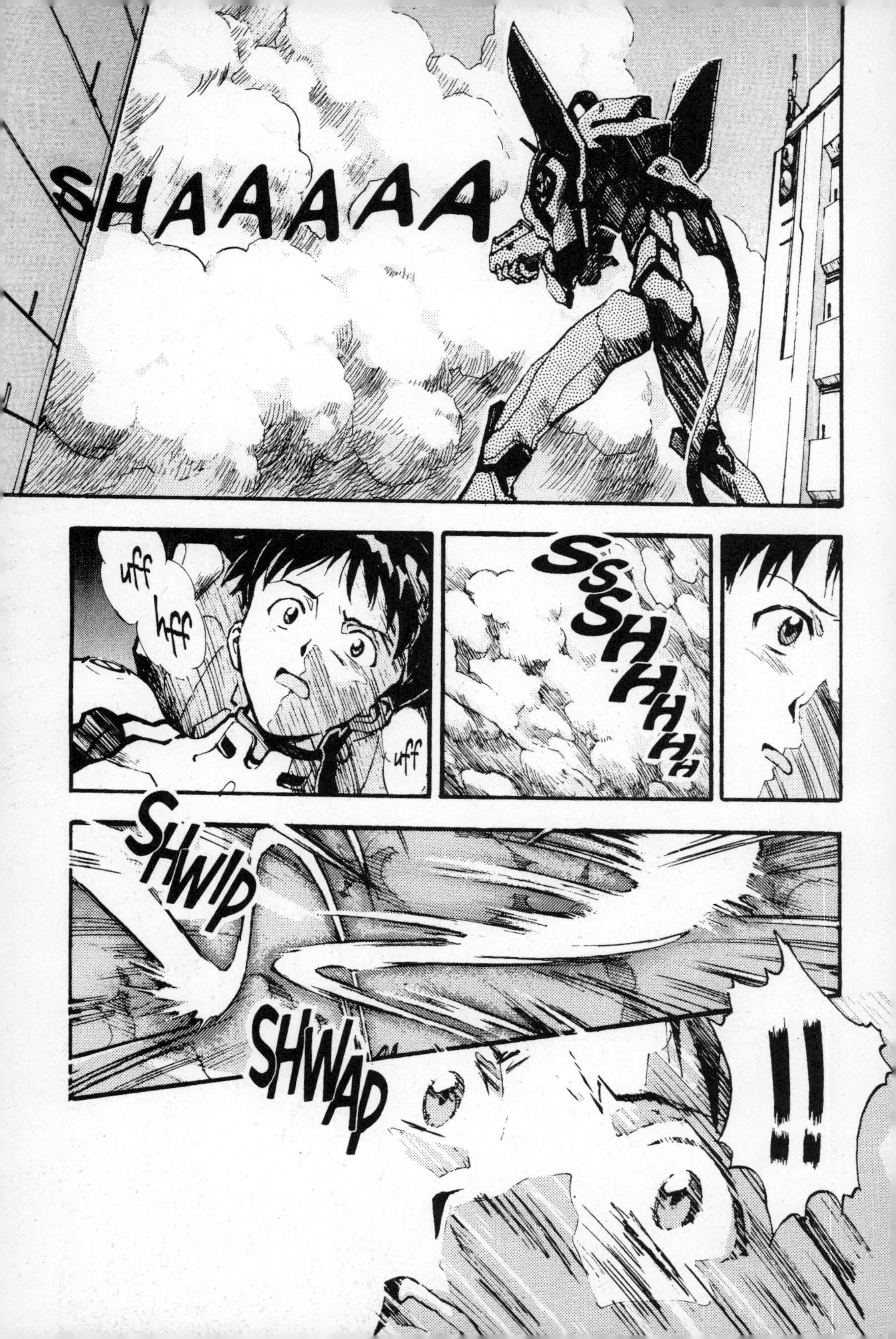
SHAAAAAA
uff
hff
uff
SSSHHHHH
SHWIP
SHWAP
!!

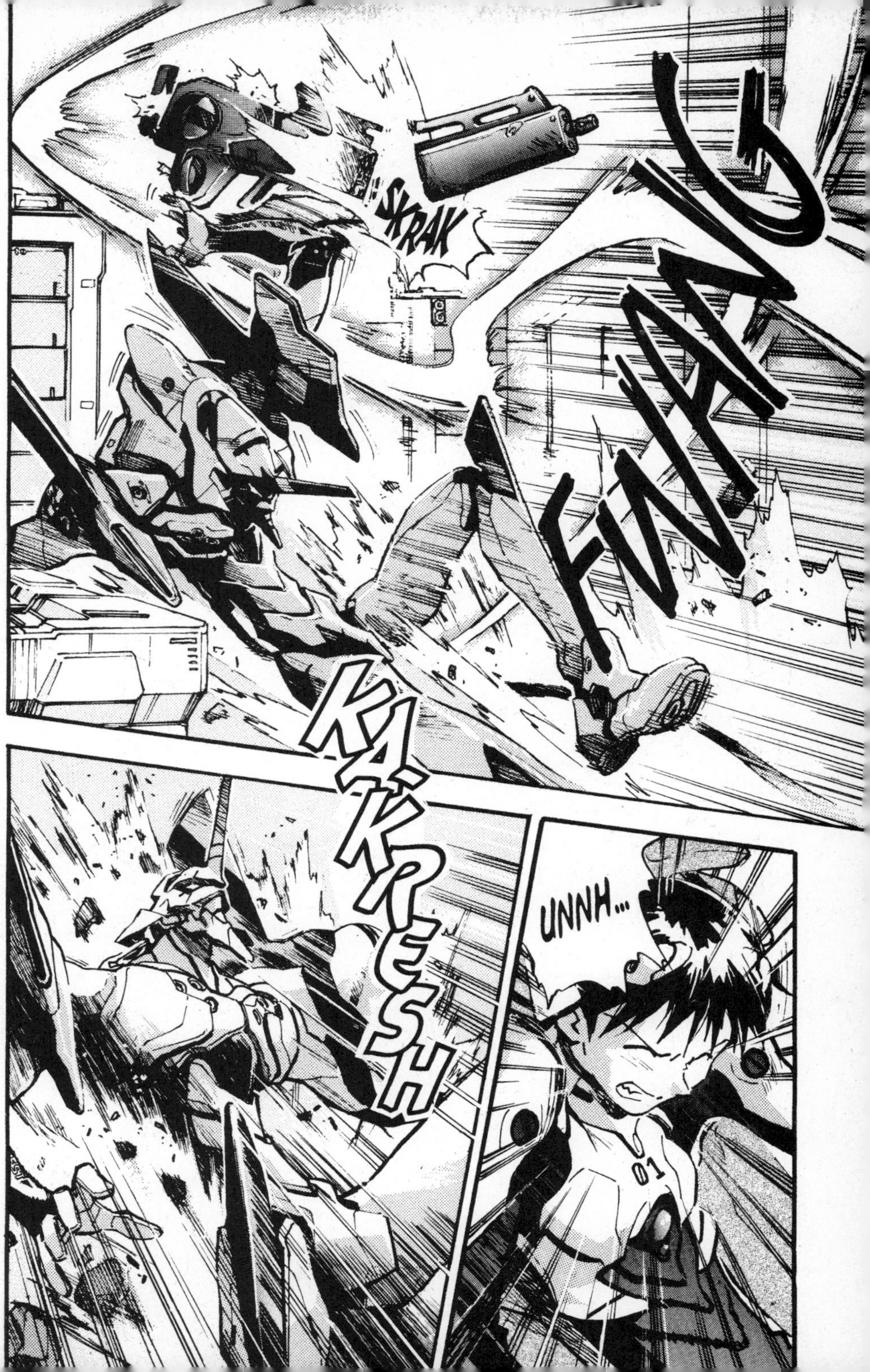
SKRAK
FZZANG
KA-KRESH
UNNH...

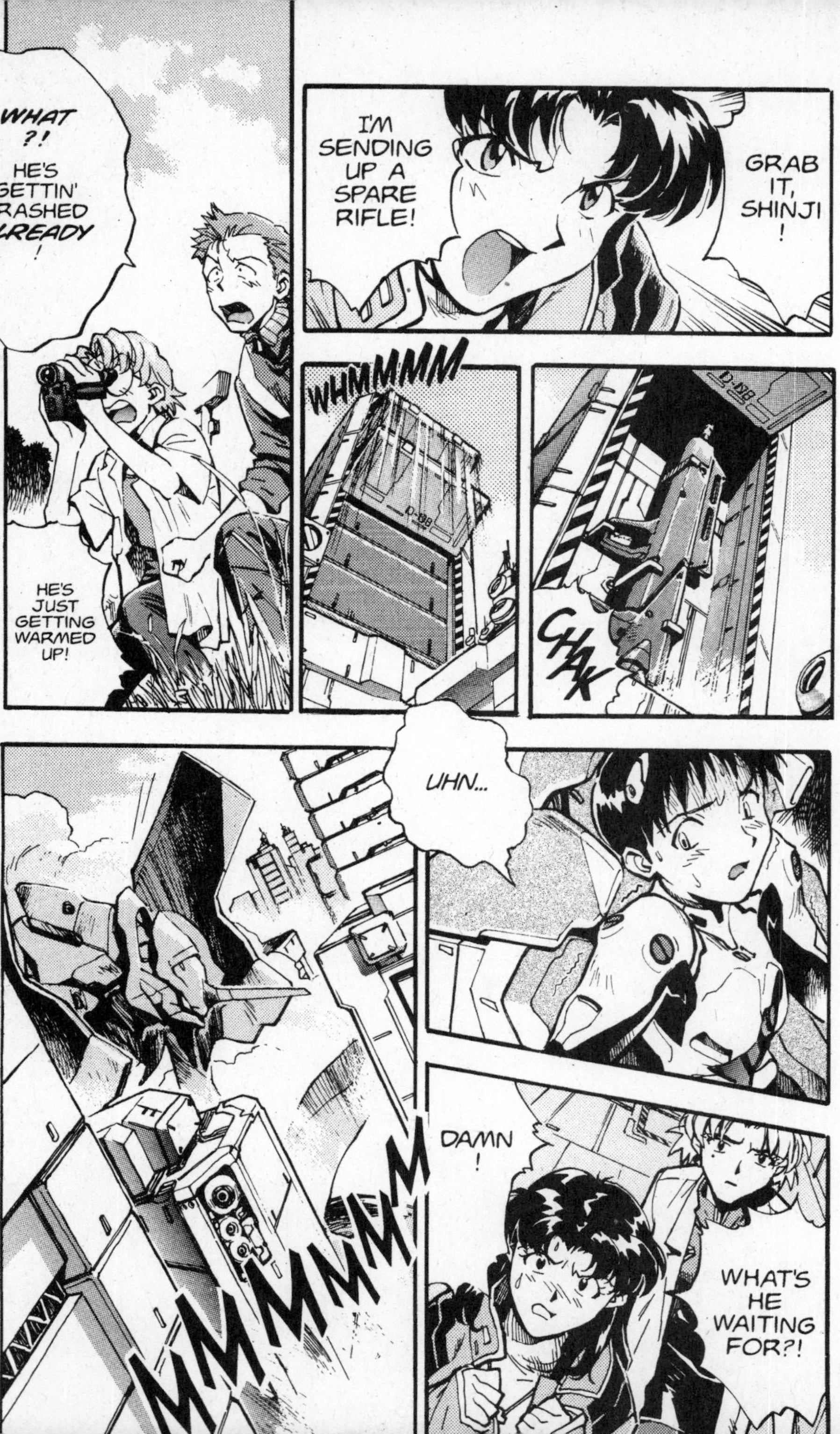
WHAT?! HE'S GETTIN' TRASHED ALREADY!
HE'S JUST GETTING WARMED UP!
I'M SENDING UP A SPARE RIFLE!
GRAB IT, SHINJI!
WHMMMMM
CHAK
MMMMMMMM
UHN...
DAMN!
WHAT'S HE WAITING FOR?!

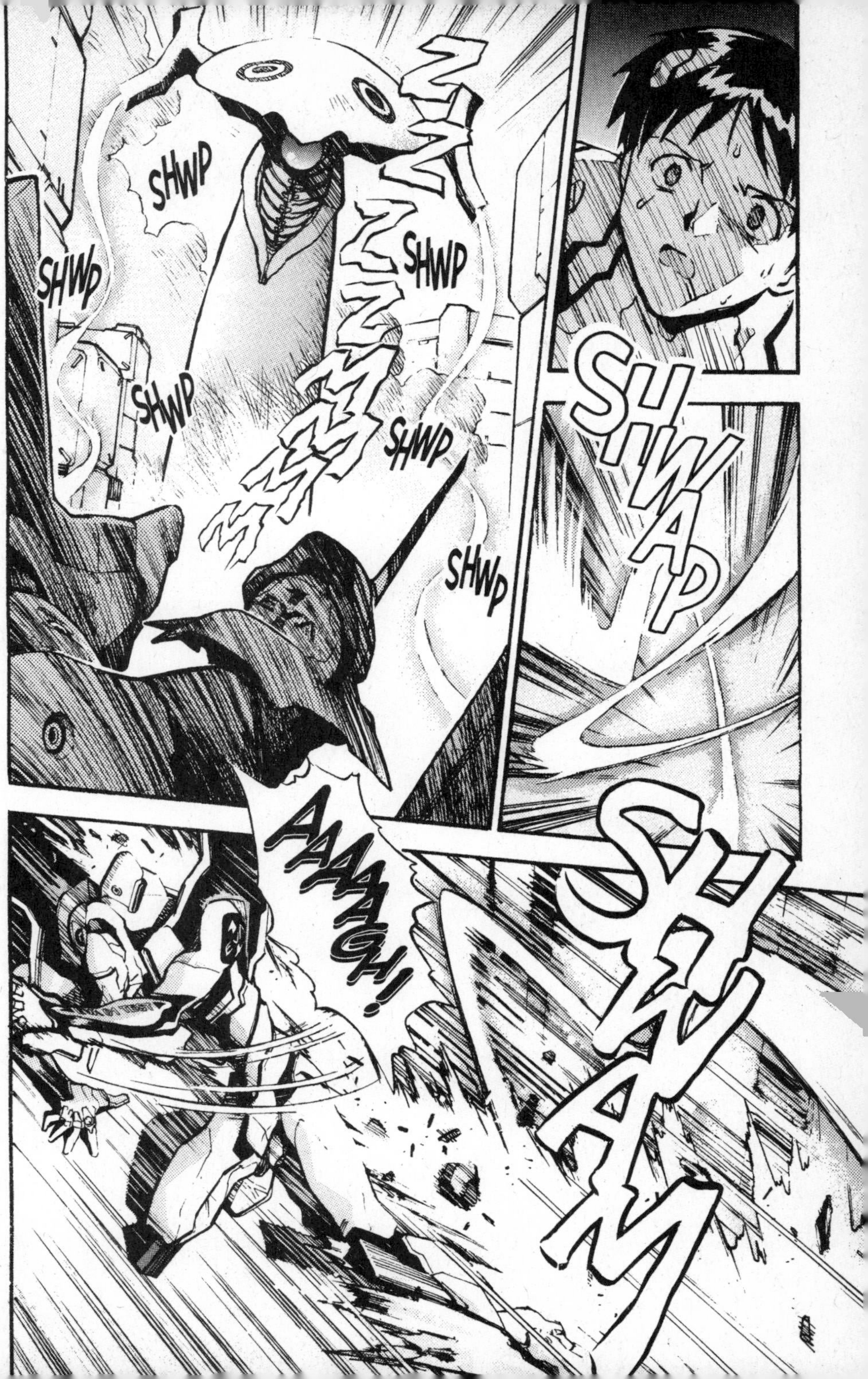
SHWP
SHWP
ZZZZZMMM
SHWP
SHWP
SHWP
SHWP
SHWAP
AAAAAGH!
SHWAM

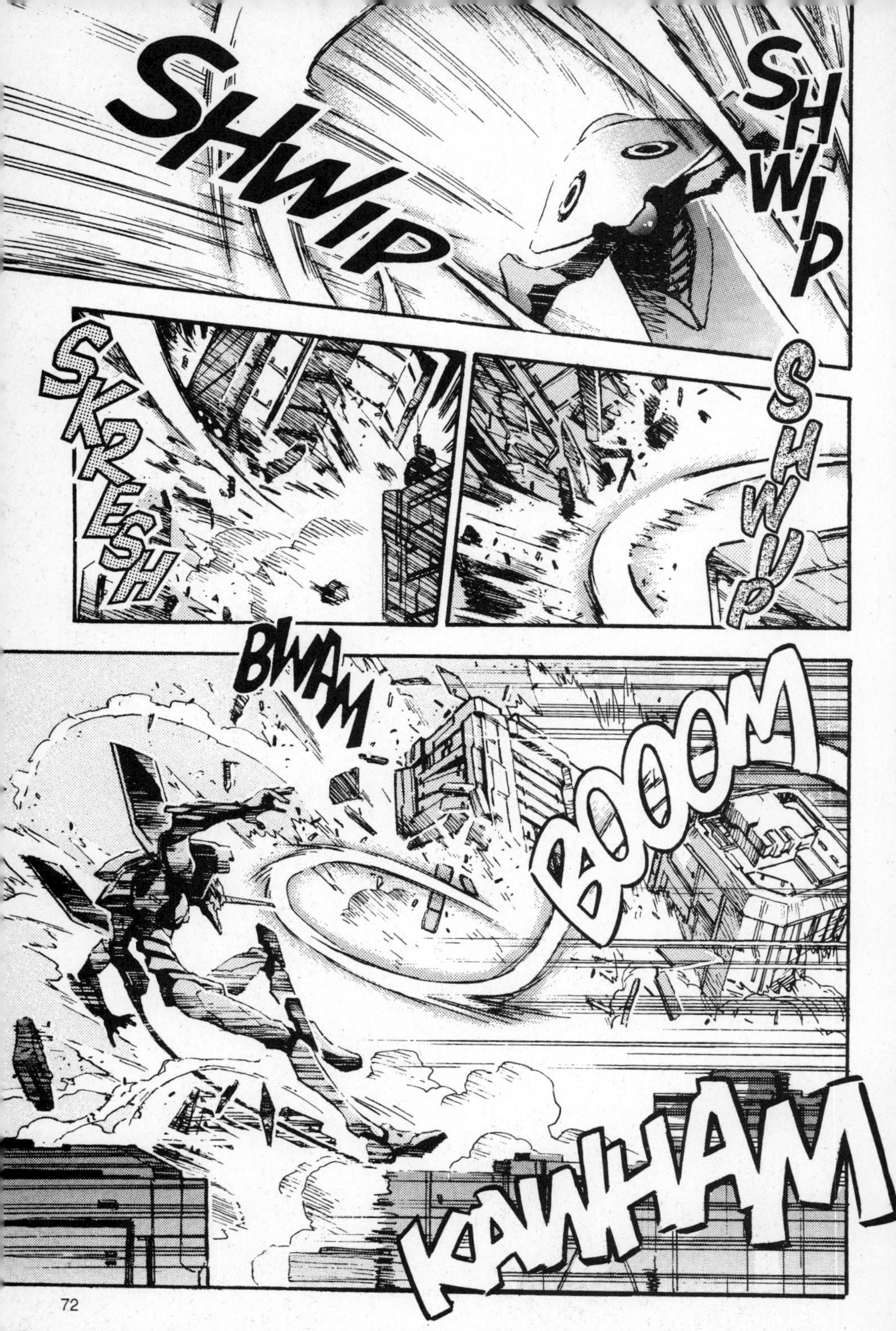
SHWIP
SHWIP
SKRESH
SHWUP
BWAM
BOOOM
KAWHAM

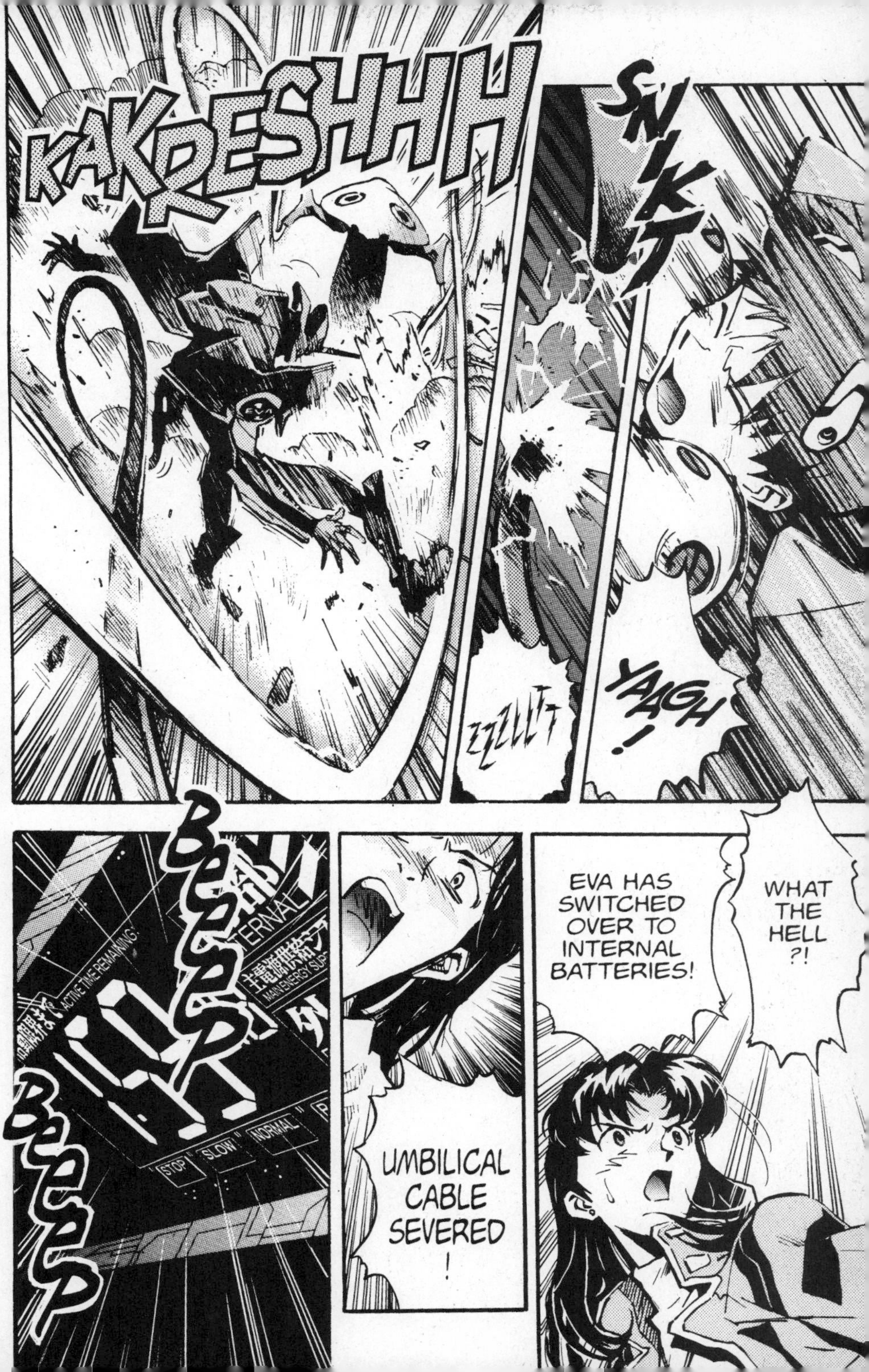
KAKRESHHH
ZZZLLTT
SNIKT
YAAGH!
Beeep
Beeep
ACTIVE TIME REMAINING:
MAIN ENERGY SUP
STOP
SLOW
NORMAL
UMBILICAL CABLE SEVERED!
EVA HAS SWITCHED OVER TO INTERNAL BATTERIES!
WHAT THE HELL?!

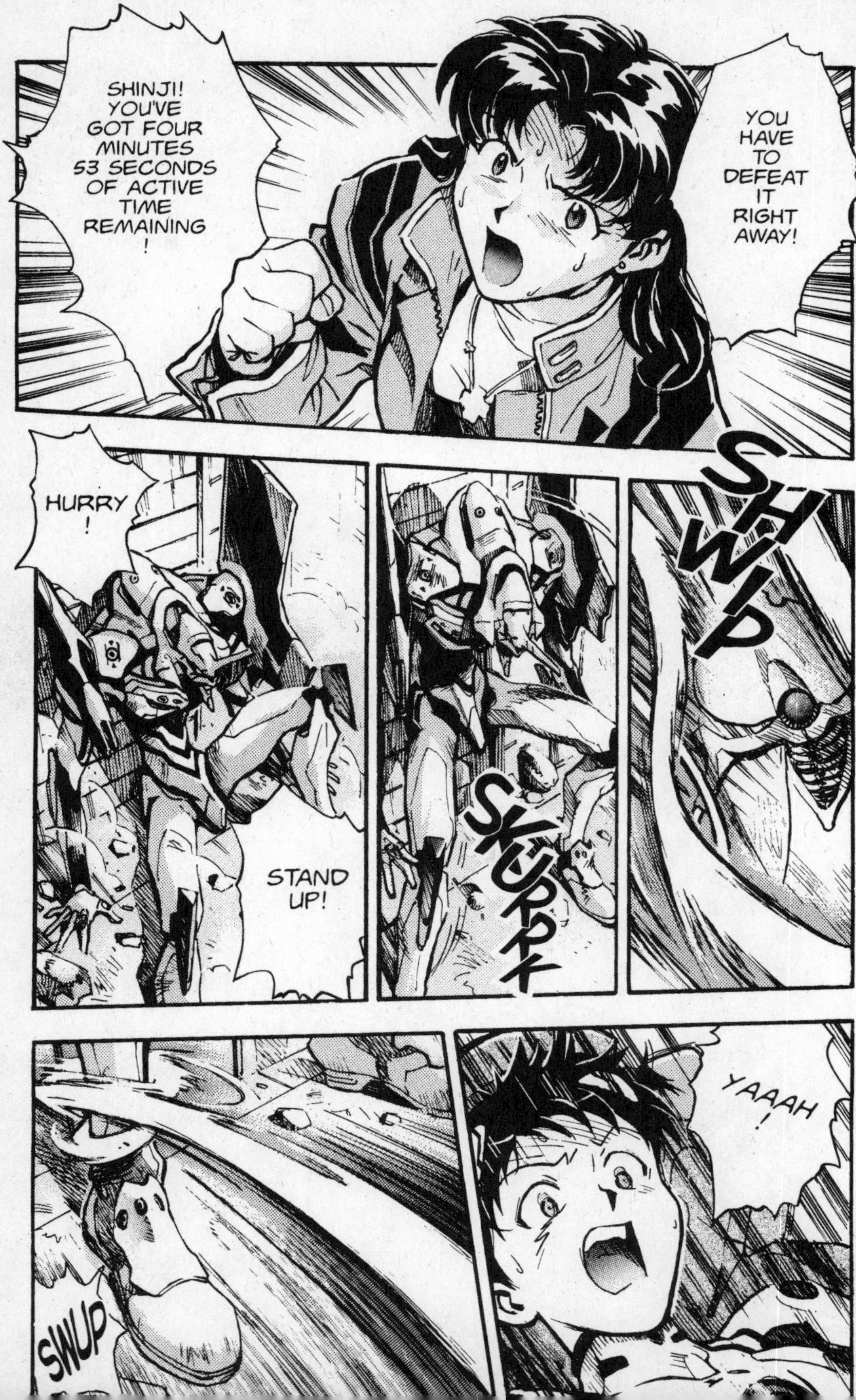
SHINJI! YOU'VE GOT FOUR MINUTES 53 SECONDS OF ACTIVE TIME REMAINING!
YOU HAVE TO DEFEAT IT RIGHT AWAY!
HURRY!
STAND UP!
SKURRK
SHWIP
SWUP
YAAAH!

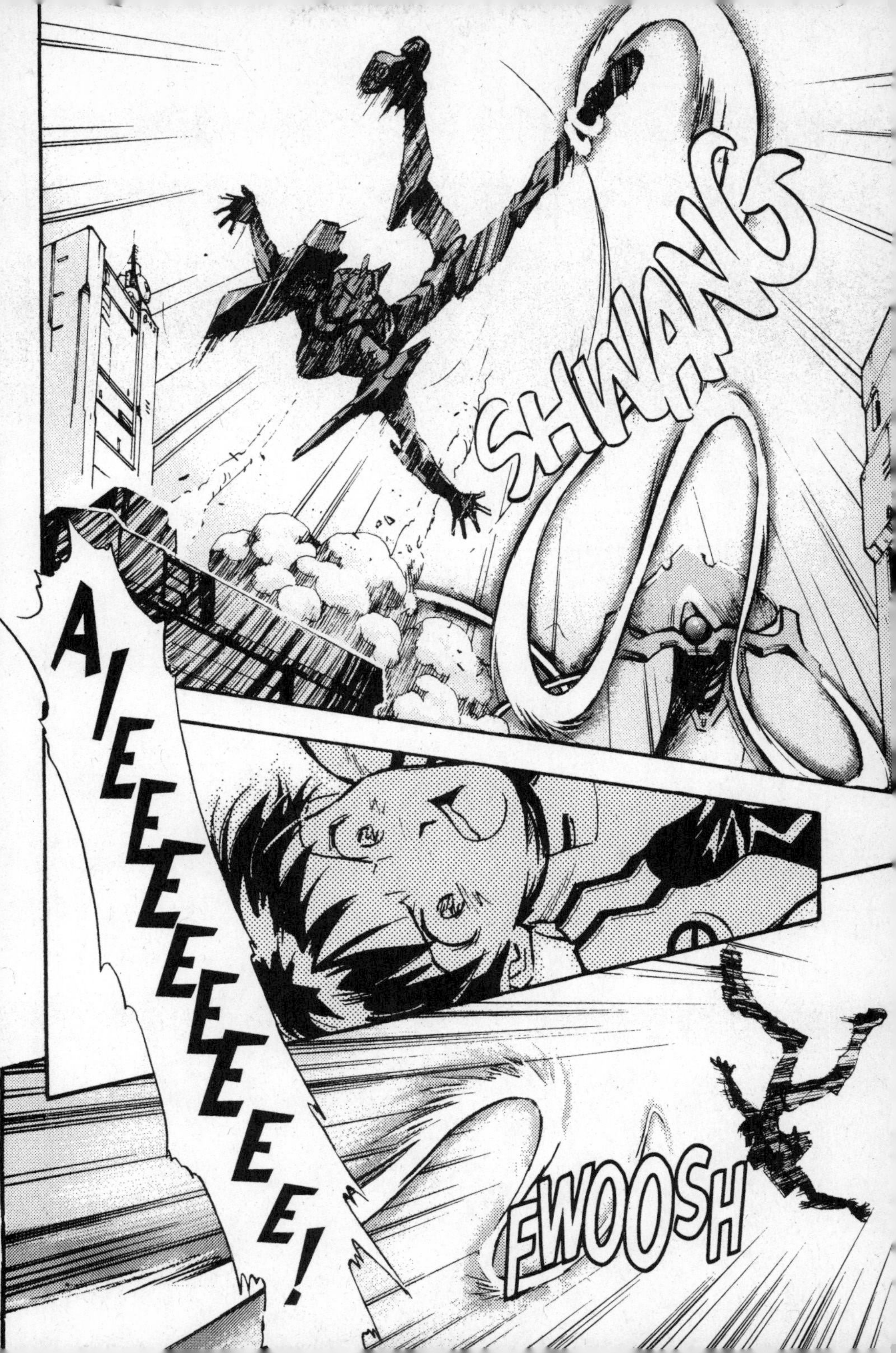
SHWANG
AIEEEEEEEEE!
FWOOSH

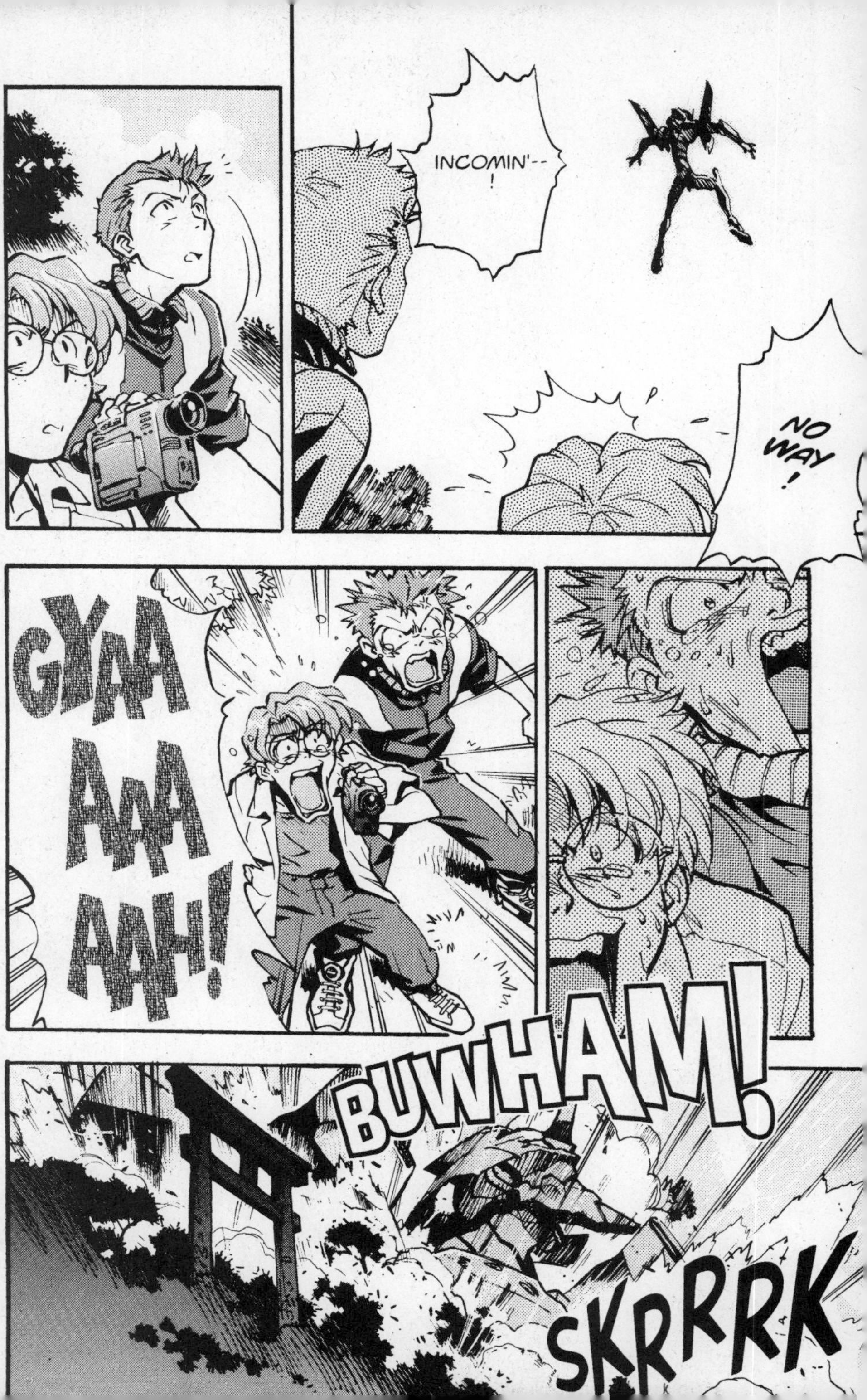
INCOMIN'-- !
NO WAY !
GYAAAAAAAAH!
BUWHAM!
SKRRRK

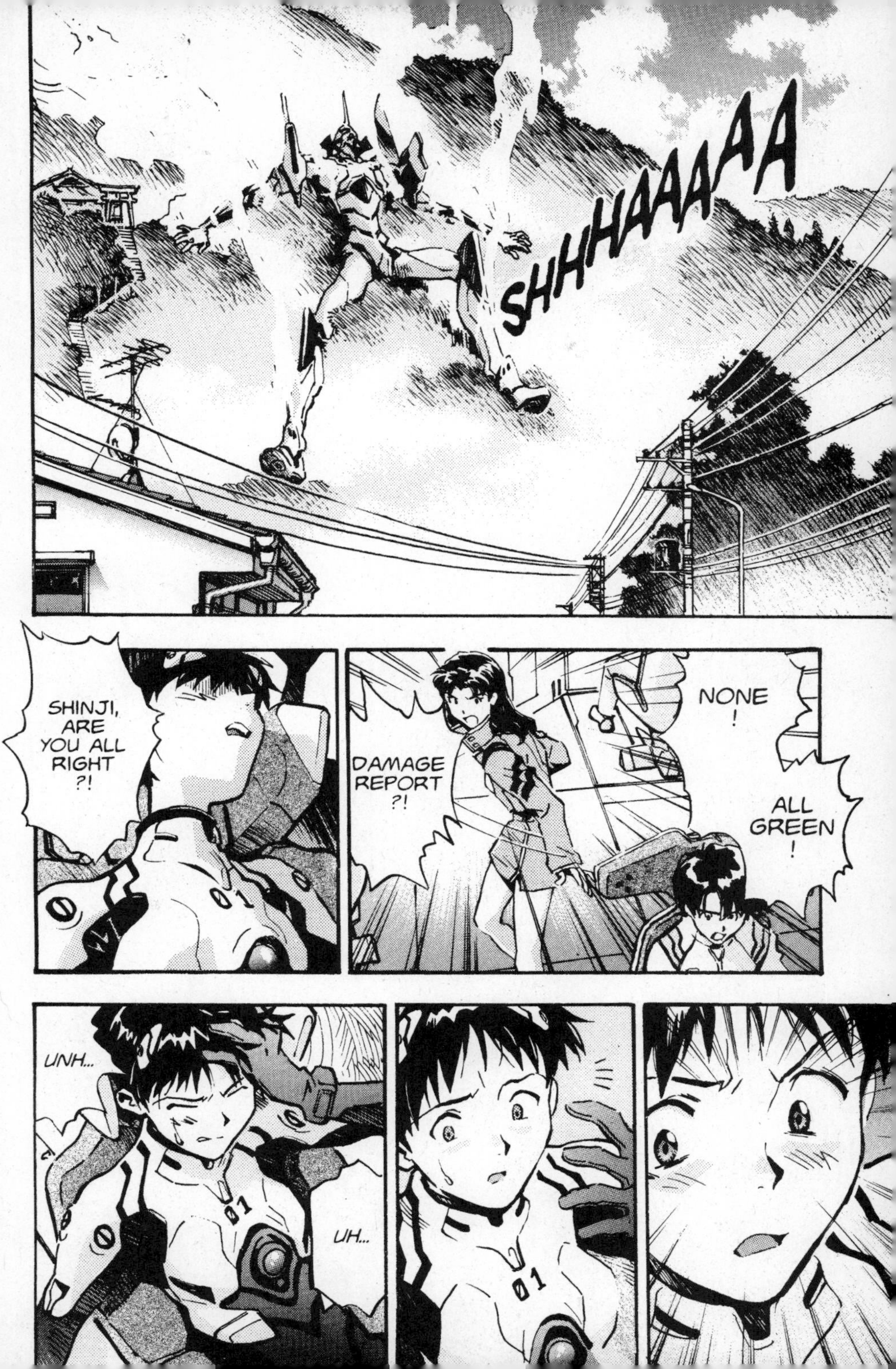
SHHHAAAAAA
SHINJI, ARE YOU ALL RIGHT ?!
DAMAGE REPORT ?!
NONE !
ALL GREEN !
UNH...
UH...

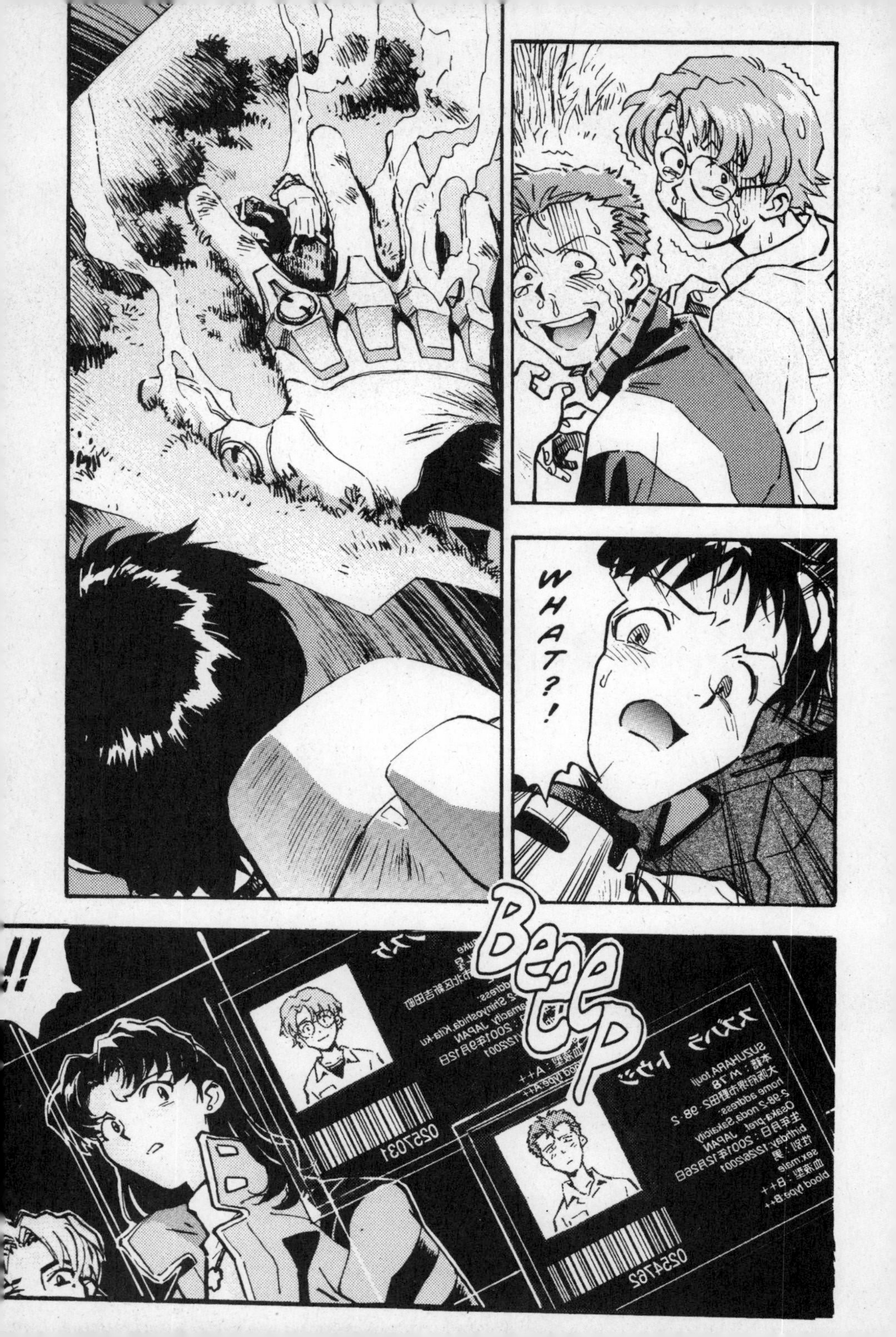
WHAT?!
Beeep
!!

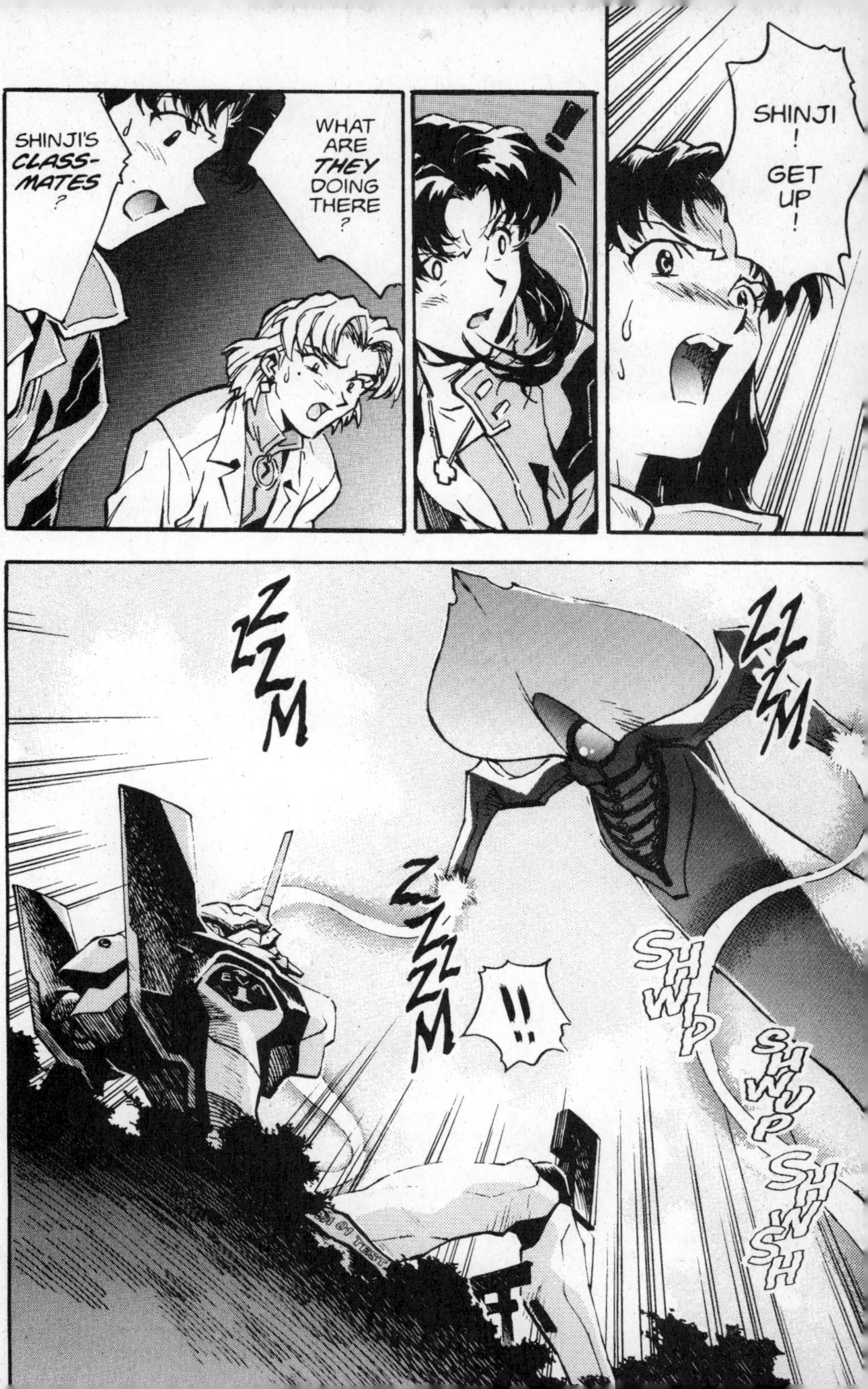
SHINJI'S *CLASS-MATES* ?
WHAT ARE *THEY* DOING THERE ?
!
SHINJI ! GET UP !
ZZZM
ZZZM
ZZZZM
!!
SHWIP
SHWUP
SHWSH

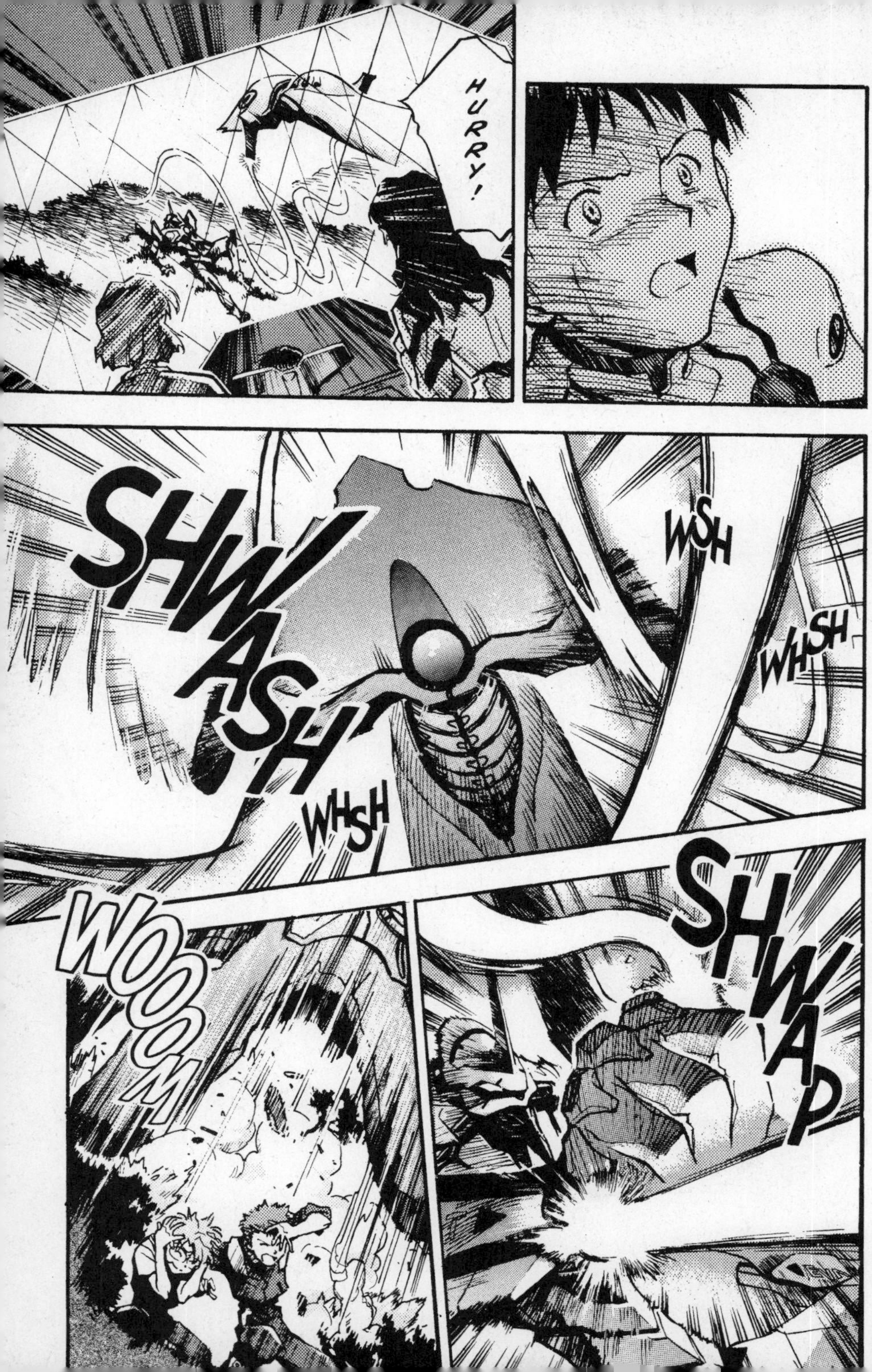
HURRY!
SHWASH
WSH
WHSH
WHSH
WOOOOM
SHWAP

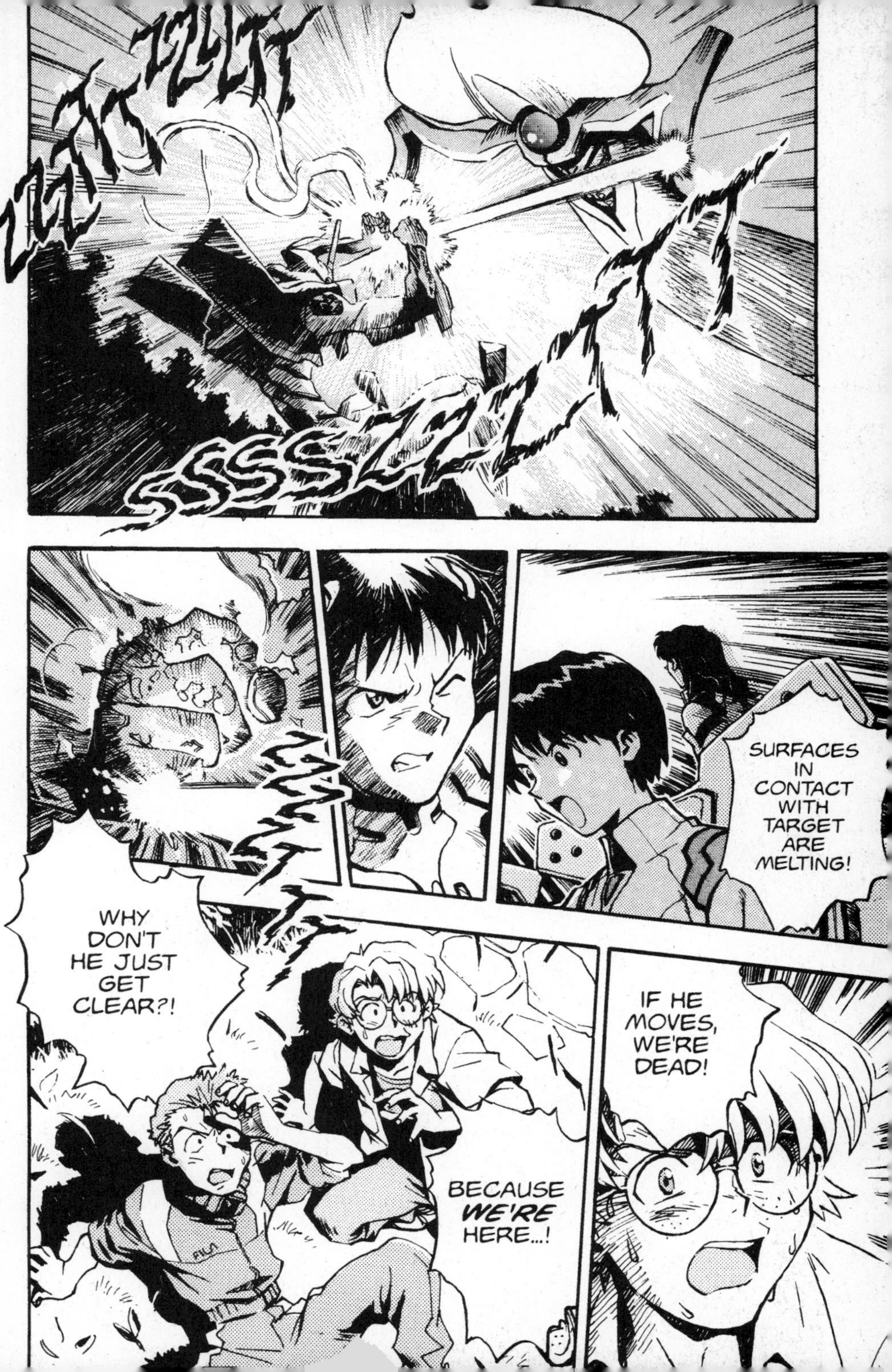
SURFACES IN CONTACT WITH TARGET ARE MELTING!
WHY DON'T HE JUST GET CLEAR?!
BECAUSE *WE'RE* HERE...!
IF HE MOVES, WE'RE DEAD!

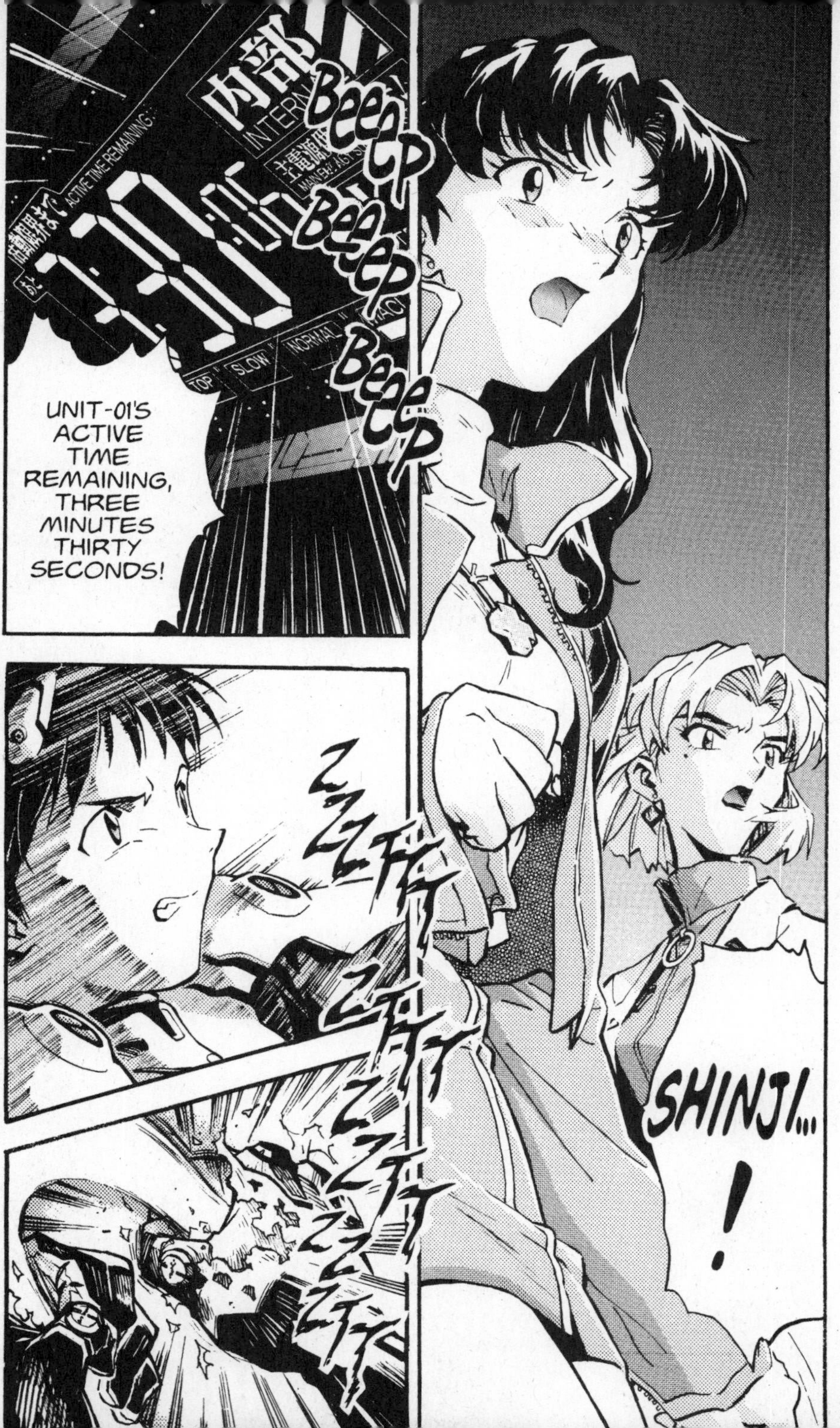

内部
INTERNAL
ACTIVE TIME REMAINING
TOP
SLOW
NORMAL
UNIT-01'S ACTIVE TIME REMAINING, THREE MINUTES THIRTY SECONDS!
Beeep
Beeep
Beeep
SHINJI...
!

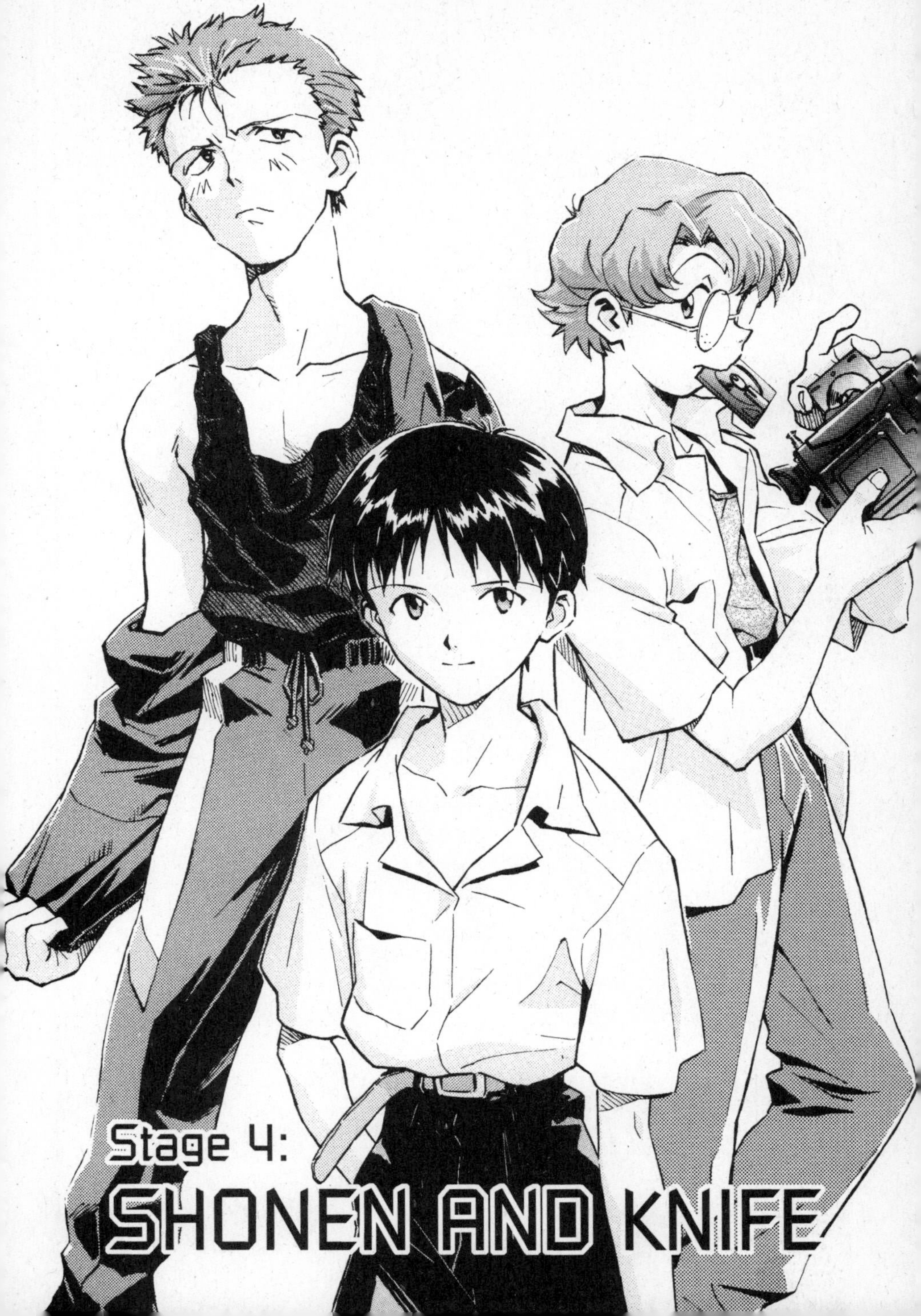
Stage 4:
SHONEN AND KNIFE

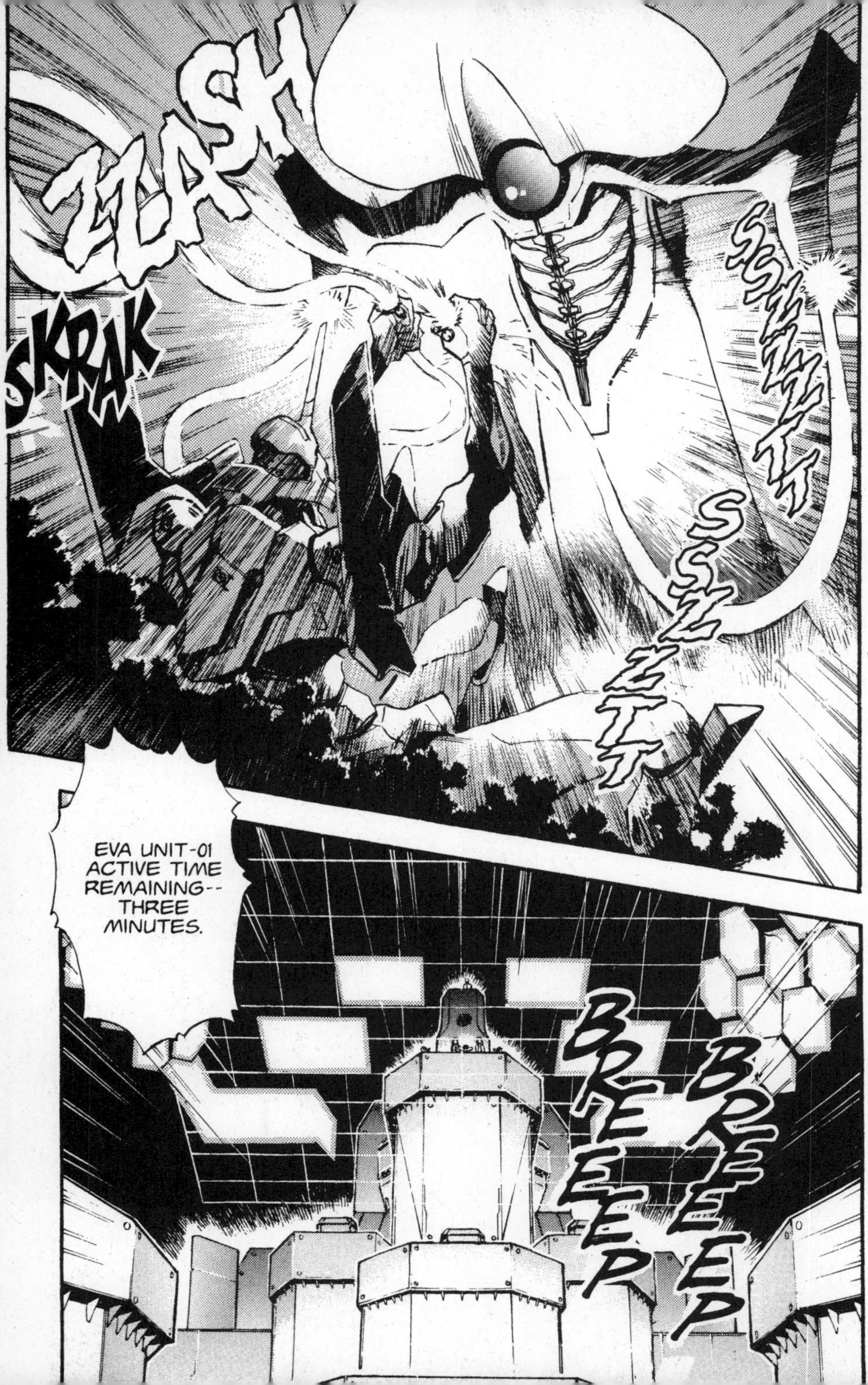
ZZASH
SKRAK
SSHNKK
SSZZTT
EVA UNIT-01 ACTIVE TIME REMAINING-- THREE MINUTES.
BREEEP
BREEEP

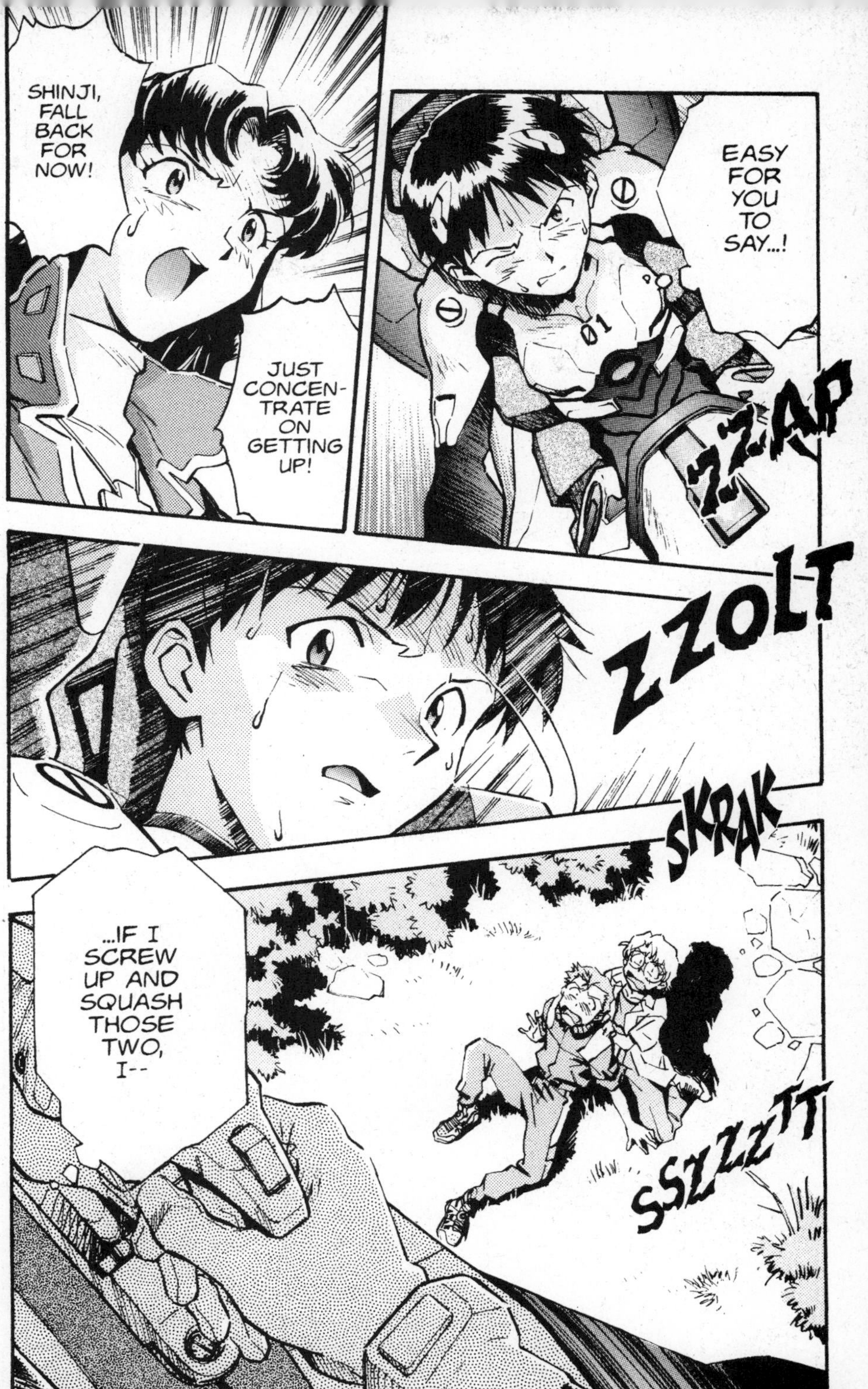
SHINJI, FALL BACK FOR NOW!
JUST CONCENTRATE ON GETTING UP!
EASY FOR YOU TO SAY...!
ZZAP
ZZOLT
SKRAK
...IF I SCREW UP AND SQUASH THOSE TWO, I--
SSZZZTT

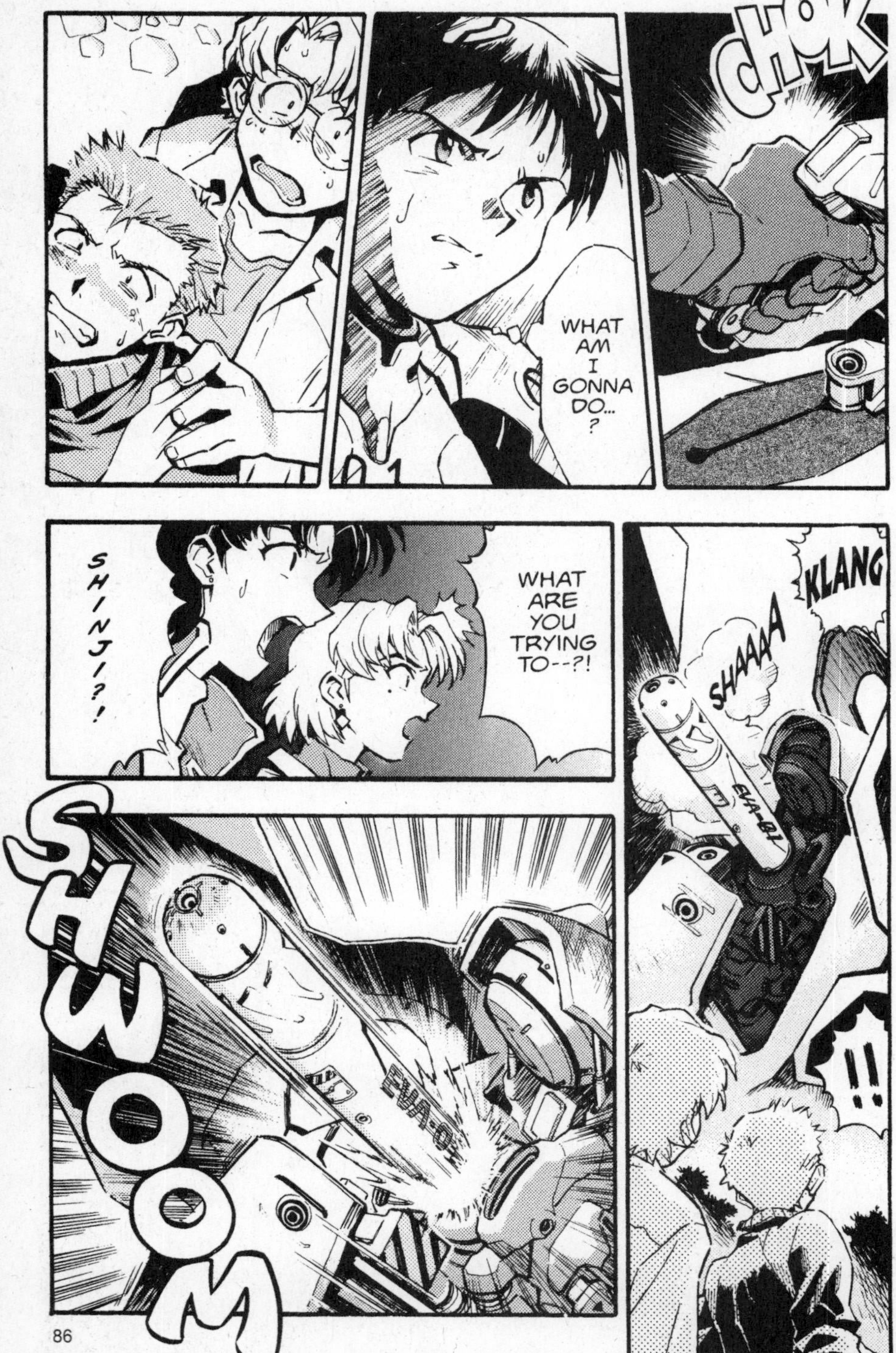
WHAT AM I GONNA DO...?
CHOK
SHINJI?!
WHAT ARE YOU TRYING TO--?!
SHWOOM
KLANG
SHAAAA
!!

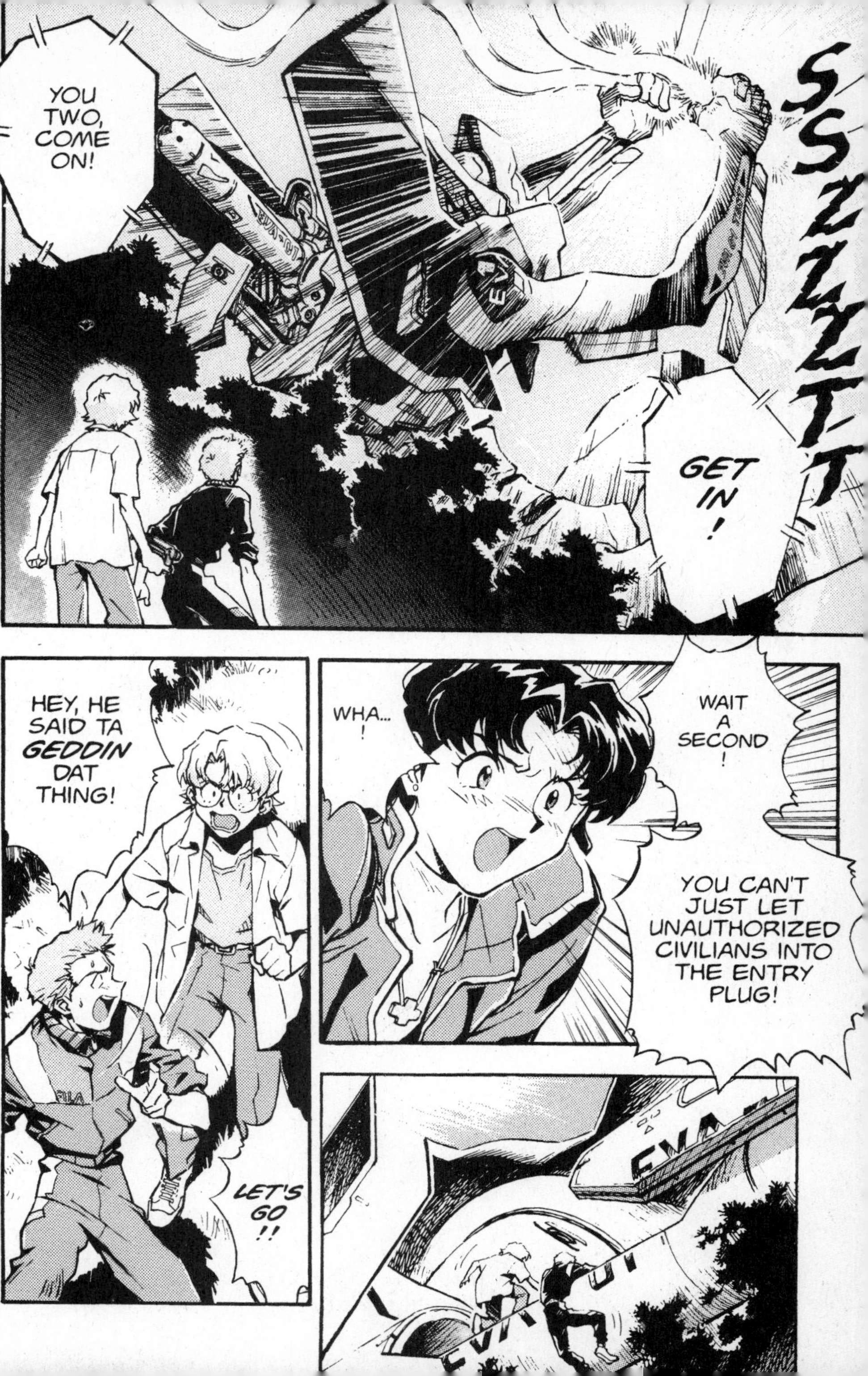
YOU TWO, COME ON!
SSZZZTT
GET IN!
HEY, HE SAID TA *GEDDIN* DAT THING!
LET'S GO!!
WHA...!
WAIT A SECOND!
YOU CAN'T JUST LET UNAUTHORIZED CIVILIANS INTO THE ENTRY PLUG!

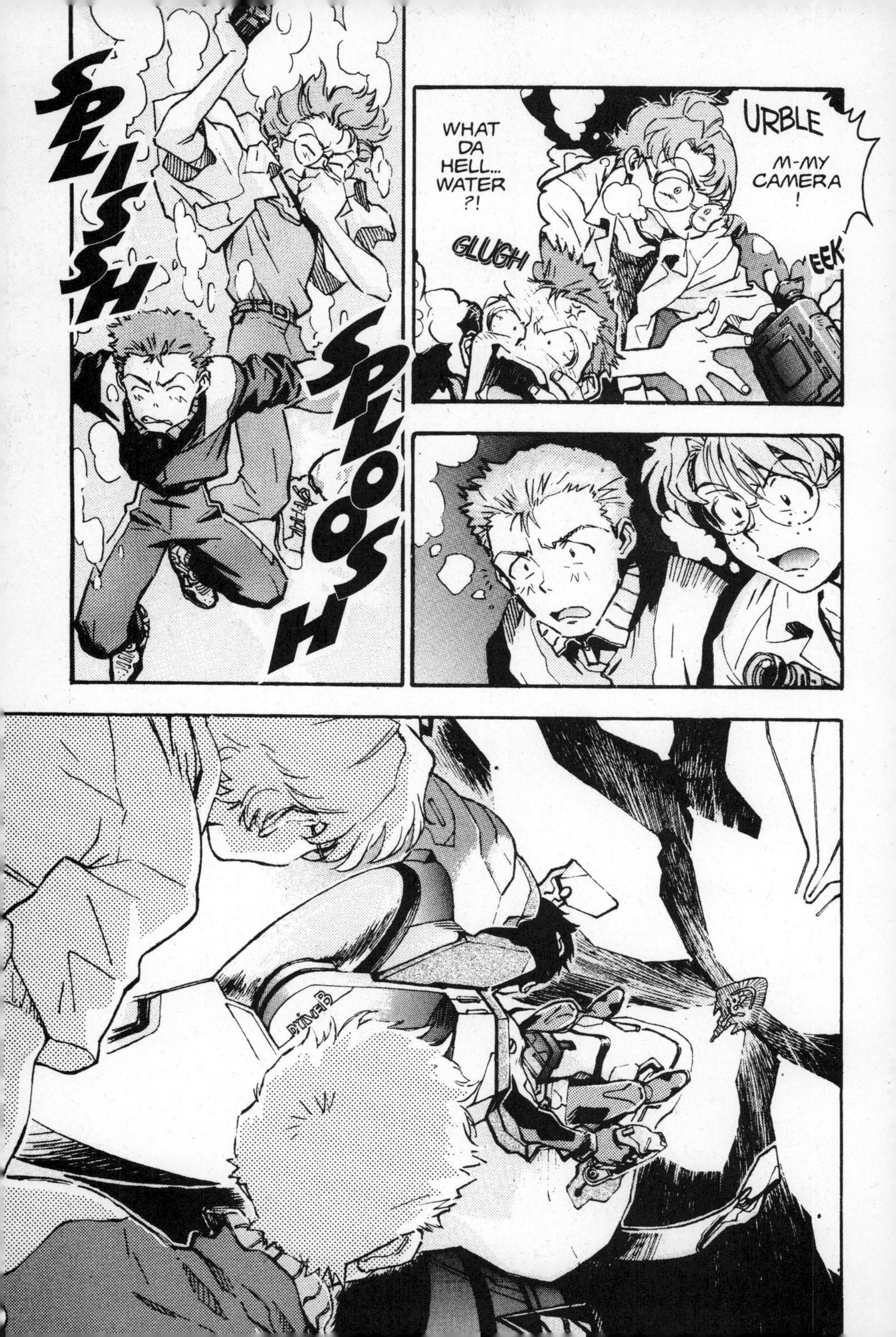

SPLISH
SPLOOSH
WHAT DA HELL... WATER ?!
URBLE
M-MY CAMERA !
GLUGH
EEK

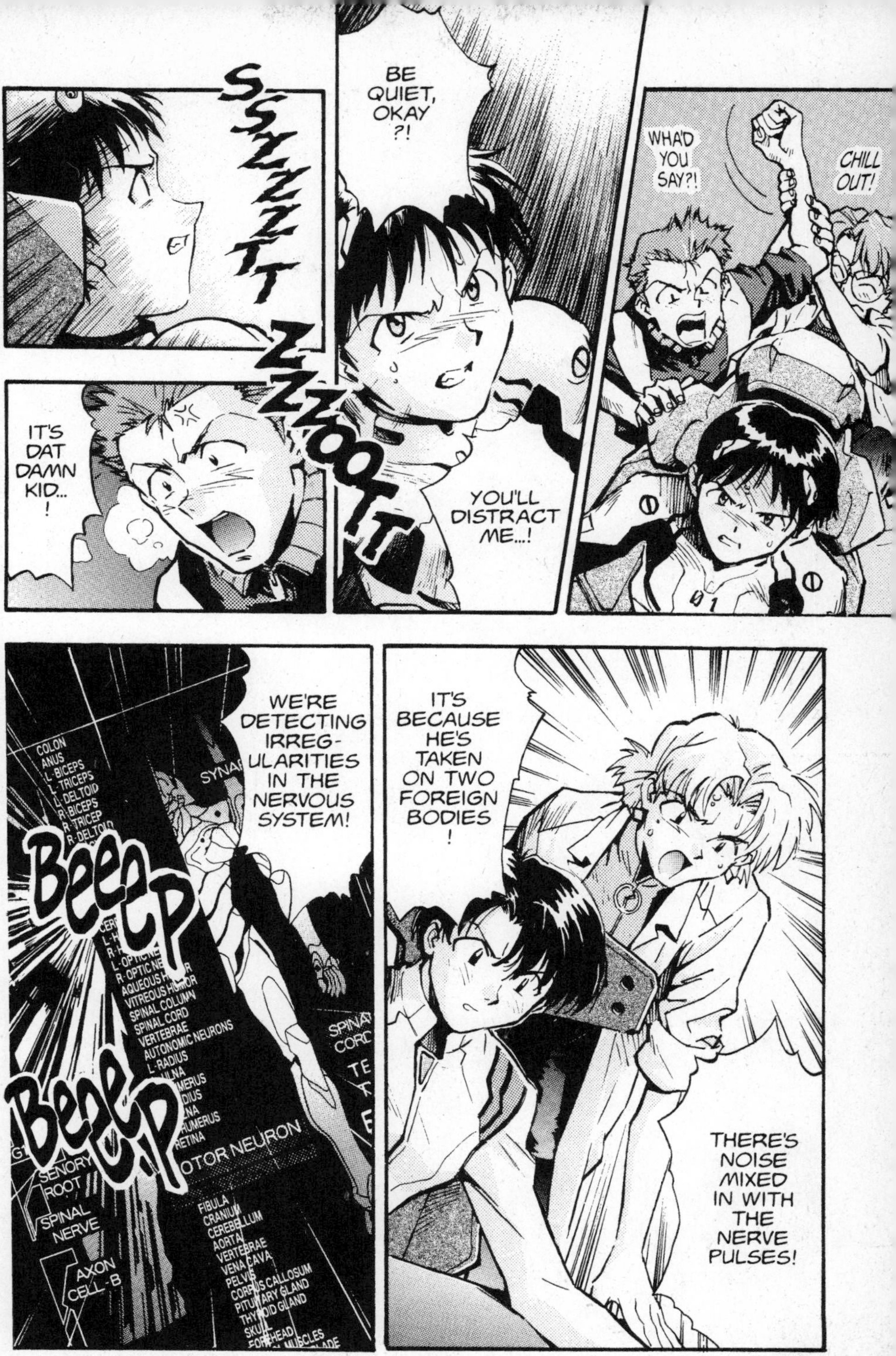
SSZZZZTTT
IT'S DAT DAMN KID...!
BE QUIET, OKAY?!
ZZZOOTT
YOU'LL DISTRACT ME...!
WHA'D YOU SAY?!
CHILL OUT!
COLON
ANUS
L-BICEPS
L-TRICEPS
L-DELTOID
R-BICEPS
R-TRICEP
R-DELTOID
Beeep
AQUEOUS HUMOR
VITREOUS HUMOR
SPINAL COLUMN
SPINAL CORD
VERTEBRAE
AUTONOMIC NEURONS
L-RADIUS
Beeep
SENORY ROOT
SPINAL NERVE
AXON
CELL-B
FIBULA
CRANIUM
CEREBELLUM
AORTA
VERTEBRAE
VENA CAVA
PELVIS
CORPUS CALLOSUM
PITUITARY GLAND
THYROID GLAND
SKULL
FOREHEAD
WE'RE DETECTING IRREG-ULARITIES IN THE NERVOUS SYSTEM!
IT'S BECAUSE HE'S TAKEN ON TWO FOREIGN BODIES!
THERE'S NOISE MIXED IN WITH THE NERVE PULSES!

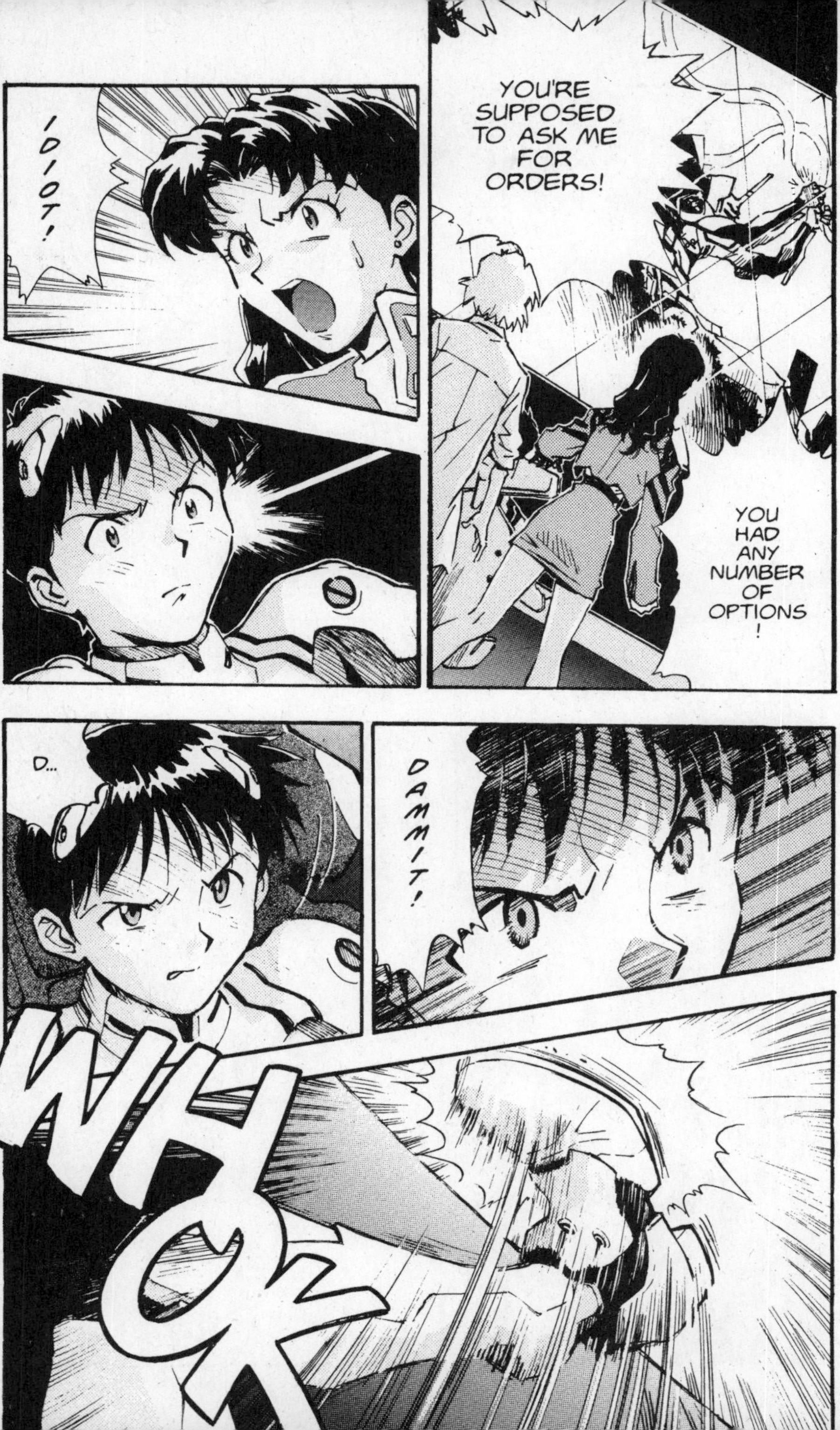
IDIOT!
YOU'RE SUPPOSED TO ASK ME FOR ORDERS!
YOU HAD ANY NUMBER OF OPTIONS!
D...
DAMMIT!
WHOK

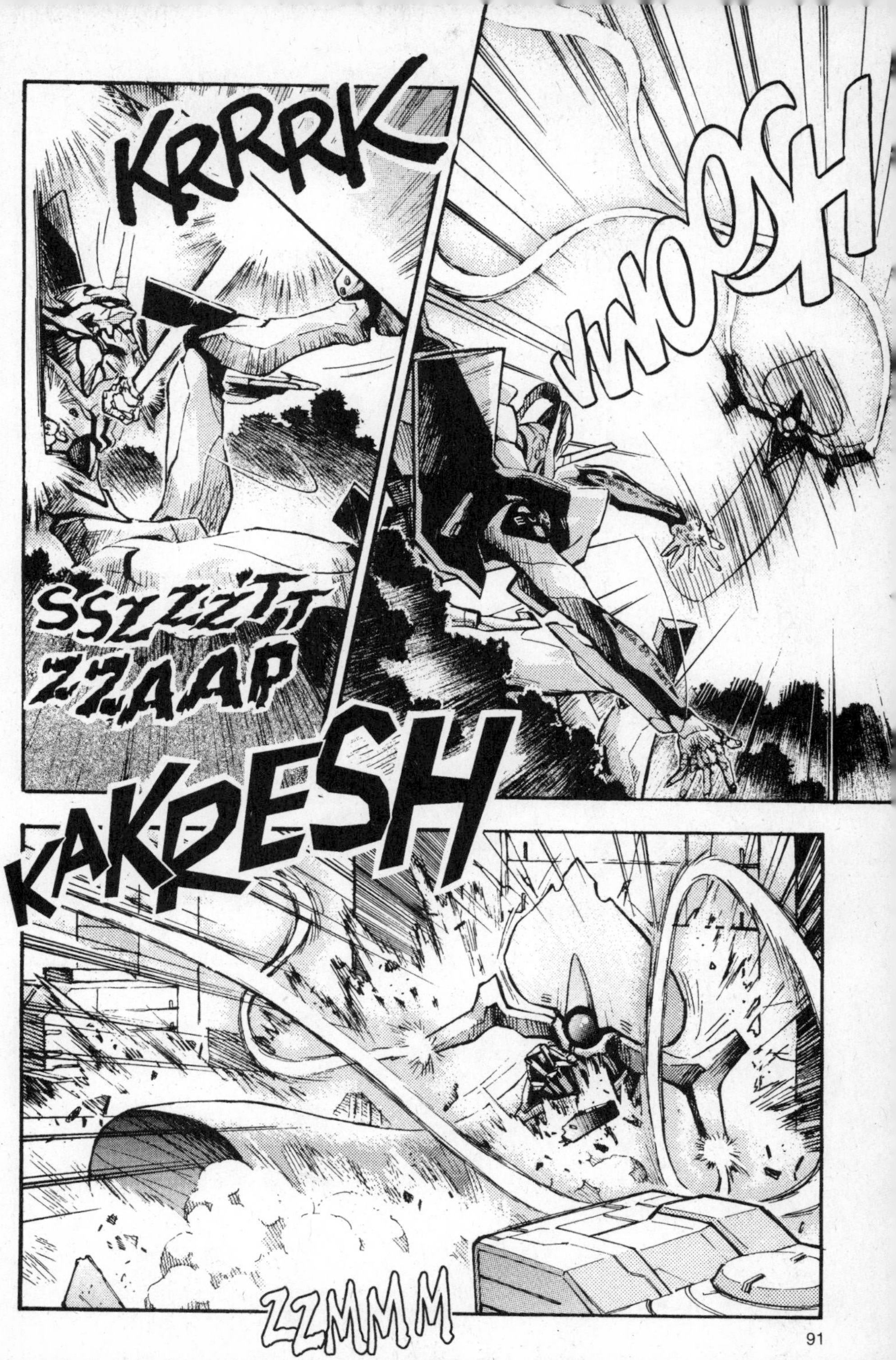
KRRRK
SSZZZTT
ZZAAP
VWOOSH
KAKRESH
ZZMMM

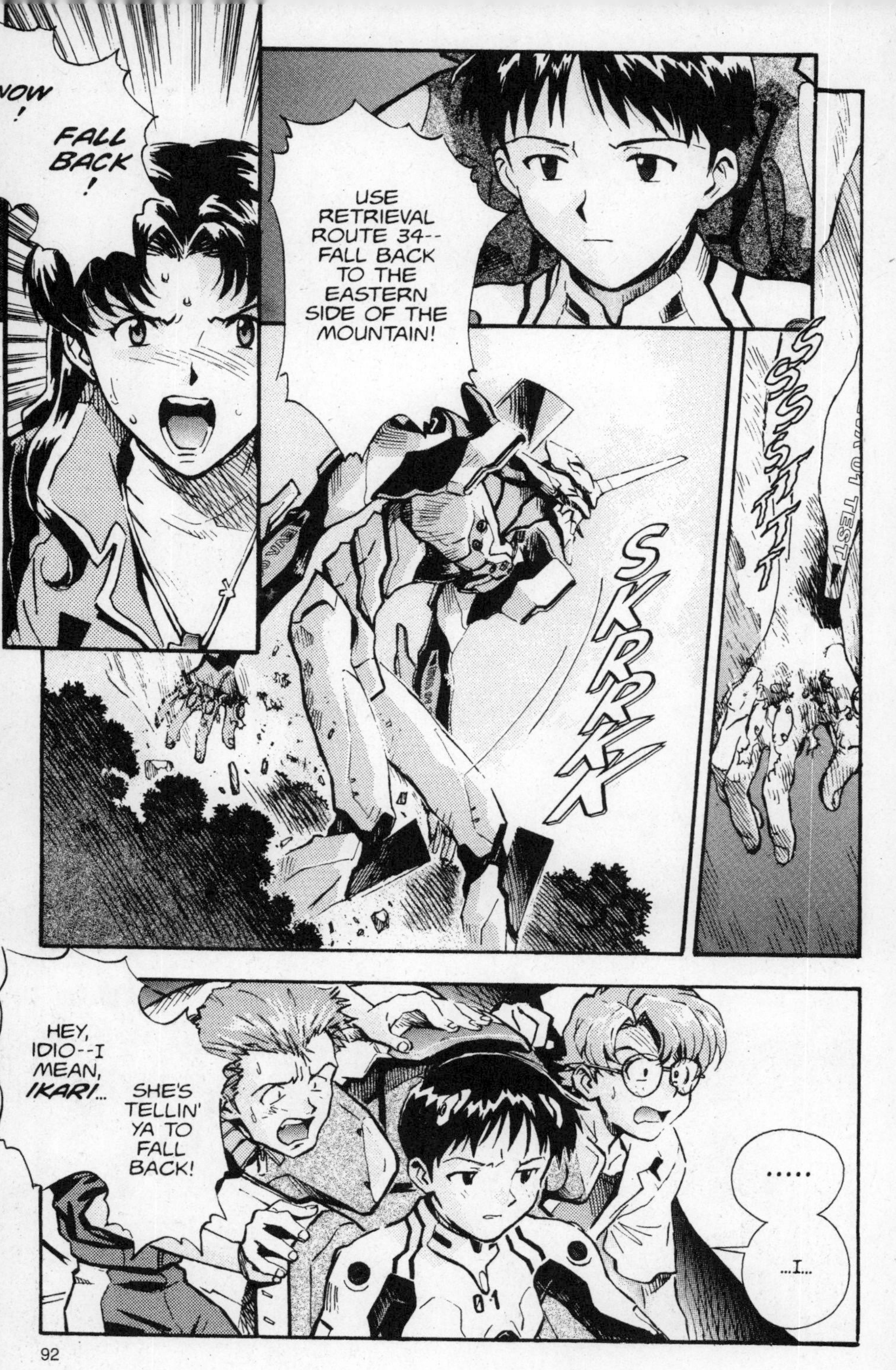
NOW! FALL BACK!
USE RETRIEVAL ROUTE 34--FALL BACK TO THE EASTERN SIDE OF THE MOUNTAIN!
SKRRRK
SSSSHTTT
01 TEST
HEY, IDIO--I MEAN, IKARI...
SHE'S TELLIN' YA TO FALL BACK!
.....
...I...

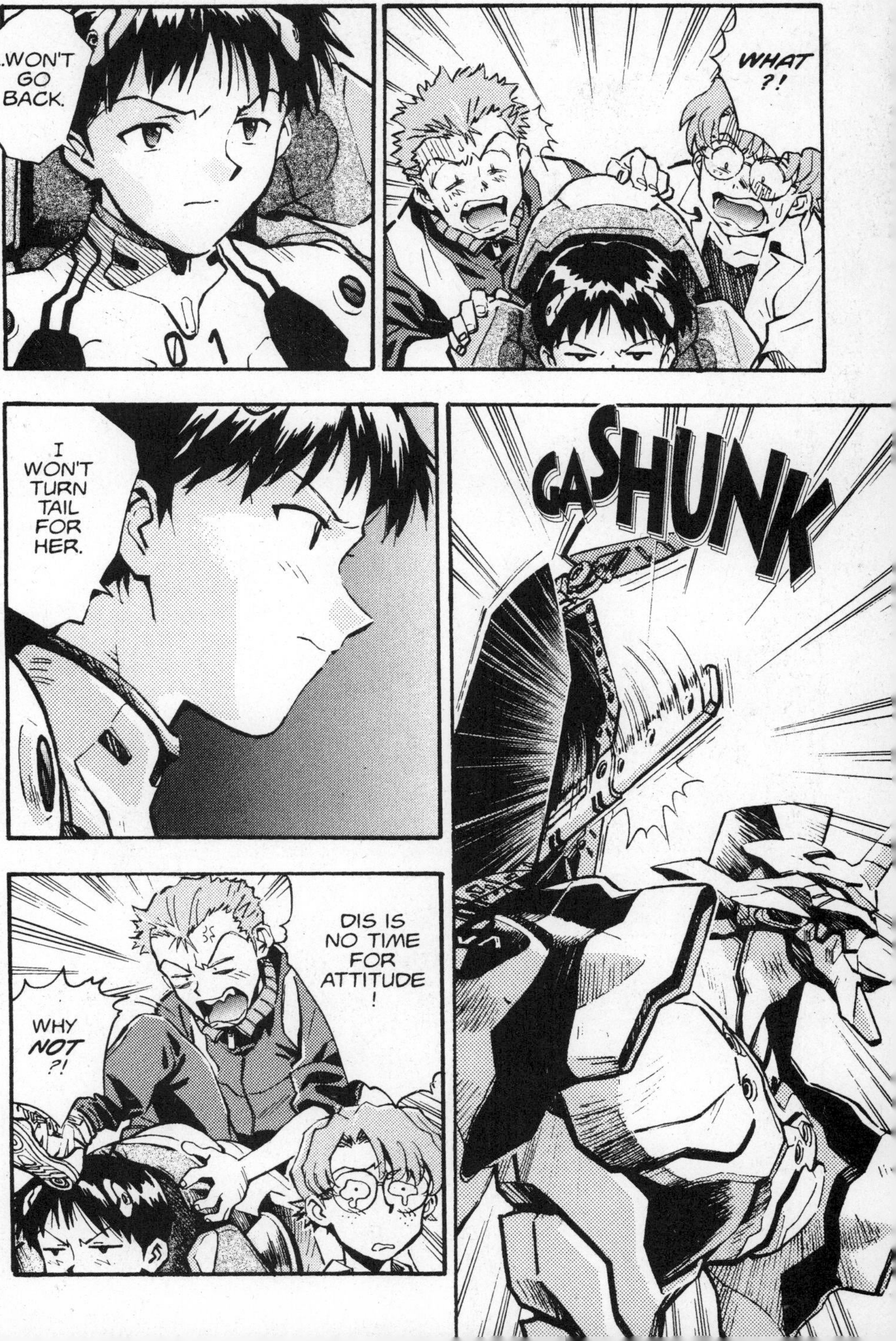
...WON'T GO BACK.
WHAT ?!
I WON'T TURN TAIL FOR HER.
GASHUNK
DIS IS NO TIME FOR ATTITUDE !
WHY NOT ?!

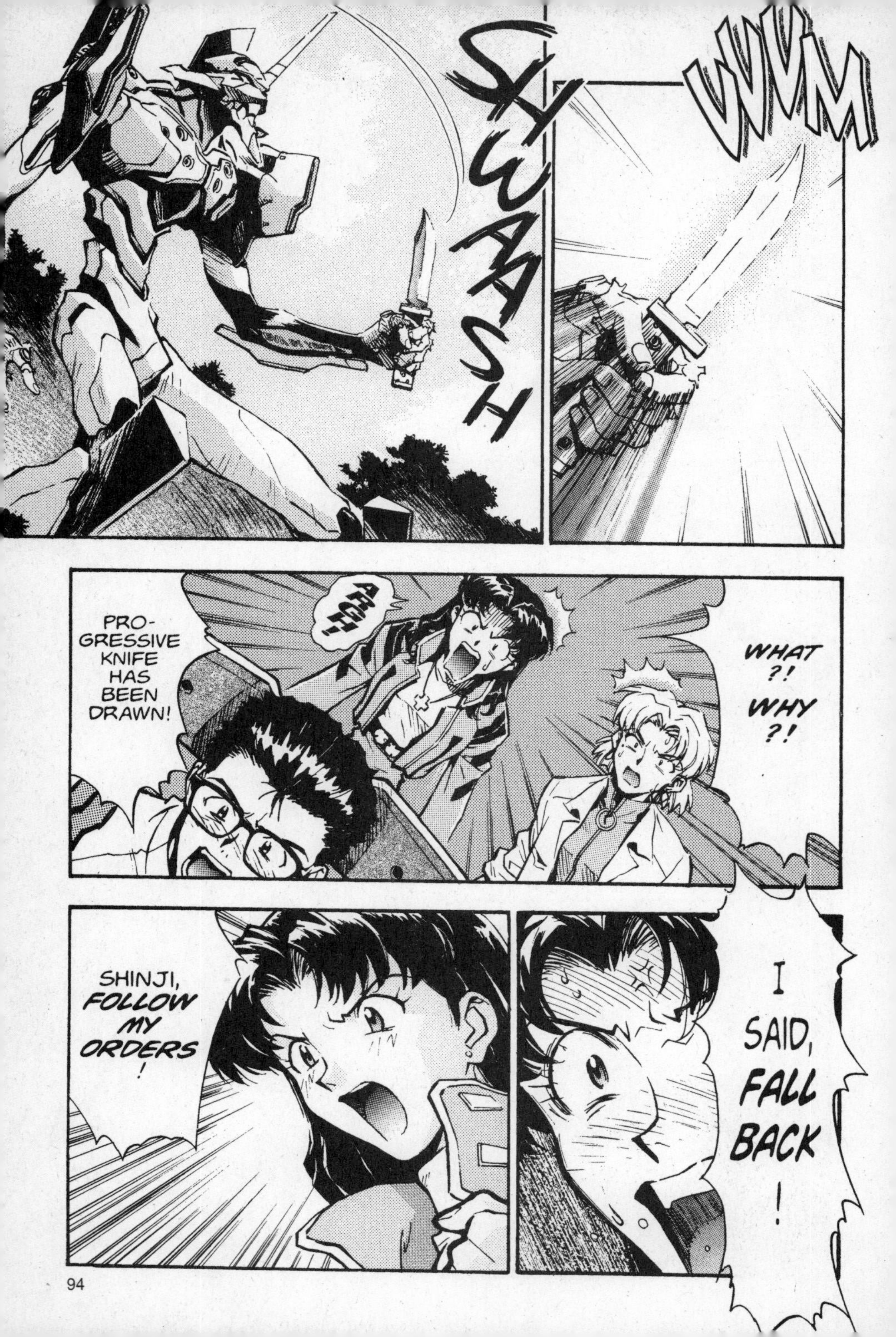
SHWASH
VVVM
PRO-GRESSIVE KNIFE HAS BEEN DRAWN!
ARGH!
WHAT?! WHY?!
SHINJI, FOLLOW MY ORDERS!
I SAID, FALL BACK!

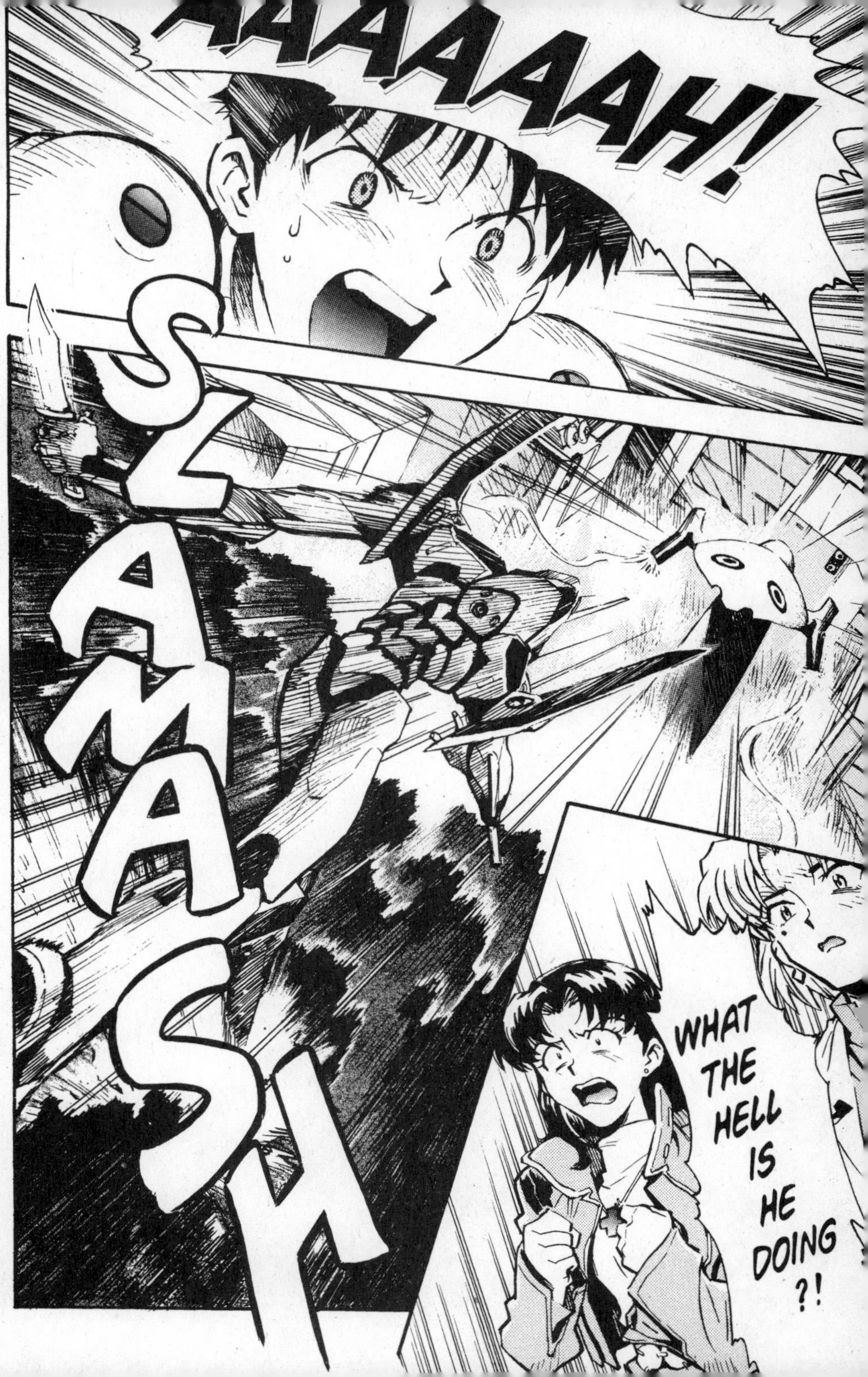
AAAAAAAH!
SLAMASH!
WHAT THE HELL IS HE DOING ?!

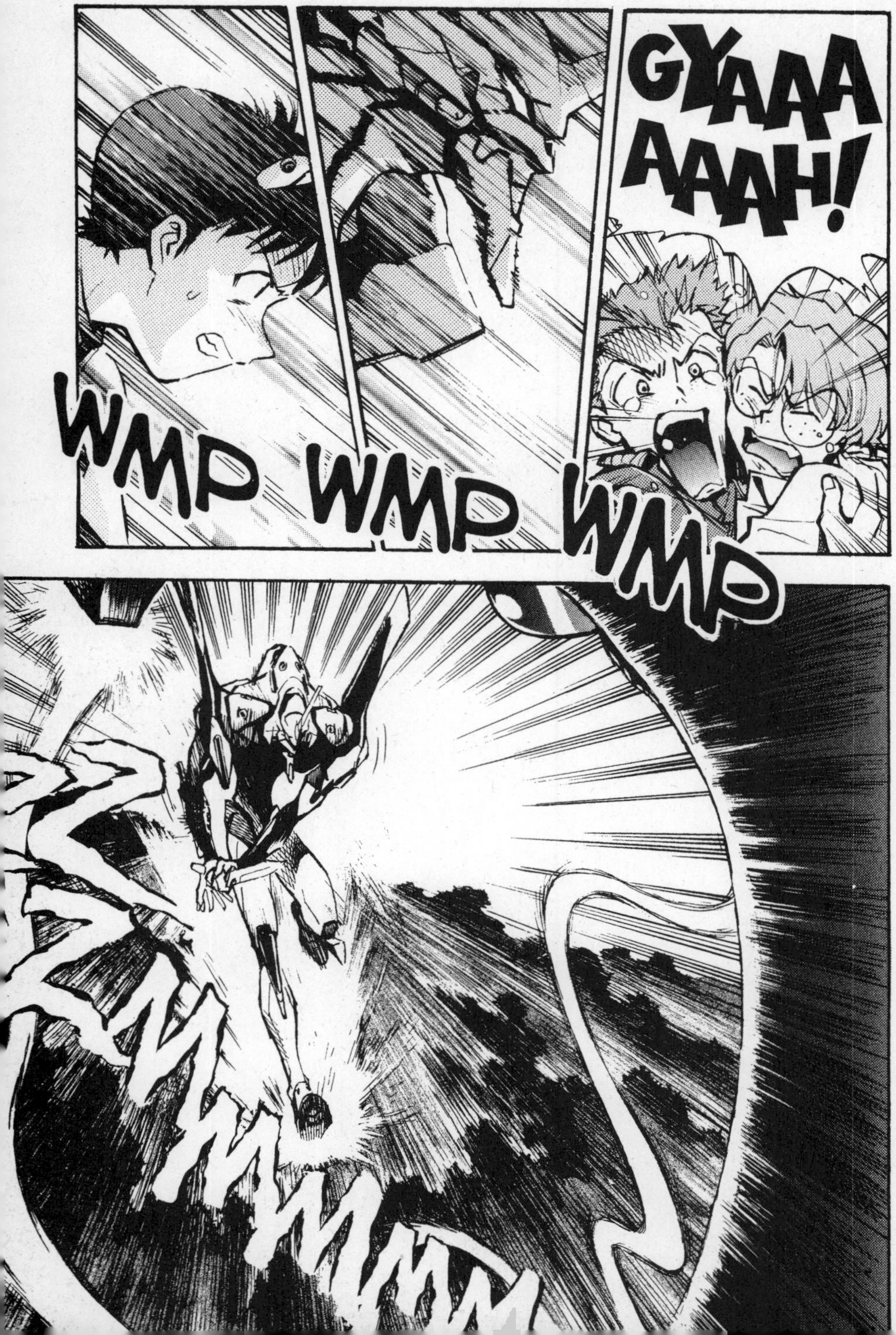
WMP
WMP
GYAAA AAAH!
WMP

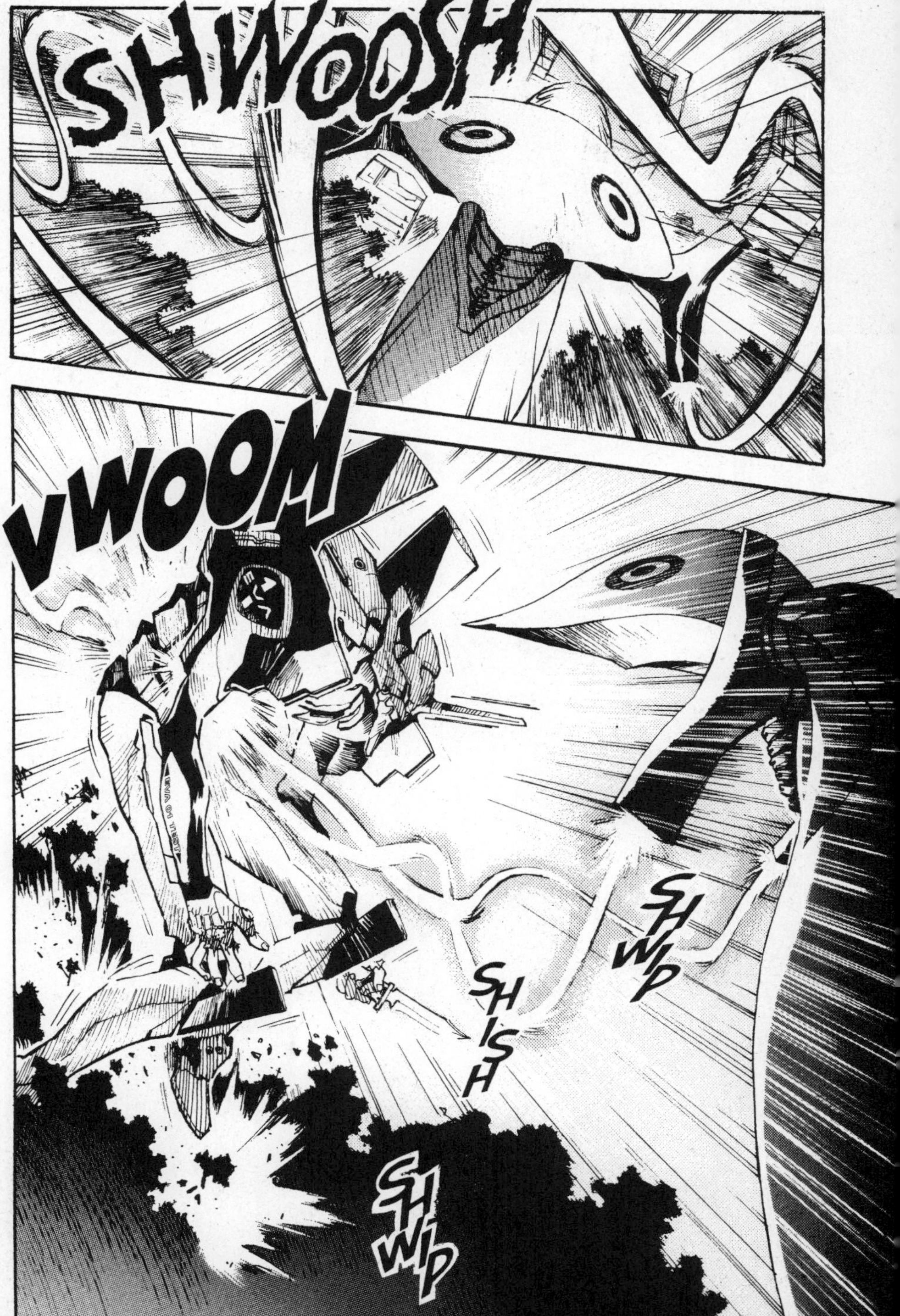
SHWOOSH
VWOOM
EVA 01 TEST
SHWIP
SHISH
SHWIP

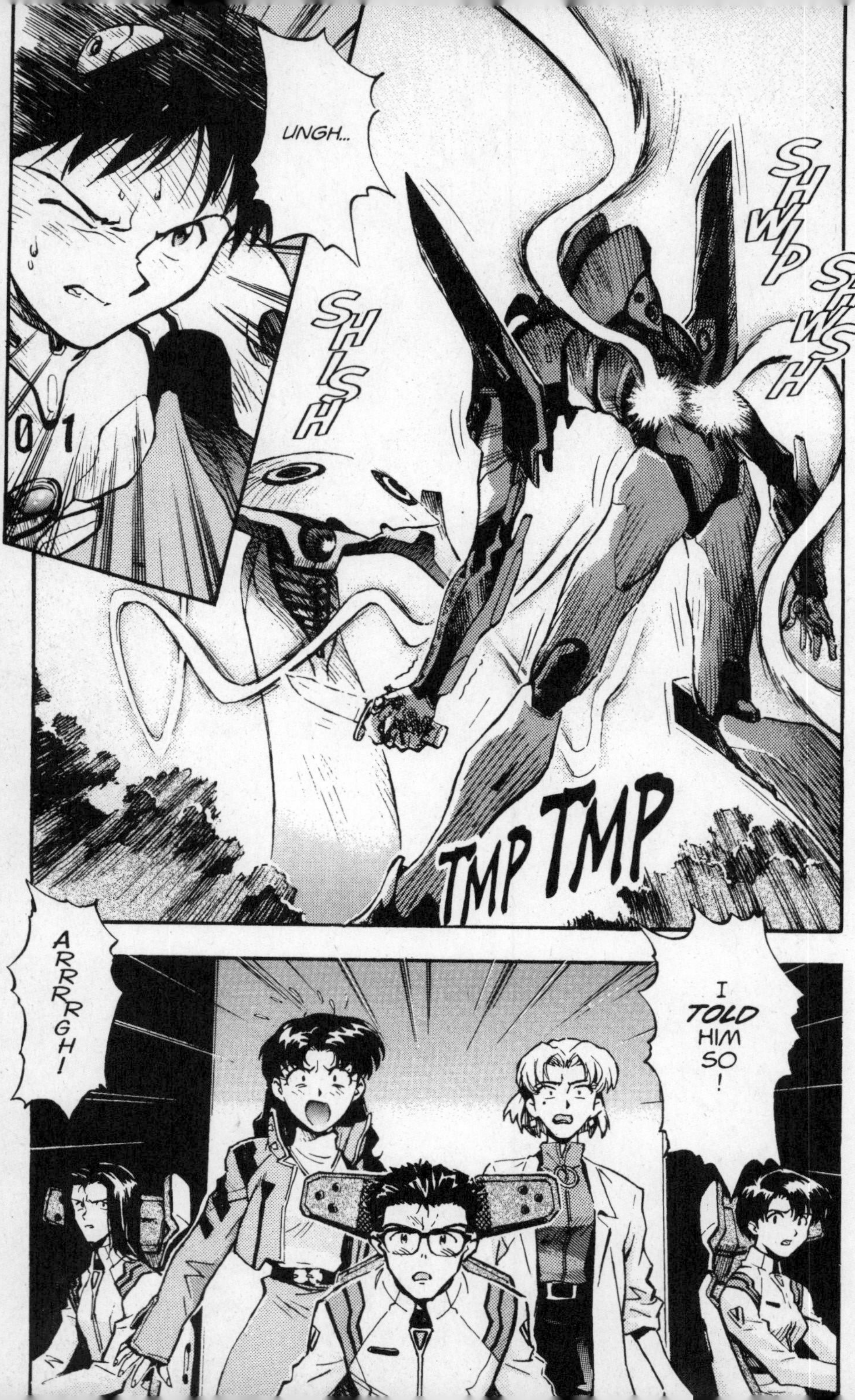
UNGH...
SHISH
SHWIP
SHWSH
TMP TMP
ARRRRGH!
I TOLD HIM SO!

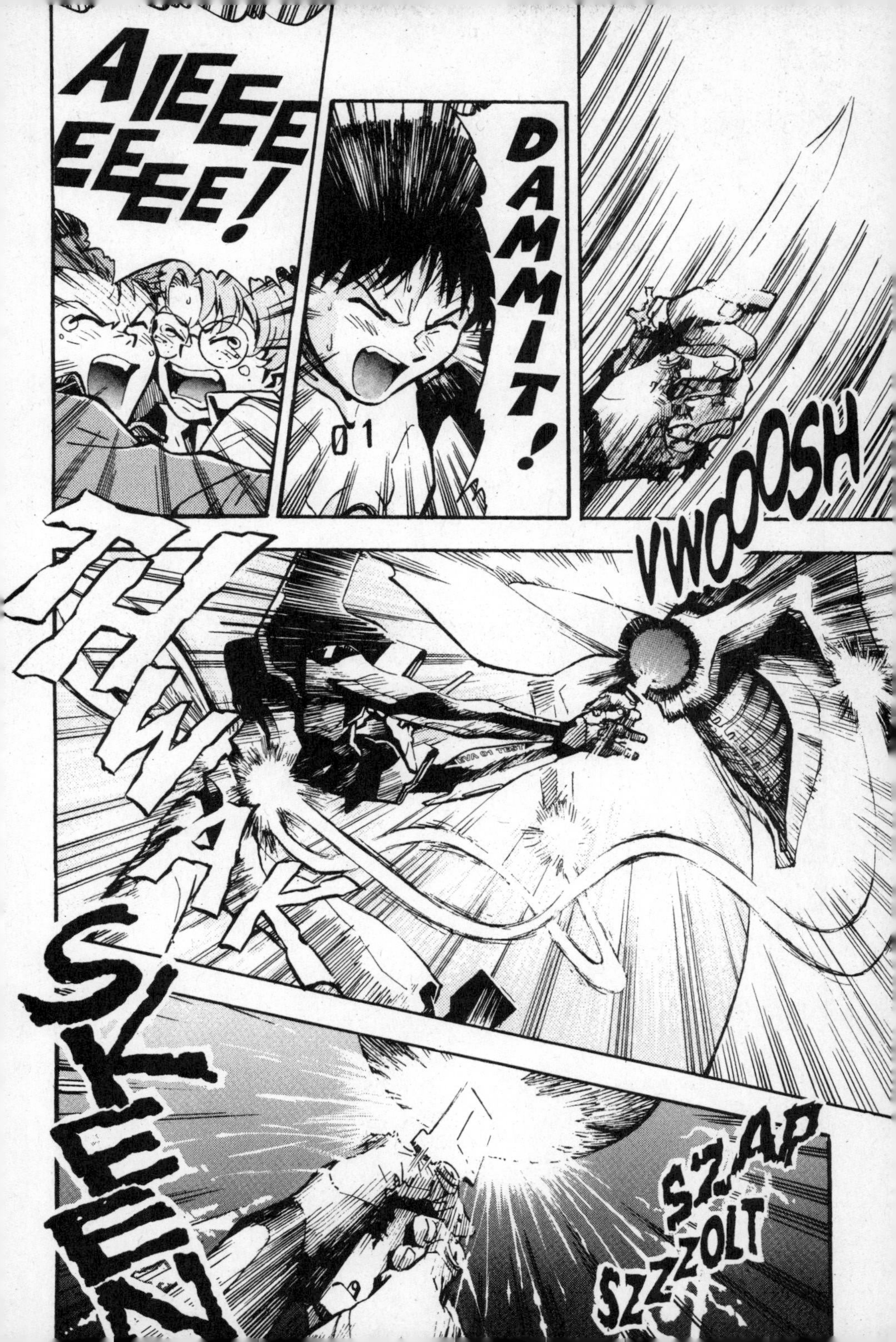

AIEEEEEEEEE!
DAMMIT!
01
VWOOOSH
THWAK
EVA 01 TEST
SKEEE
SZZAP
SZZZOLT

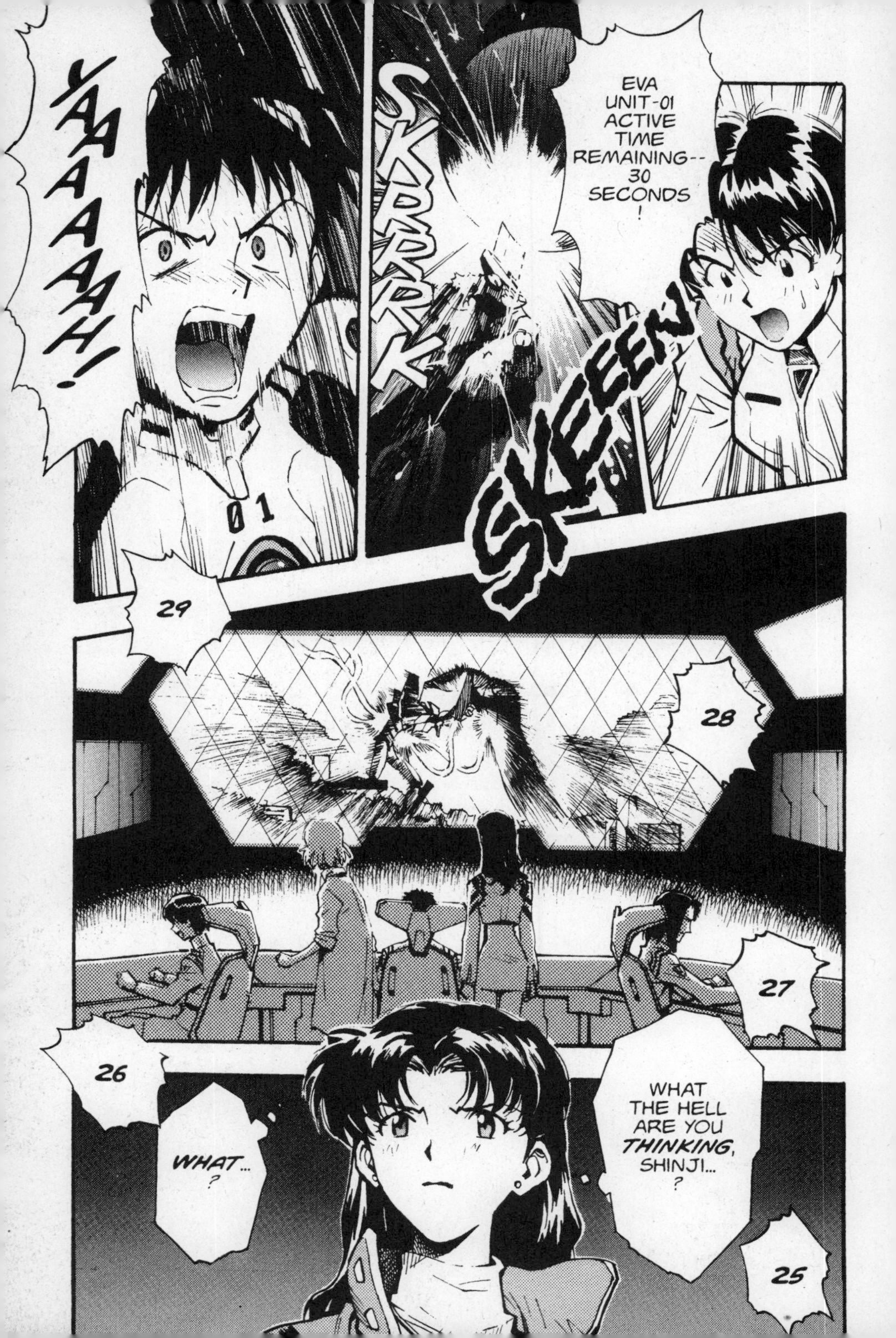
YAAAAAAAH!
SKRRRK
EVA UNIT-01 ACTIVE TIME REMAINING-- 30 SECONDS !
SKEEEN
29
28
27
26
WHAT... ?
WHAT THE HELL ARE YOU THINKING, SHINJI... ?
25

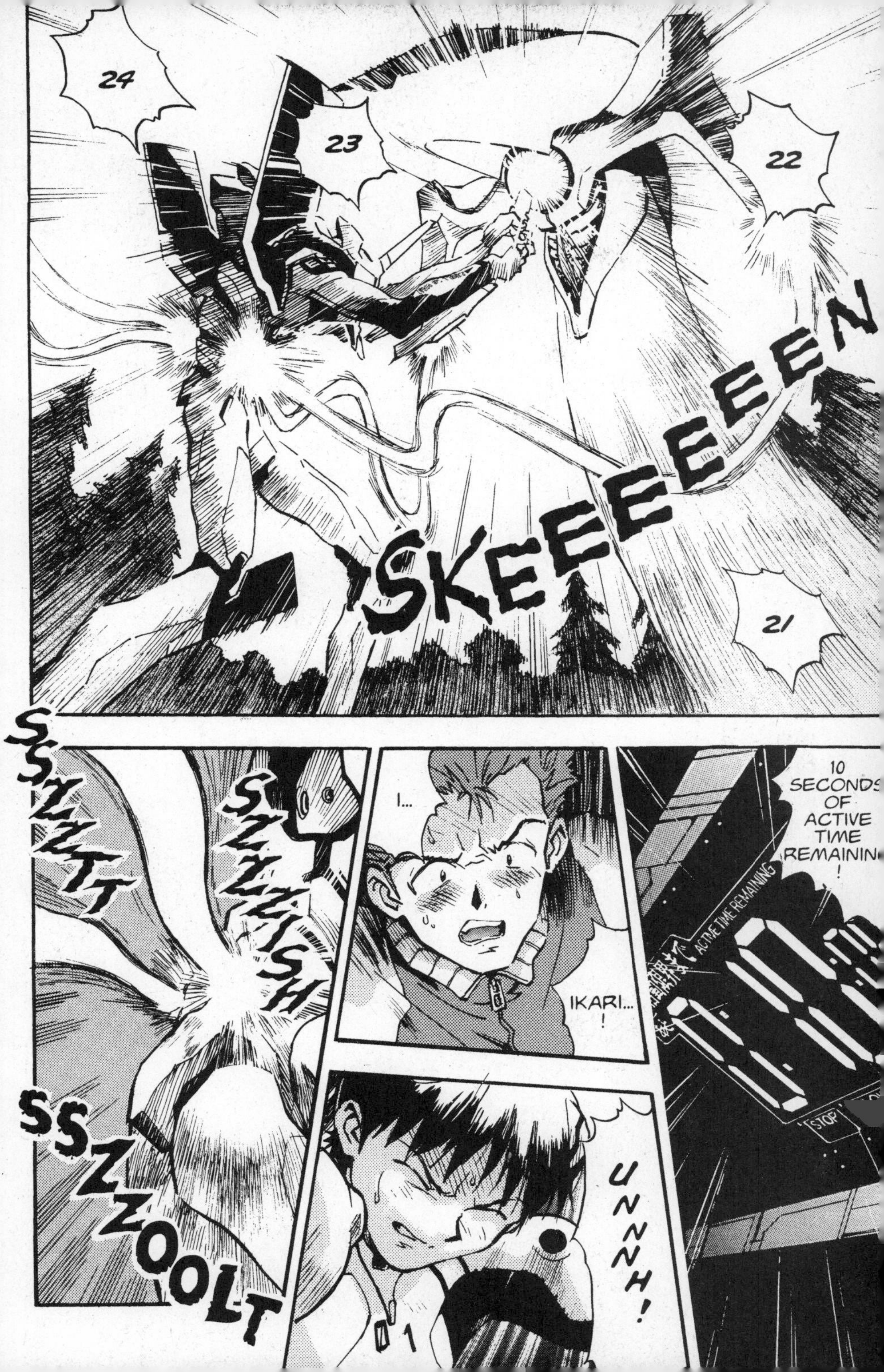

24
23
22
SKEEEEEEEN
21
SSZZZTT
SSZZZUISH
SSZZOOLT
I...
IKARI... !
UNNNH!
10 SECONDS OF ACTIVE TIME REMAININ !
ACTIVE TIME REMAINING
STOP

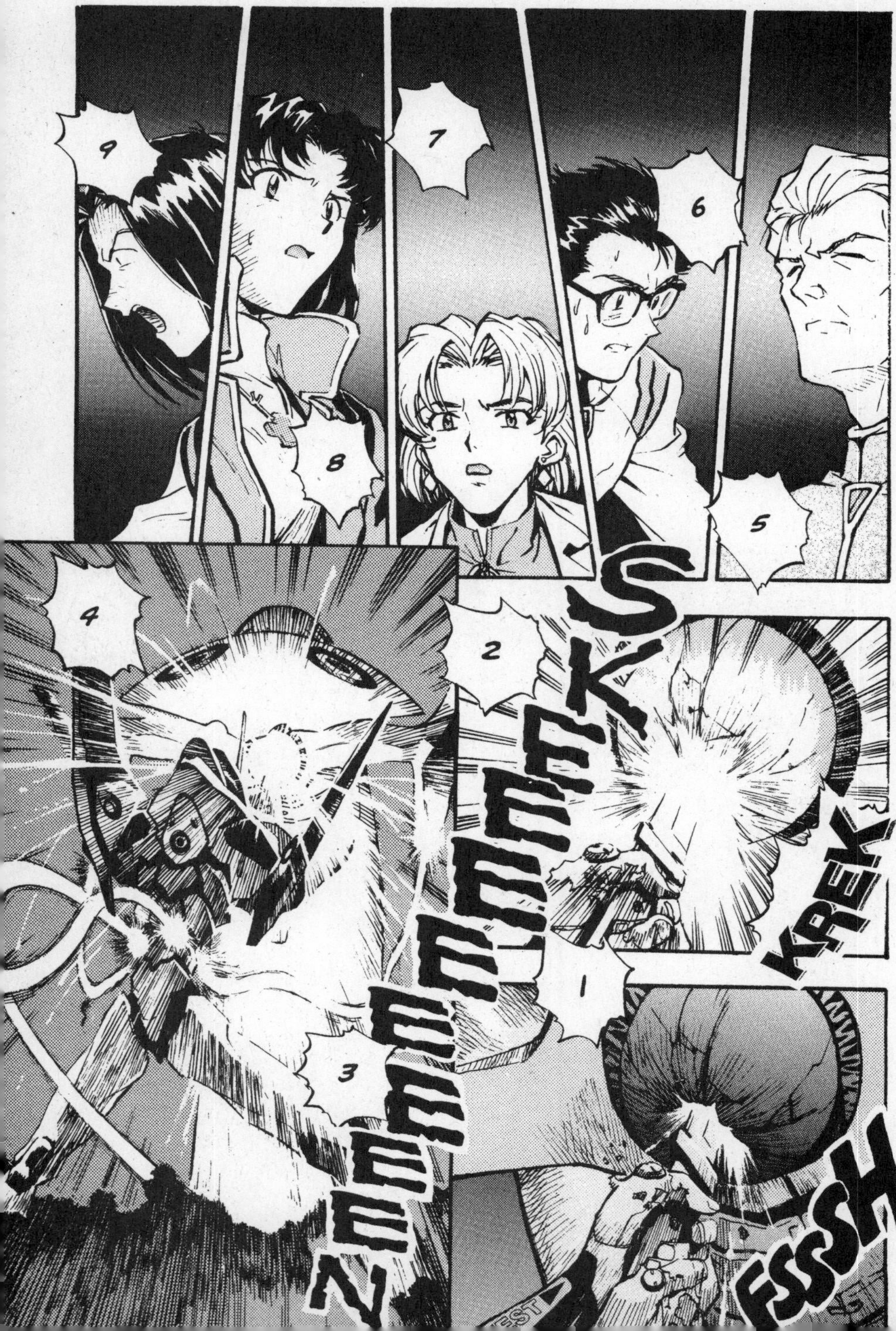
9
8
7
6
5
4
3
SKEEEEEEEEN
2
1
KREK
FSSSH

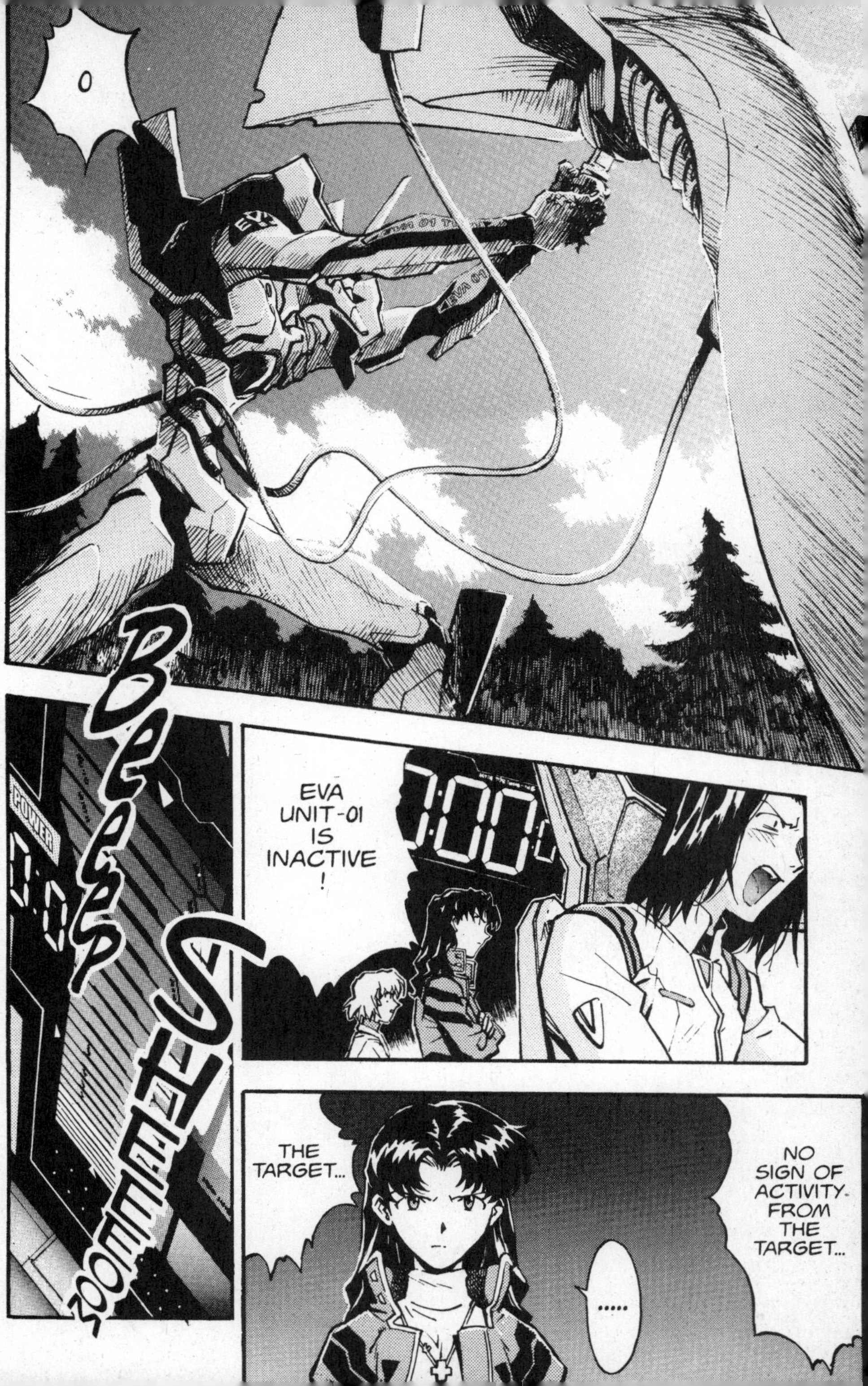

O
Beeeep
EVA UNIT-01 IS INACTIVE!
POWER
THE TARGET...
NO SIGN OF ACTIVITY FROM THE TARGET...
......

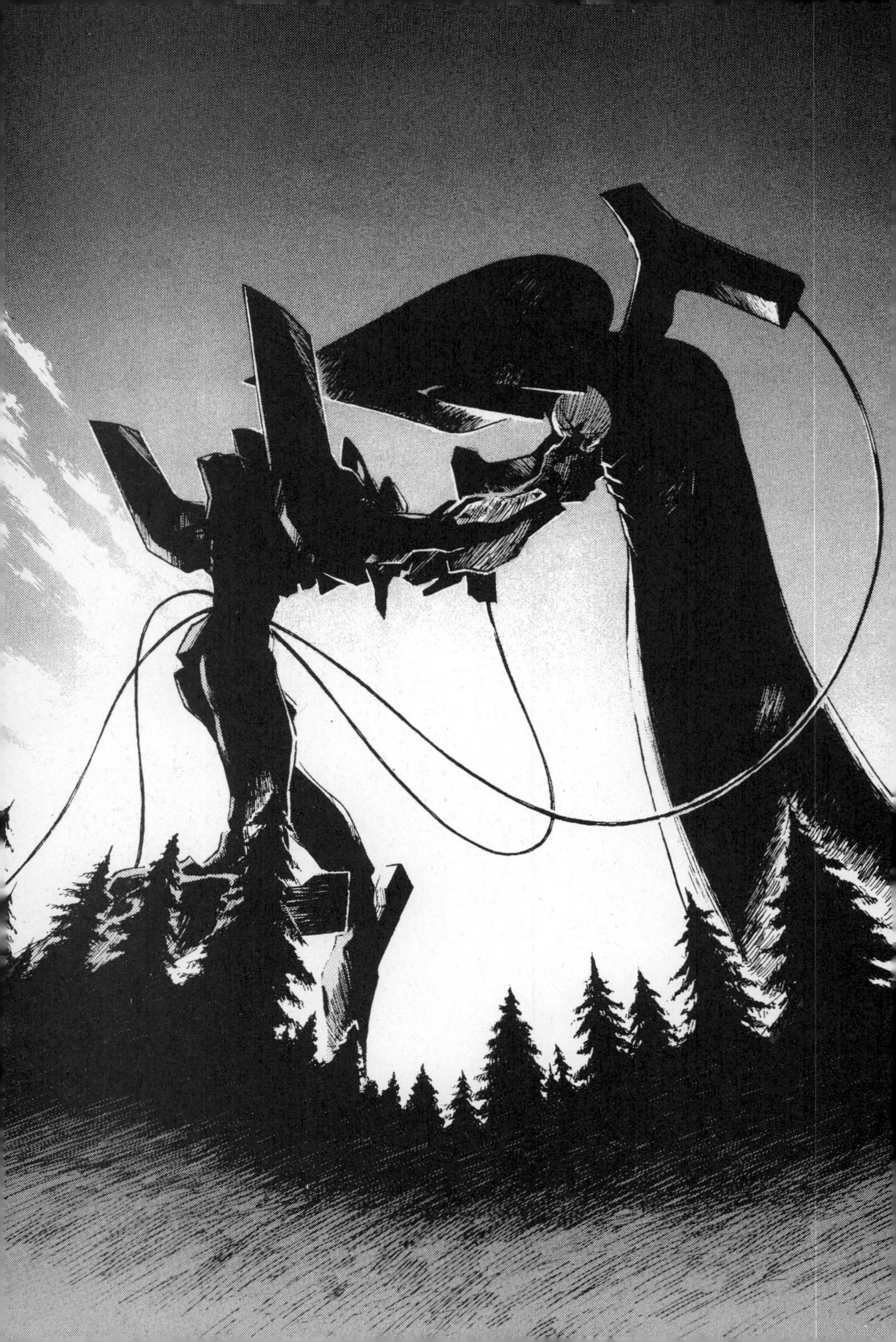

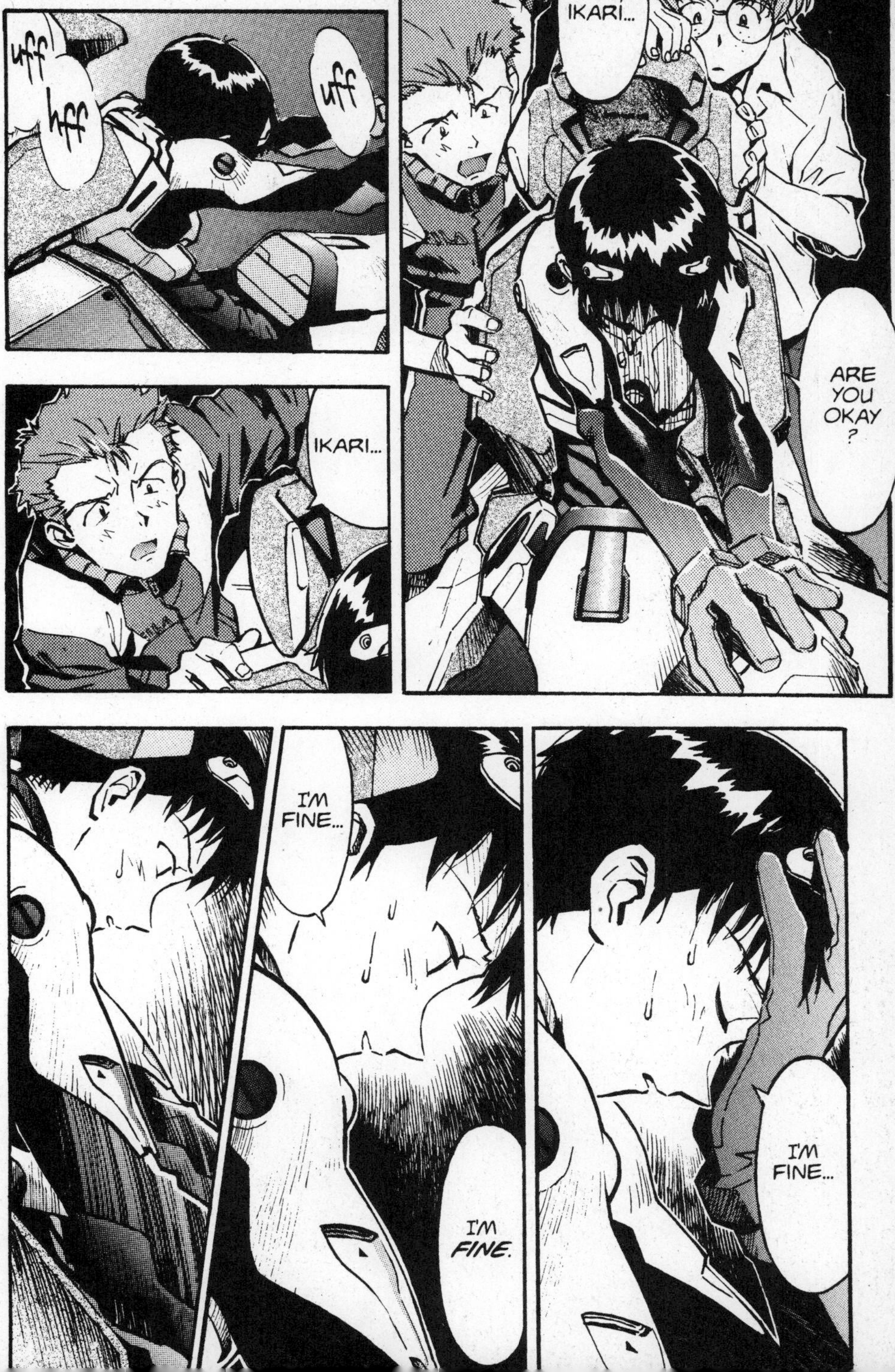
uff
hff
uff
IKARI...
HEY, IKARI...
ARE YOU OKAY?
I'M FINE...
I'M *FINE*.
I'M FINE...

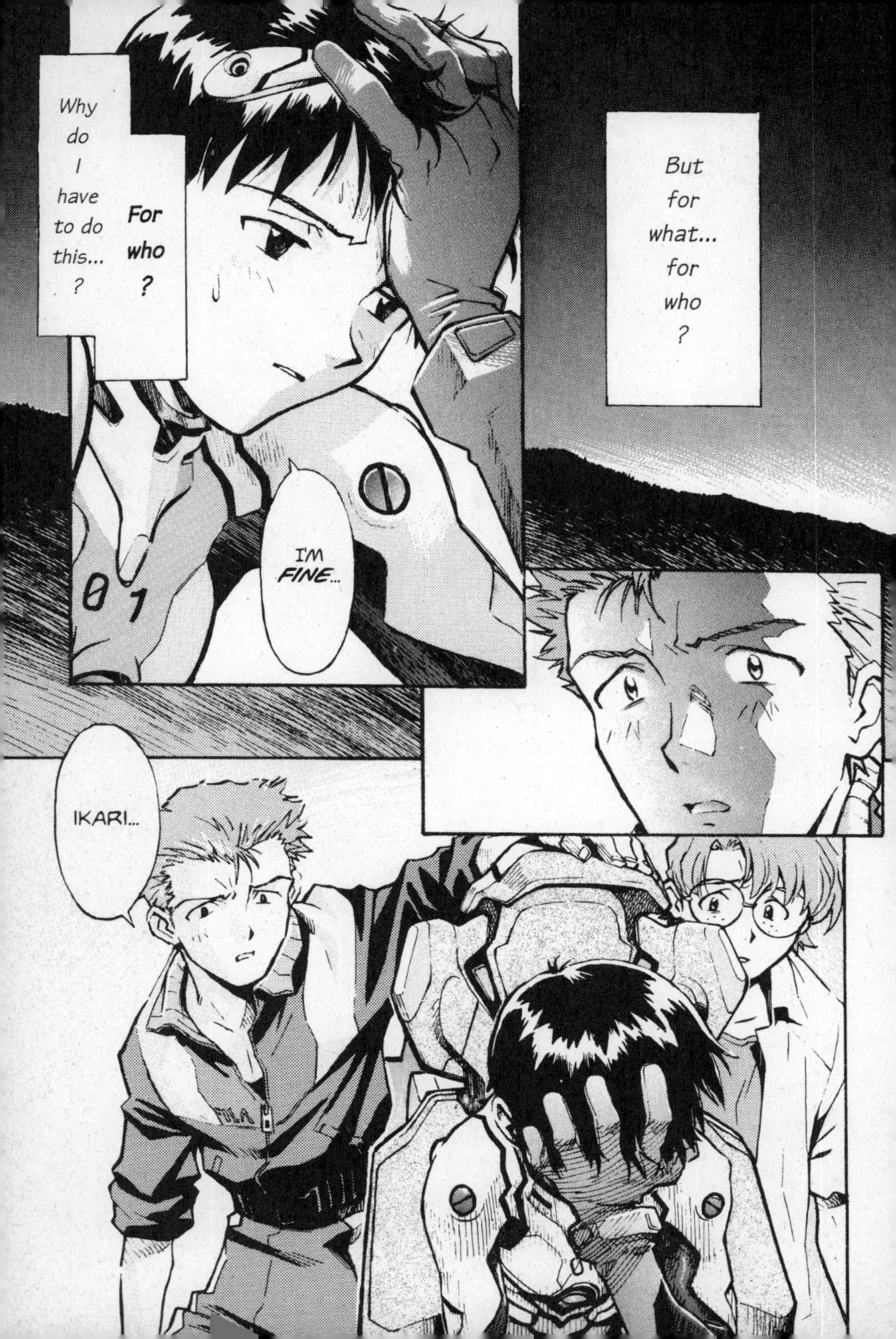

Why do I have to do this... ?
For who ?
I'M FINE...
But for what... for who ?
IKARI...

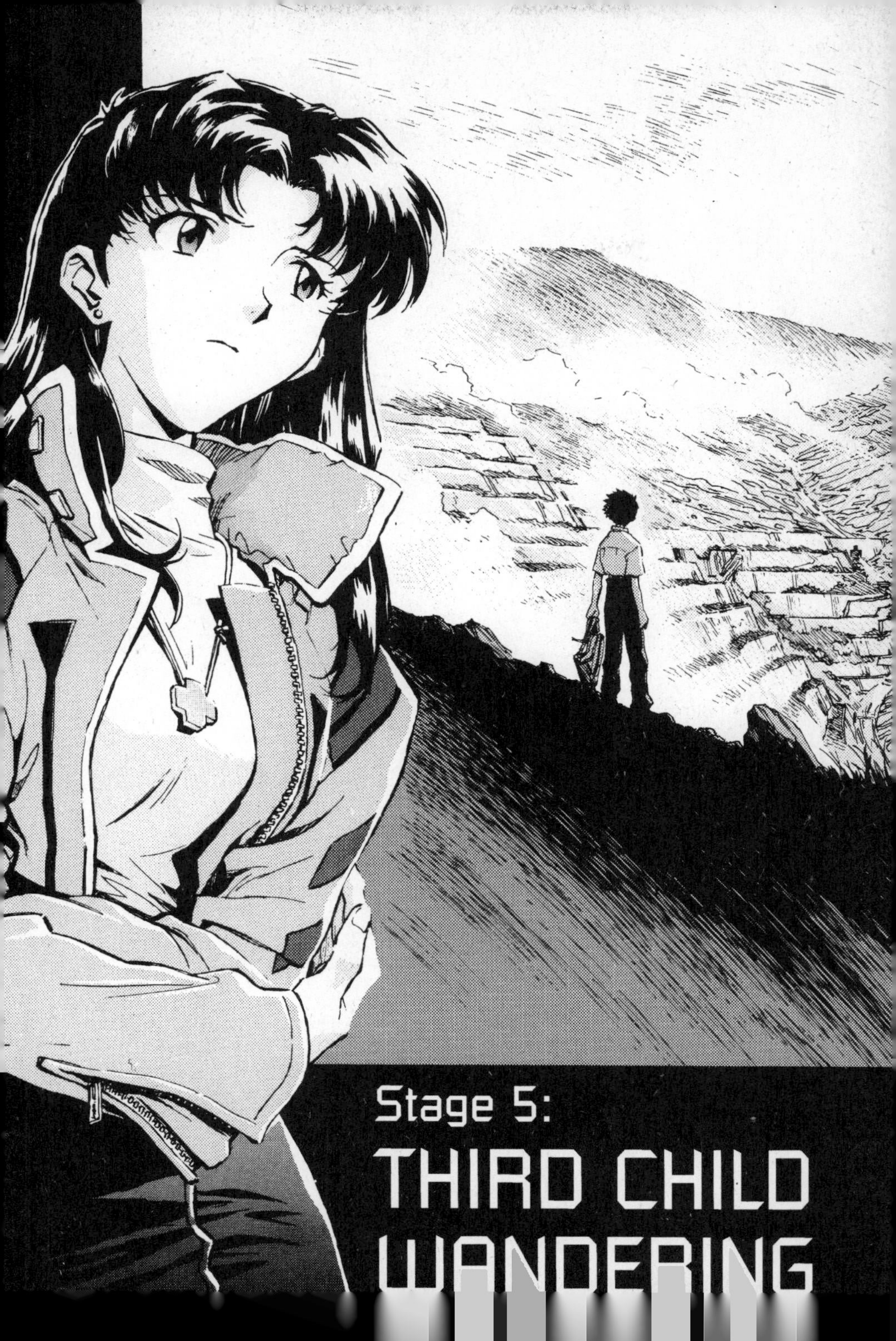

Stage 5: THIRD CHILD WANDERING

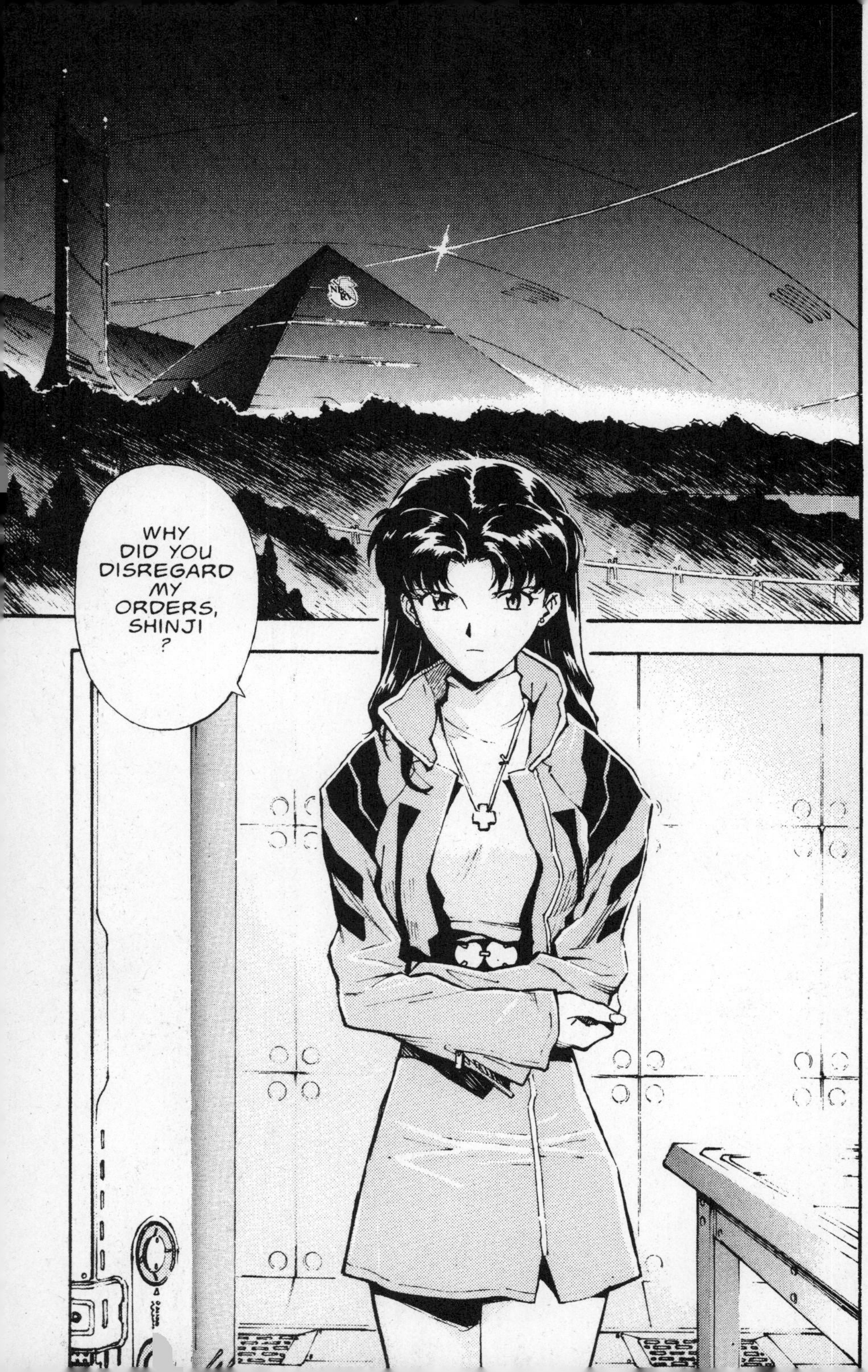
WHY DID YOU DISREGARD MY ORDERS, SHINJI?

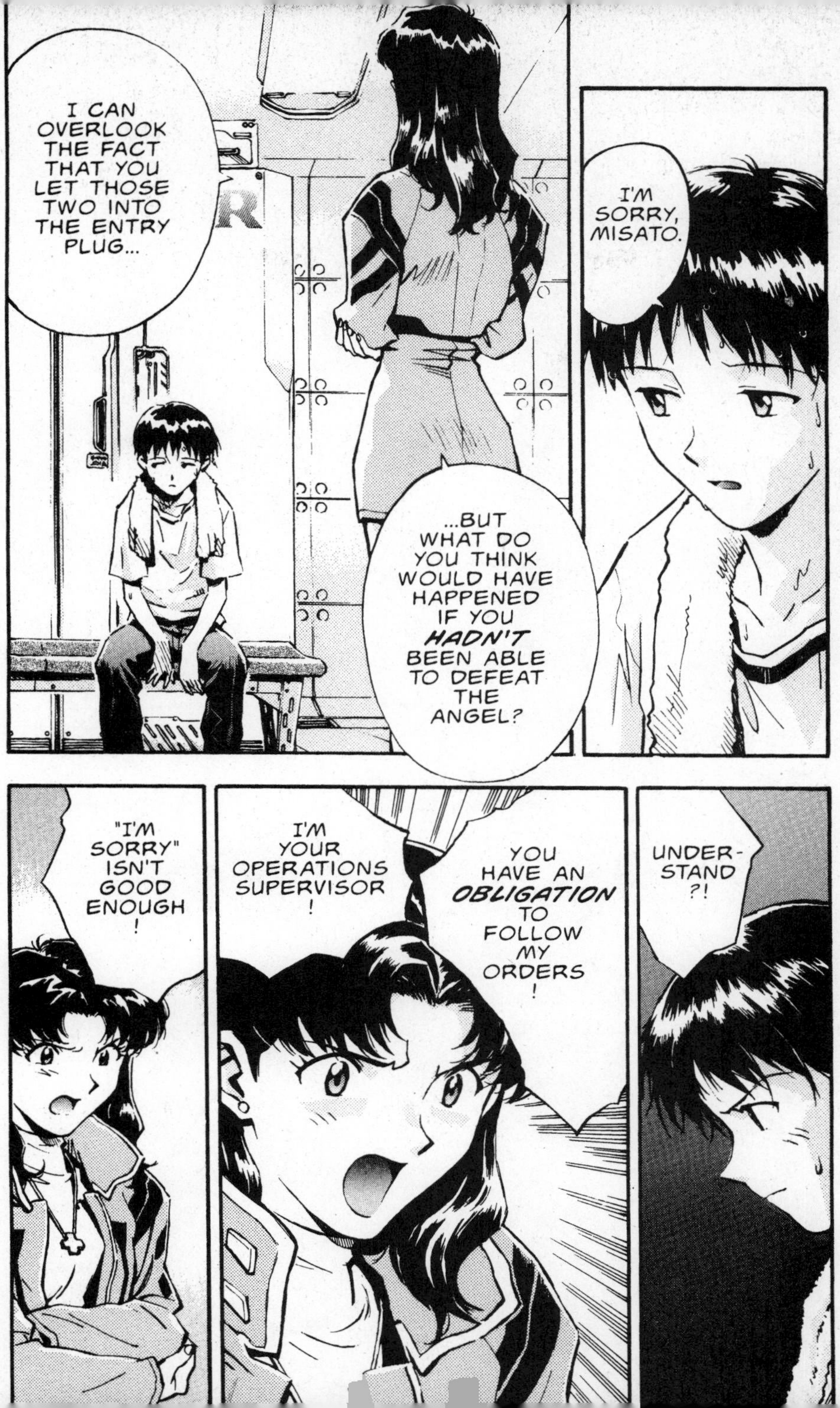
I CAN OVERLOOK THE FACT THAT YOU LET THOSE TWO INTO THE ENTRY PLUG...
...BUT WHAT DO YOU THINK WOULD HAVE HAPPENED IF YOU *HADN'T* BEEN ABLE TO DEFEAT THE ANGEL?
I'M SORRY, MISATO.
"I'M SORRY" ISN'T GOOD ENOUGH!
I'M YOUR OPERATIONS SUPERVISOR!
YOU HAVE AN *OBLIGATION* TO FOLLOW *MY* ORDERS!
UNDERSTAND?!

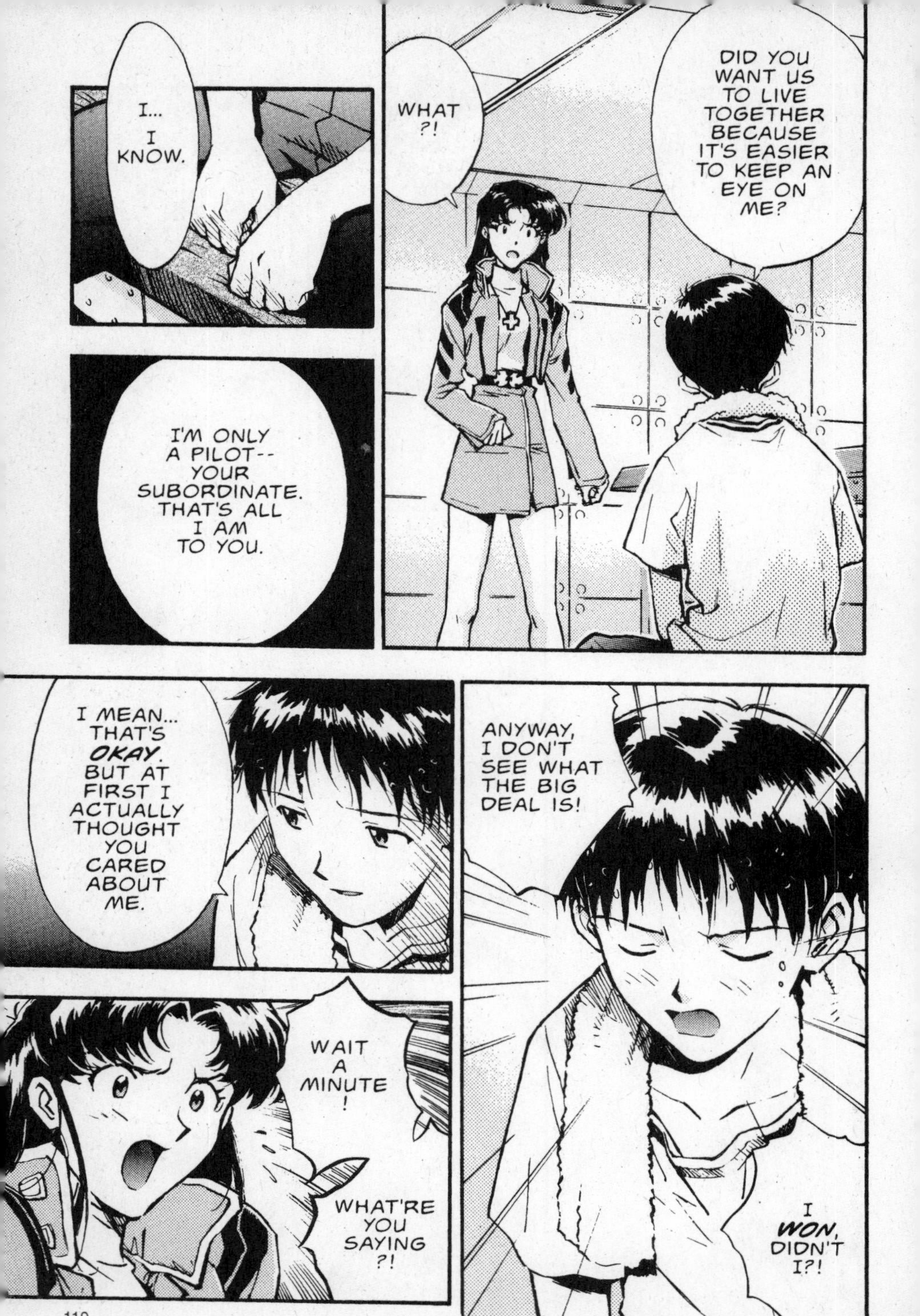
I... I KNOW.
I'M ONLY A PILOT-- YOUR SUBORDINATE. THAT'S ALL I AM TO YOU.
WHAT ?!
DID YOU WANT US TO LIVE TOGETHER BECAUSE IT'S EASIER TO KEEP AN EYE ON ME?
I MEAN... THAT'S *OKAY*. BUT AT FIRST I ACTUALLY THOUGHT YOU CARED ABOUT ME.
WAIT A MINUTE !
WHAT'RE YOU SAYING ?!
ANYWAY, I DON'T SEE WHAT THE BIG DEAL IS!
I *WON*, DIDN'T I?!

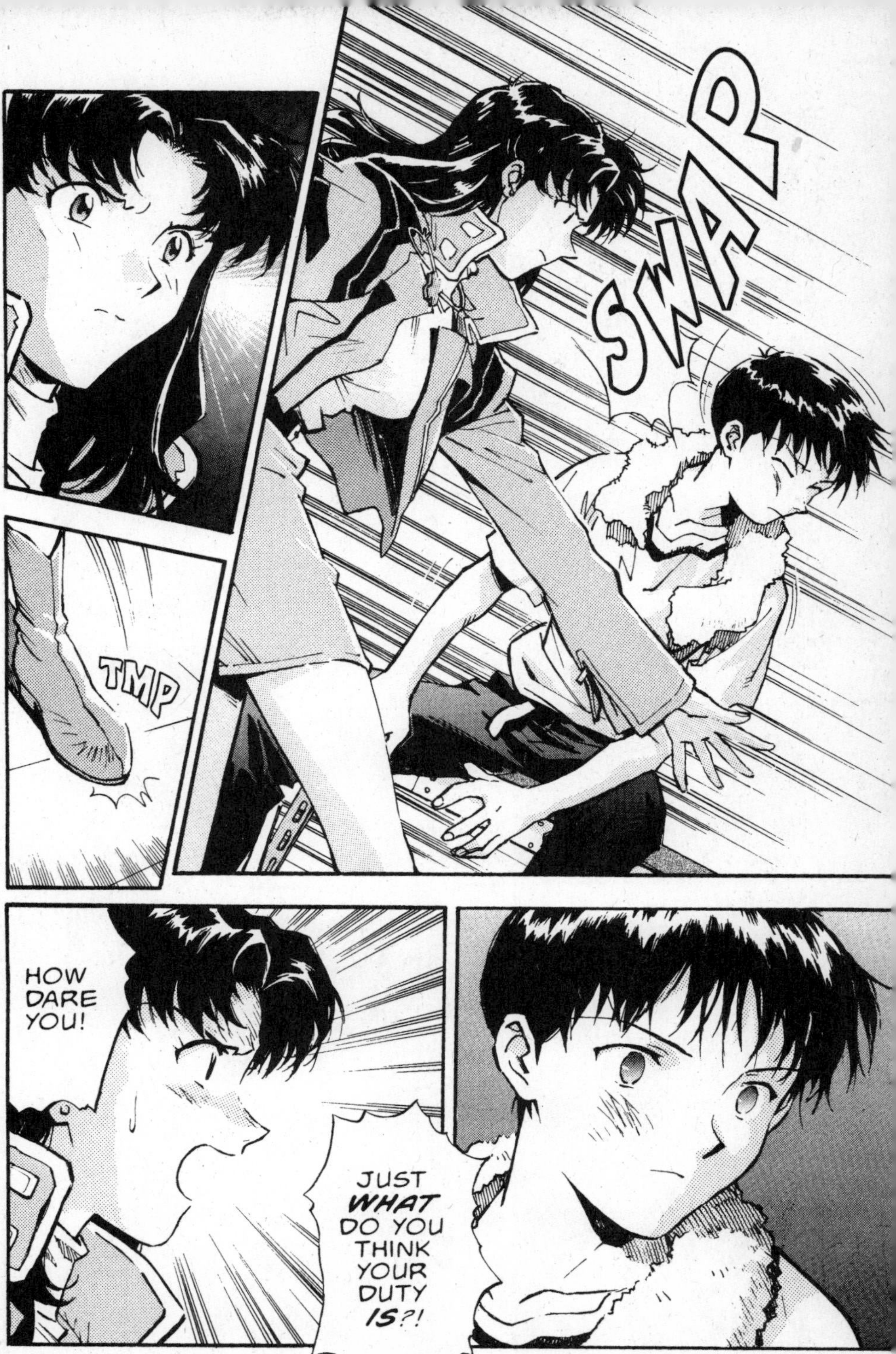
SWAP
TMP
HOW DARE YOU!
JUST WHAT DO YOU THINK YOUR DUTY IS?!

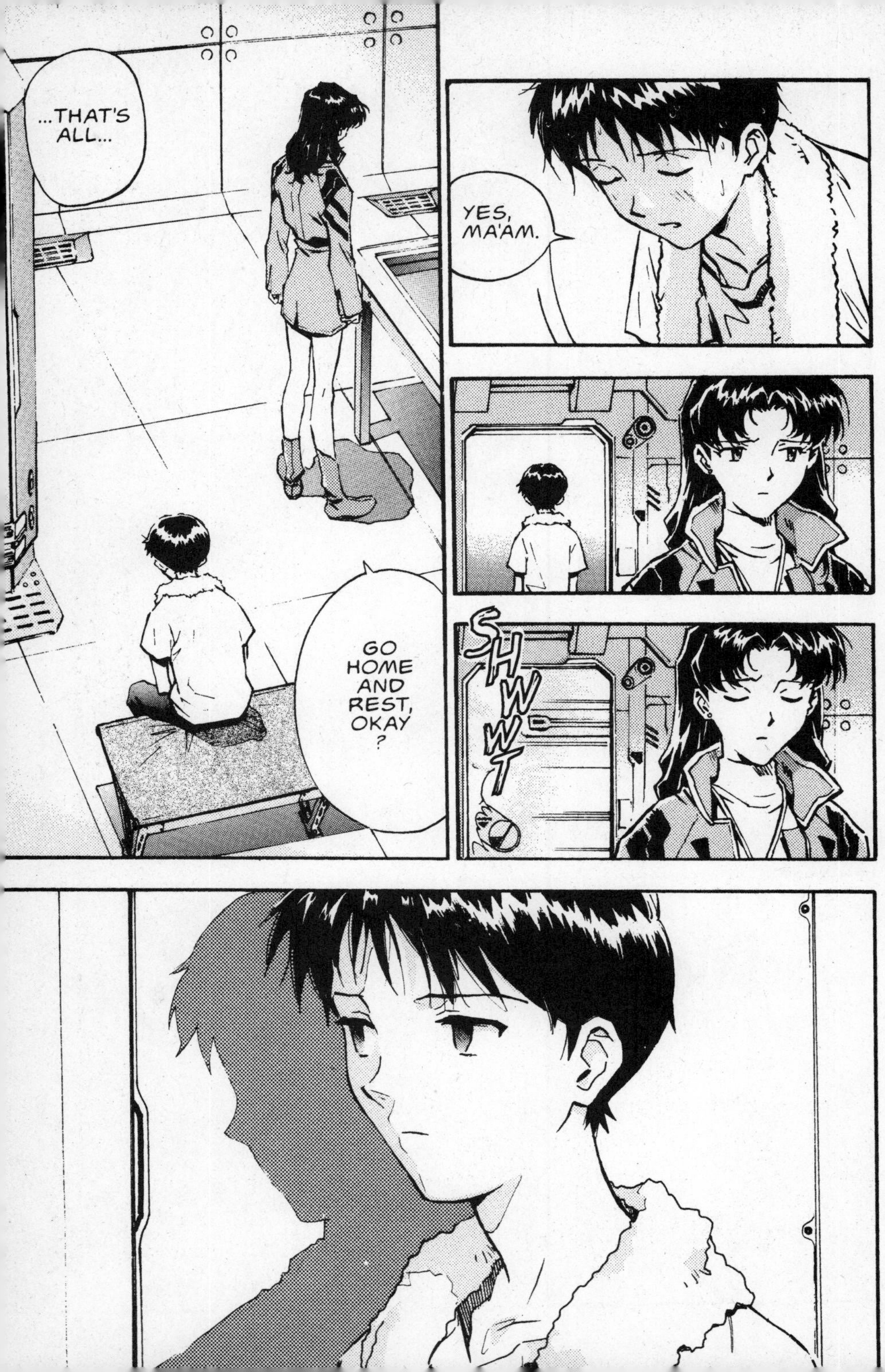
...THAT'S ALL...
GO HOME AND REST, OKAY?
YES, MA'AM.
SHWWT

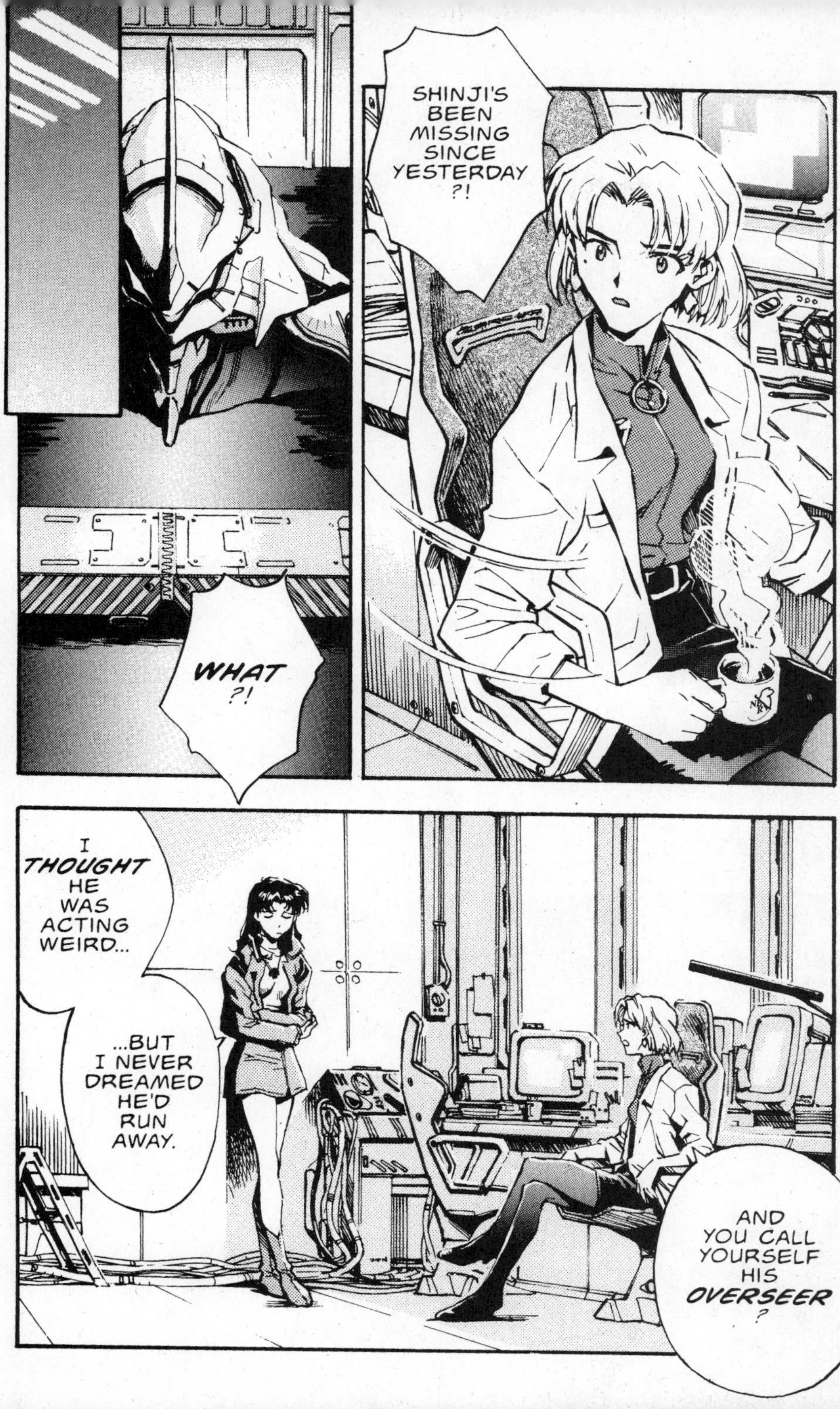

SHINJI'S BEEN MISSING SINCE YESTERDAY ?!
WHAT ?!
I THOUGHT HE WAS ACTING WEIRD...
...BUT I NEVER DREAMED HE'D RUN AWAY.
AND YOU CALL YOURSELF HIS OVERSEER ?

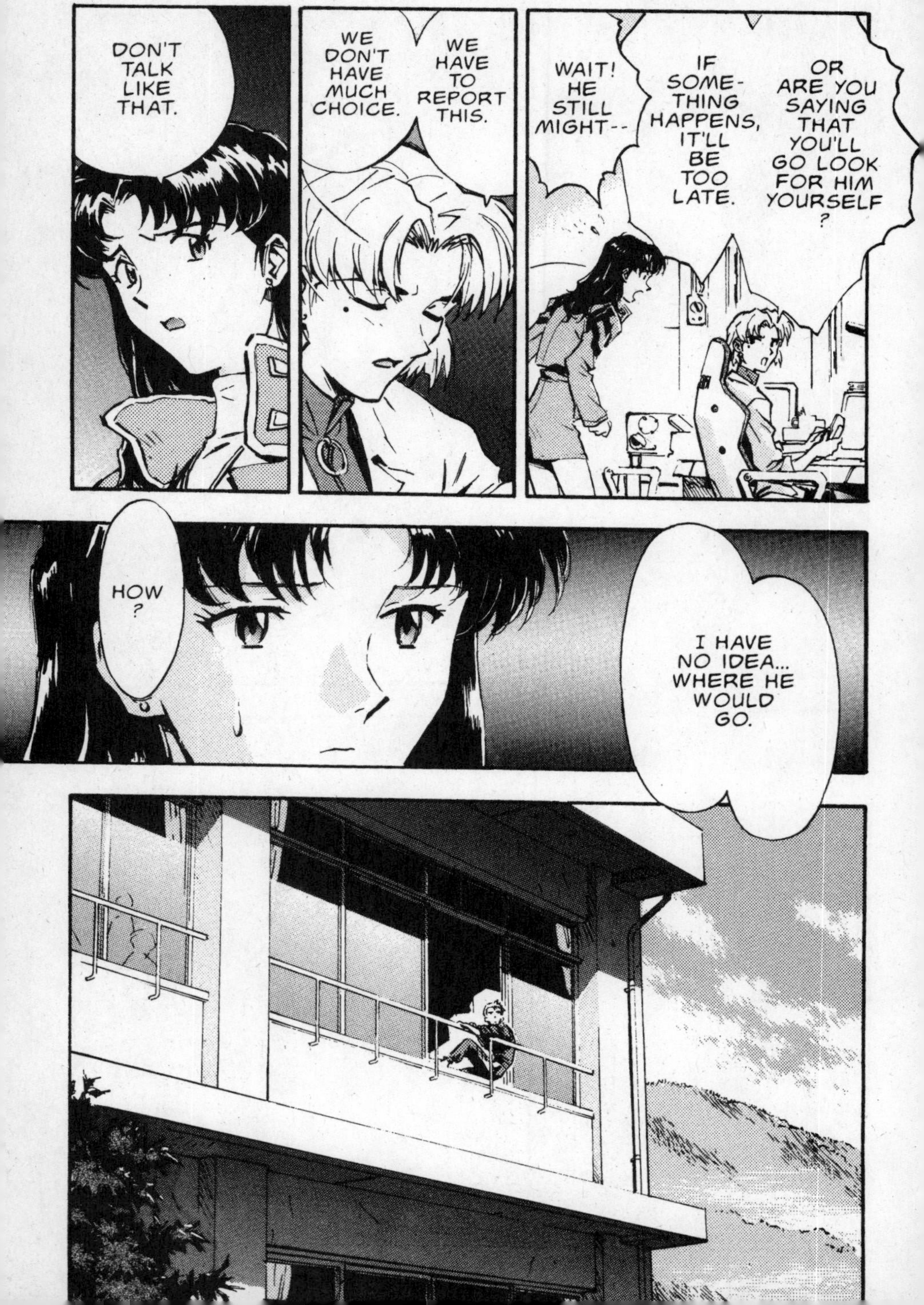
DON'T TALK LIKE THAT.
WE DON'T HAVE MUCH CHOICE.
WE HAVE TO REPORT THIS.
WAIT! HE STILL MIGHT--
IF SOMETHING HAPPENS, IT'LL BE TOO LATE.
OR ARE YOU SAYING THAT YOU'LL GO LOOK FOR HIM YOURSELF?
HOW?
I HAVE NO IDEA... WHERE HE WOULD GO.

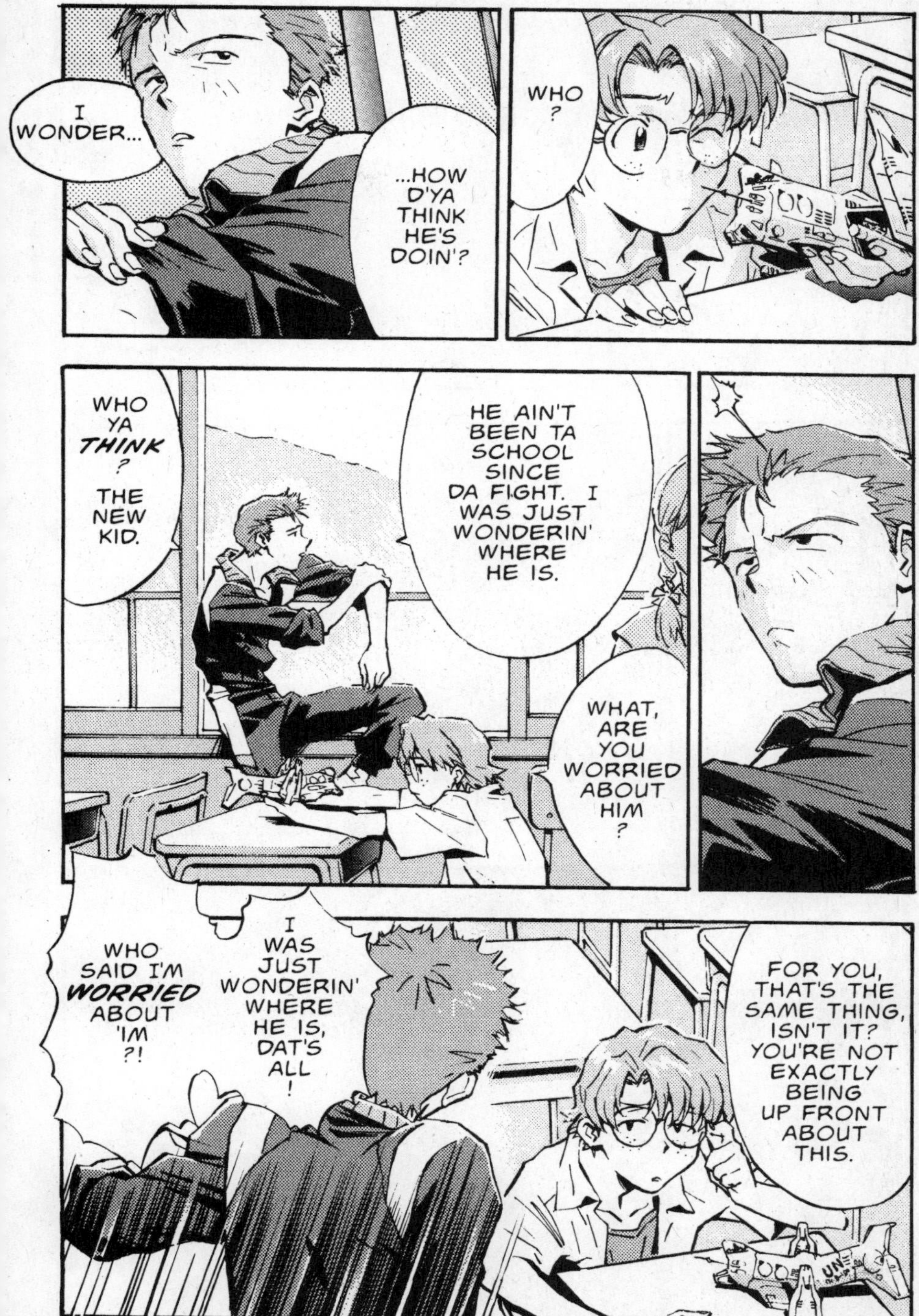
I WONDER...
...HOW D'YA THINK HE'S DOIN'?
WHO?
WHO YA *THINK*? THE NEW KID.
HE AIN'T BEEN TA SCHOOL SINCE DA FIGHT. I WAS JUST WONDERIN' WHERE HE IS.
WHAT, ARE YOU WORRIED ABOUT HIM?
WHO SAID I'M *WORRIED* ABOUT 'IM?!
I WAS JUST WONDERIN' WHERE HE IS, DAT'S ALL!
FOR YOU, THAT'S THE SAME THING, ISN'T IT? YOU'RE NOT EXACTLY BEING UP FRONT ABOUT THIS.

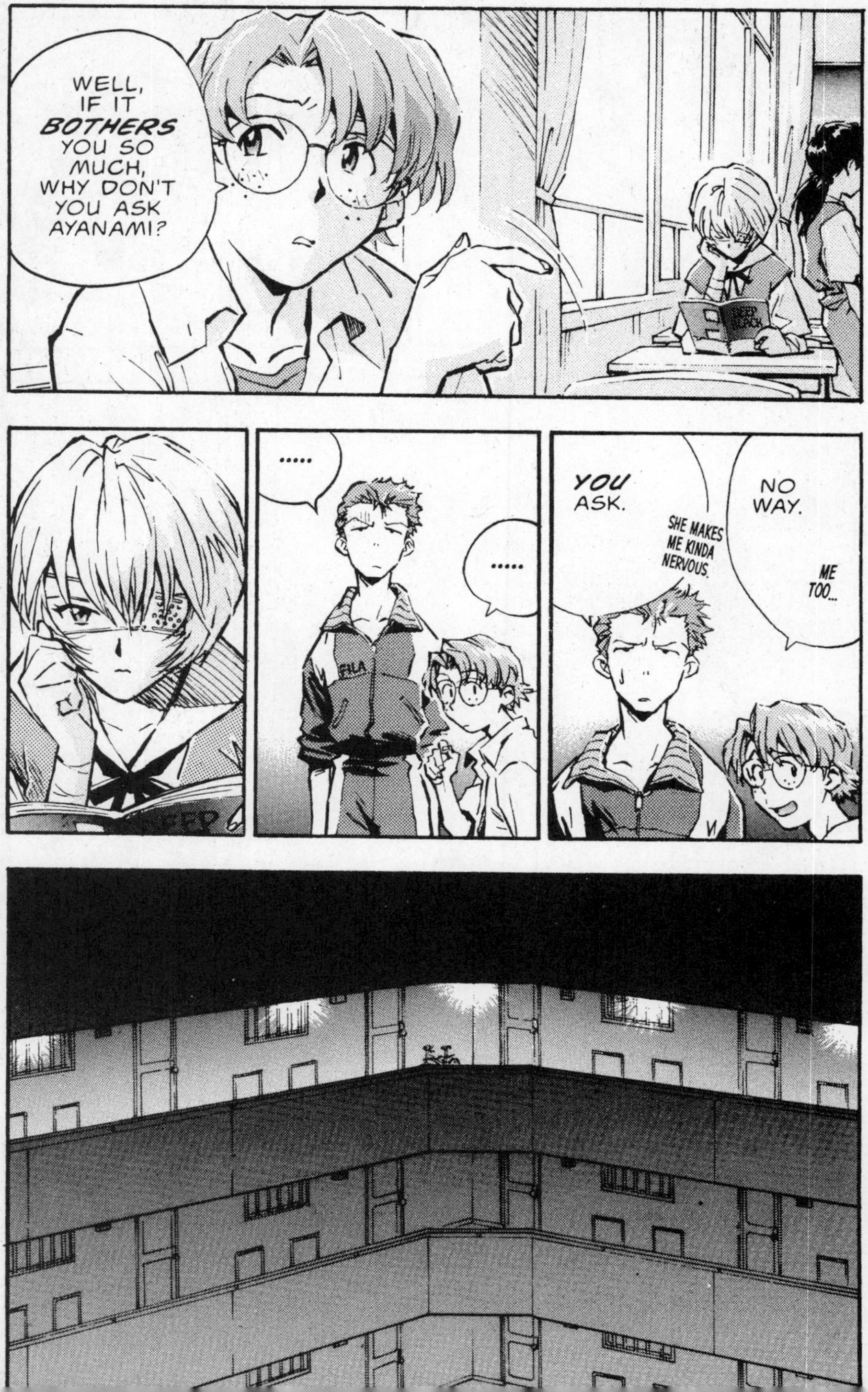
WELL, IF IT ***BOTHERS*** YOU SO MUCH, WHY DON'T YOU ASK AYANAMI?
.....
.....
FILA
YOU ASK.
SHE MAKES ME KINDA NERVOUS.
NO WAY.
ME TOO...

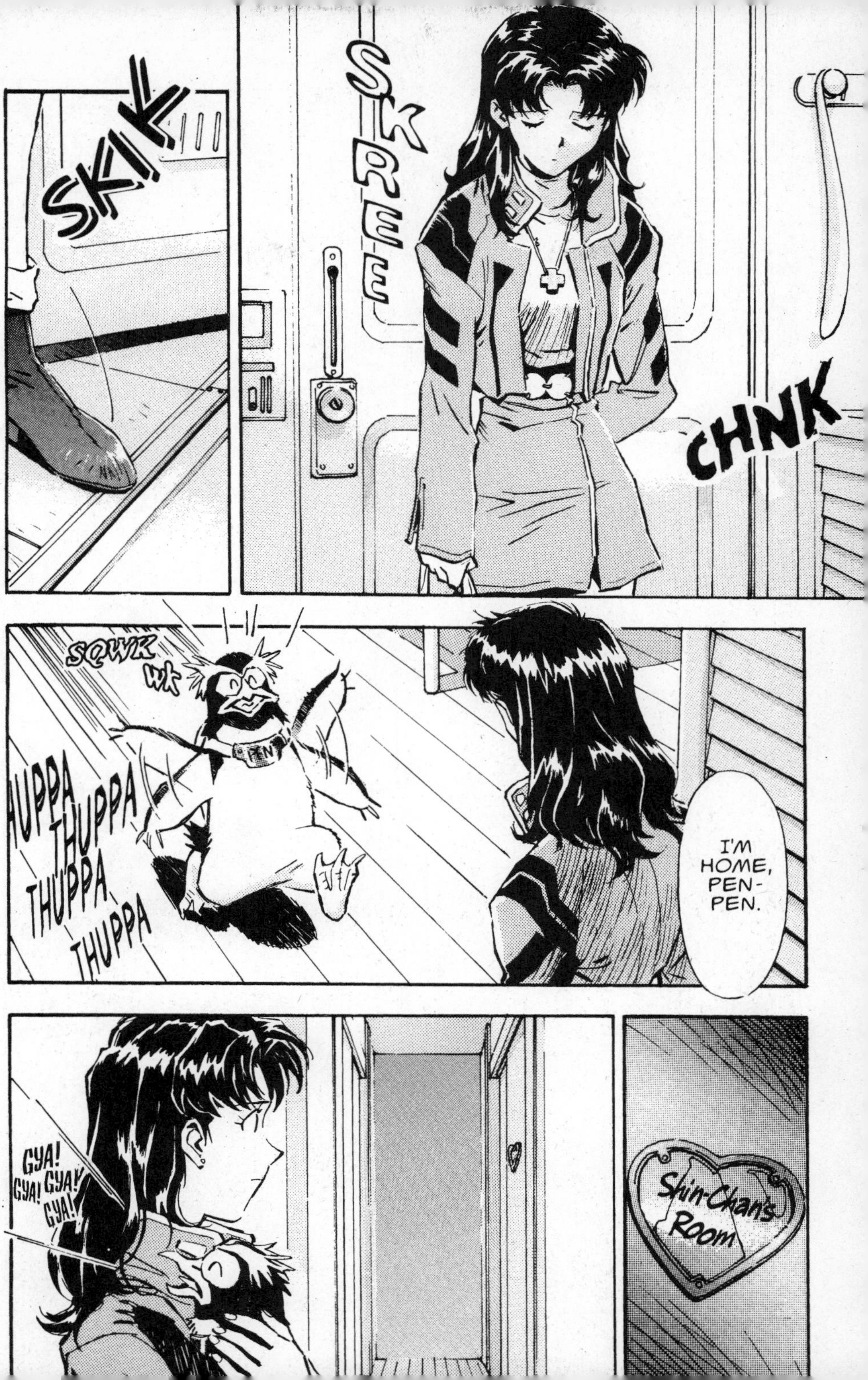
SKIK
SKREE
CHNK
SQWK
WK
THUPPA
THUPPA
THUPPA
THUPPA
I'M HOME, PEN-PEN.
GYA! GYA! GYA! GYA!
Shin-Chan's Room

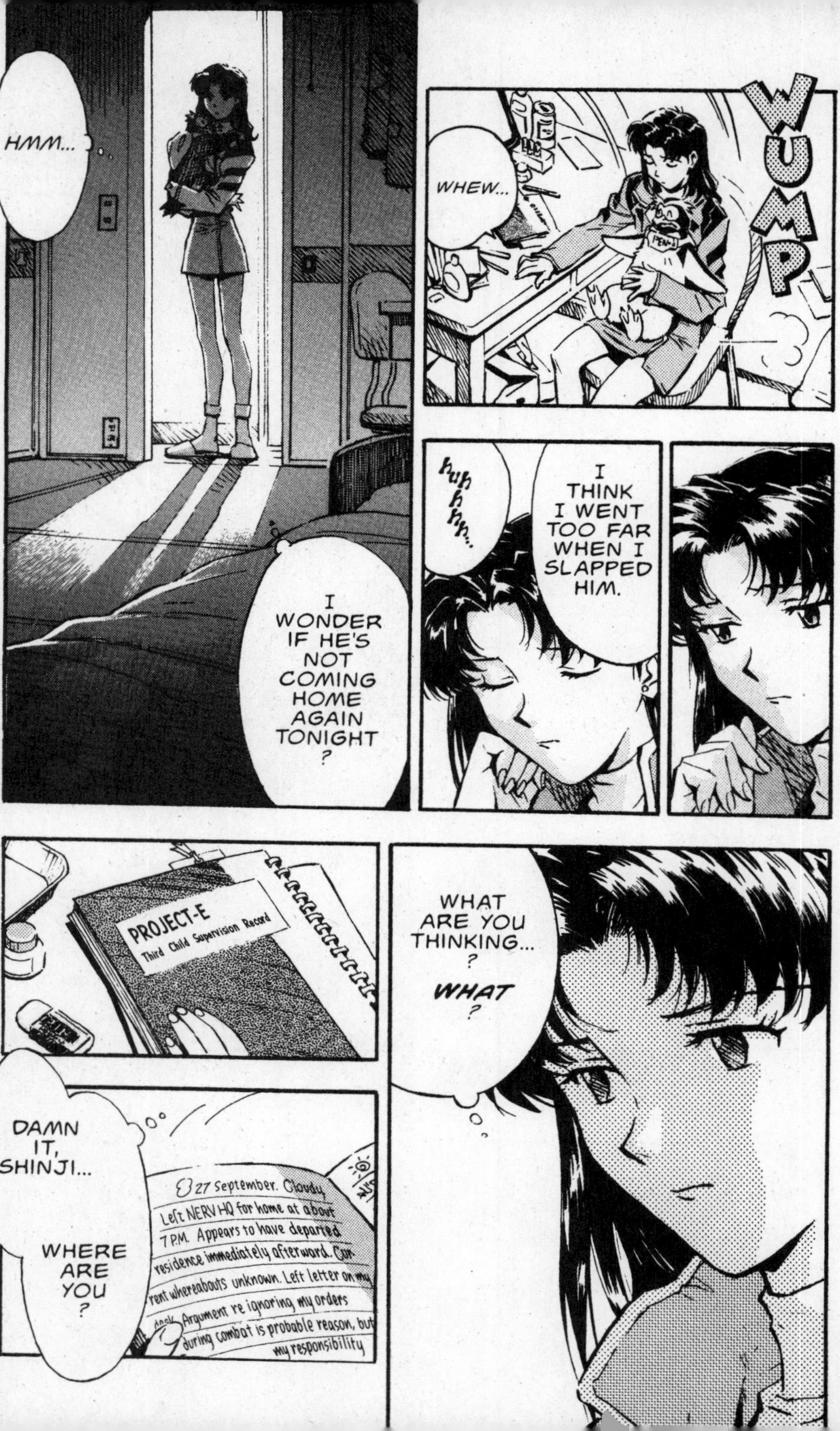

HMM...
I WONDER IF HE'S NOT COMING HOME AGAIN TONIGHT?
WHEW...
WUMP
huhhhh...
I THINK I WENT TOO FAR WHEN I SLAPPED HIM.
PROJECT-E
Third Child Supervision Record
DAMN IT, SHINJI...
27 September. Cloudy
Left NERV HQ for home at about
7 P.M. Appears to have departed
residence immediately afterword. Cur-
rent whereabouts unknown. Left letter on my
desk. Argument re ignoring my orders
during combat is probable reason, but
my responsibility
WHERE ARE YOU?
WHAT ARE YOU THINKING...?
WHAT?

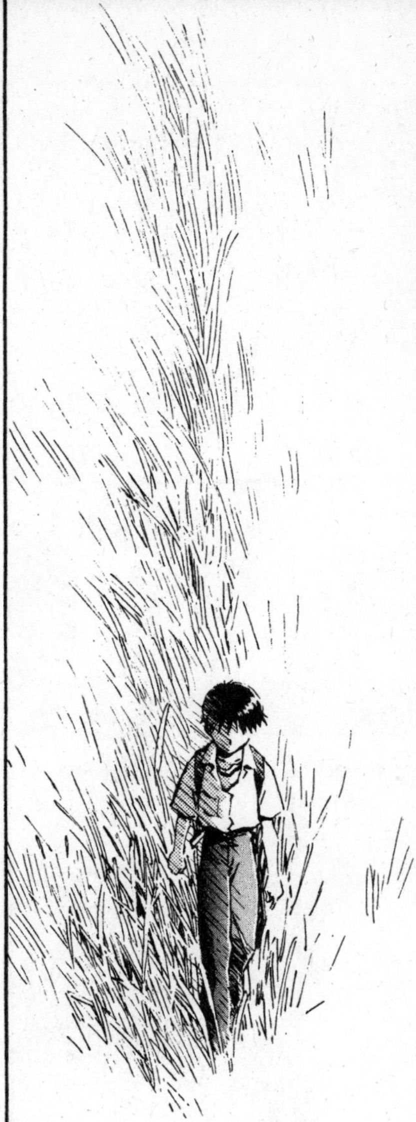

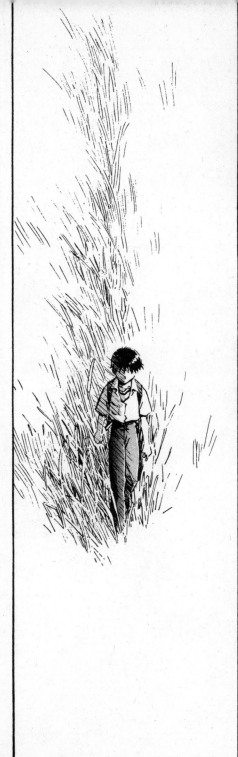

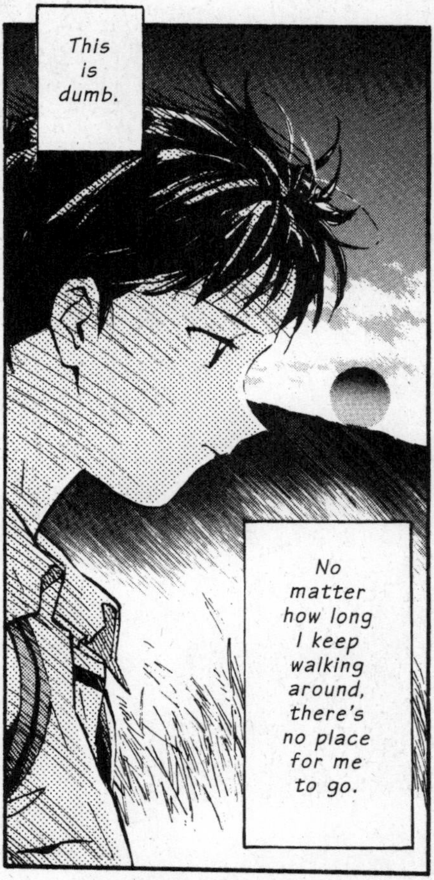
This is dumb.
No matter how long I keep walking around, there's no place for me to go.

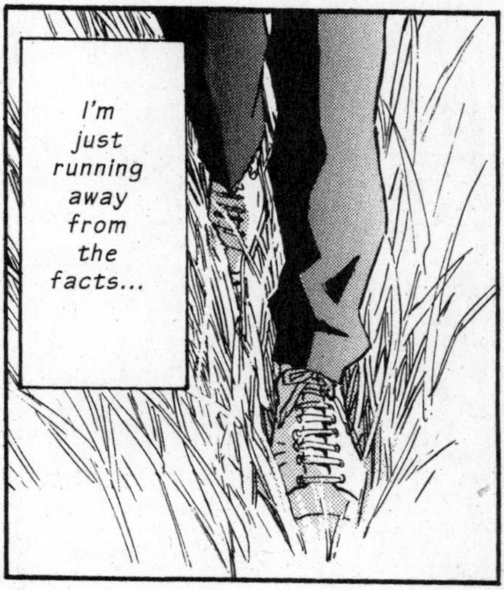
I'm just running away from the facts...

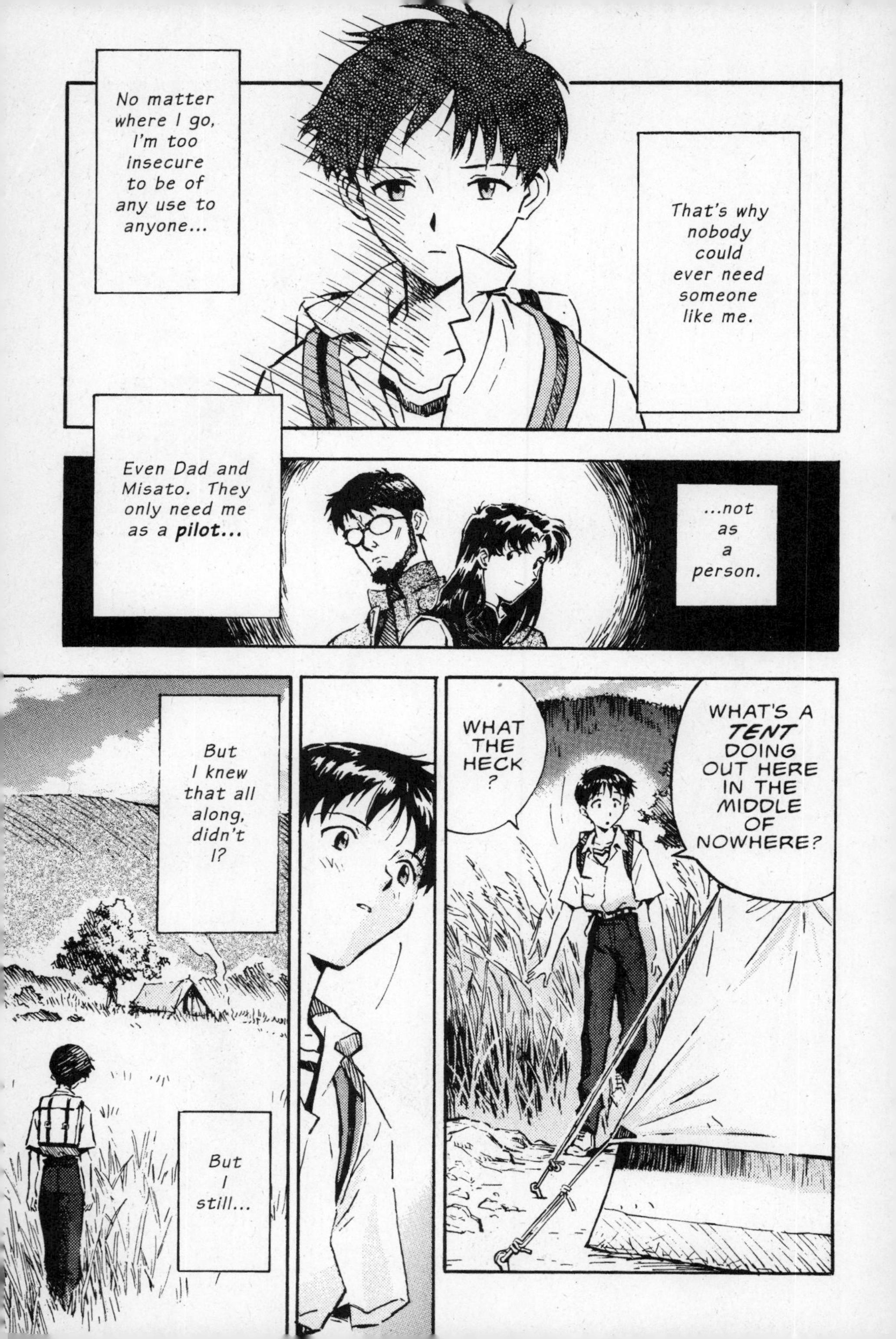
No matter where I'm go, I'm too insecure to be of any use to anyone...
That's why nobody could ever need someone like me.
Even Dad and Misato. They only need me as a **pilot**...
...not as a person.
But I knew that all along, didn't I?
But I still...
WHAT THE HECK?
WHAT'S A *TENT* DOING OUT HERE IN THE MIDDLE OF NOWHERE?

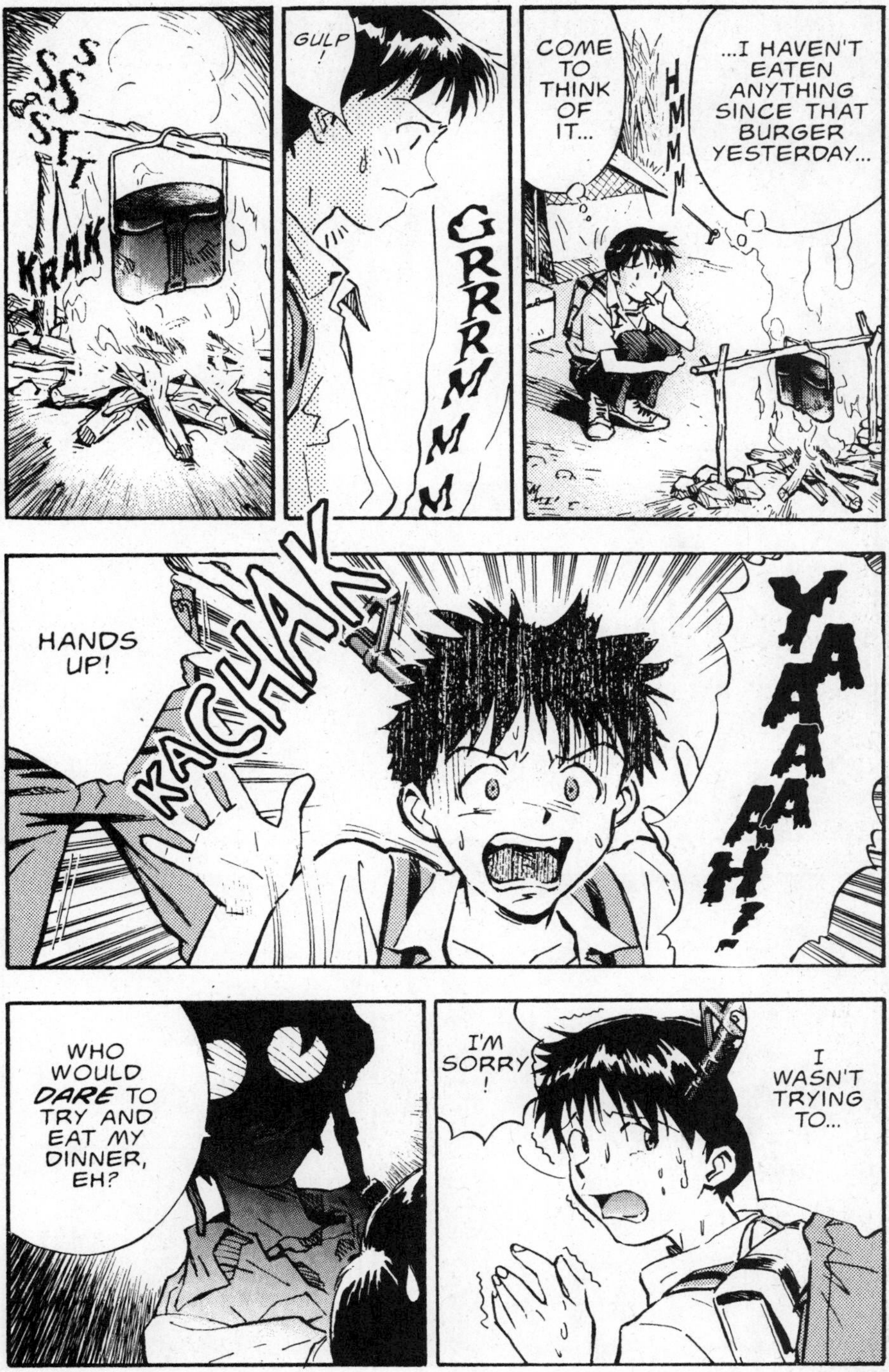
SSSS
SSTT
KRAK
GULP!
GRRRRMMMM
COME TO THINK OF IT...
HMMM
...I HAVEN'T EATEN ANYTHING SINCE THAT BURGER YESTERDAY...
HANDS UP!
KACHAK
YAAAAAH!
WHO WOULD *DARE* TO TRY AND EAT MY DINNER, EH?
I'M SORRY!
I WASN'T TRYING TO...

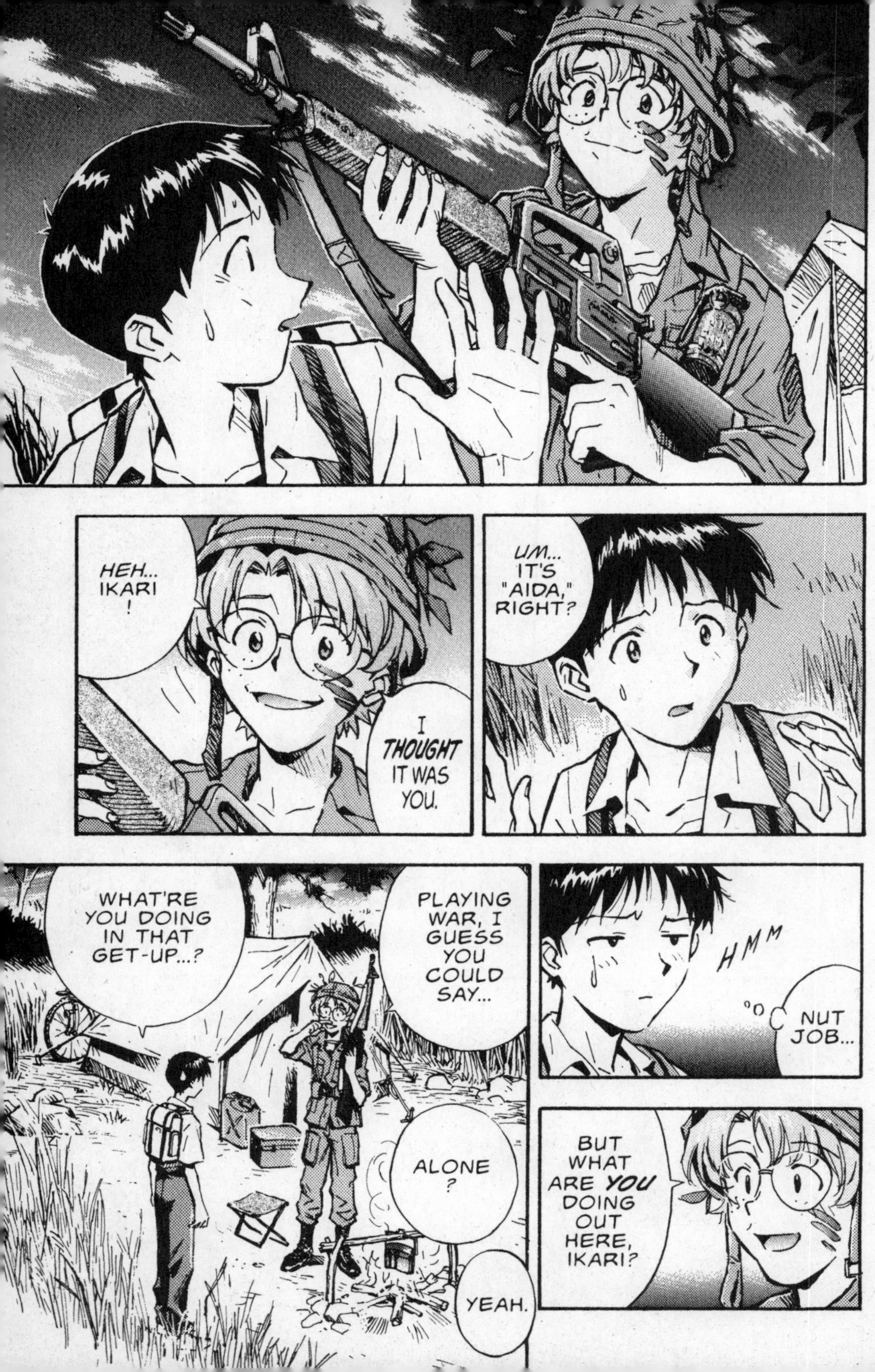
HEH... IKARI!
I *THOUGHT* IT WAS YOU.
UM... IT'S "AIDA," RIGHT?
WHAT'RE YOU DOING IN THAT GET-UP...?
PLAYING WAR, I GUESS YOU COULD SAY...
ALONE?
YEAH.
HMMM
NUT JOB...
BUT WHAT ARE *YOU* DOING OUT HERE, IKARI?

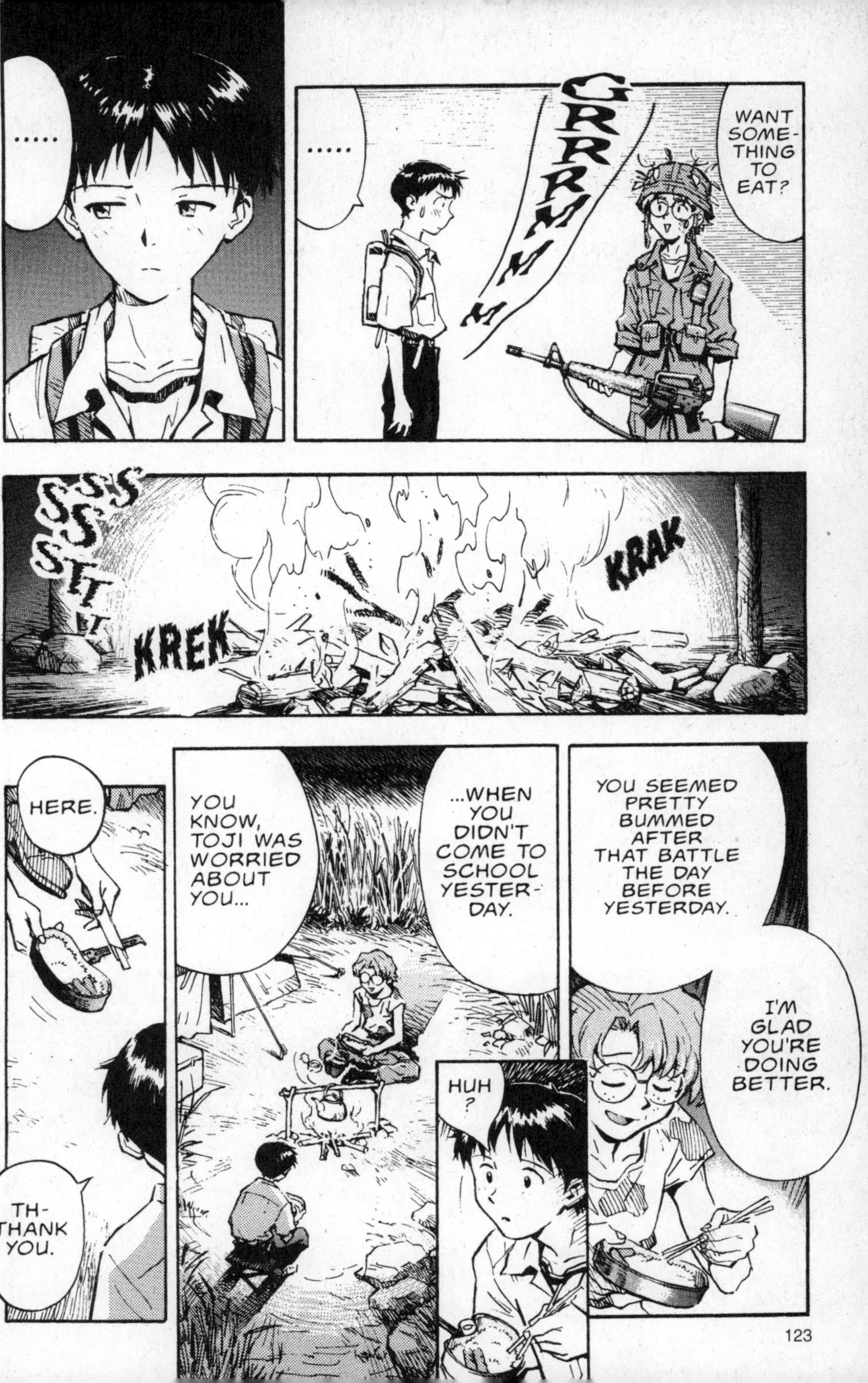
......
......
GRRRMMM
WANT SOME-THING TO EAT?
SSSSSTTT
KREK
KRAK
HERE.
TH-THANK YOU.
YOU KNOW, TOJI WAS WORRIED ABOUT YOU...
...WHEN YOU DIDN'T COME TO SCHOOL YESTER-DAY.
YOU SEEMED PRETTY BUMMED AFTER THAT BATTLE THE DAY BEFORE YESTERDAY.
I'M GLAD YOU'RE DOING BETTER.
HUH?

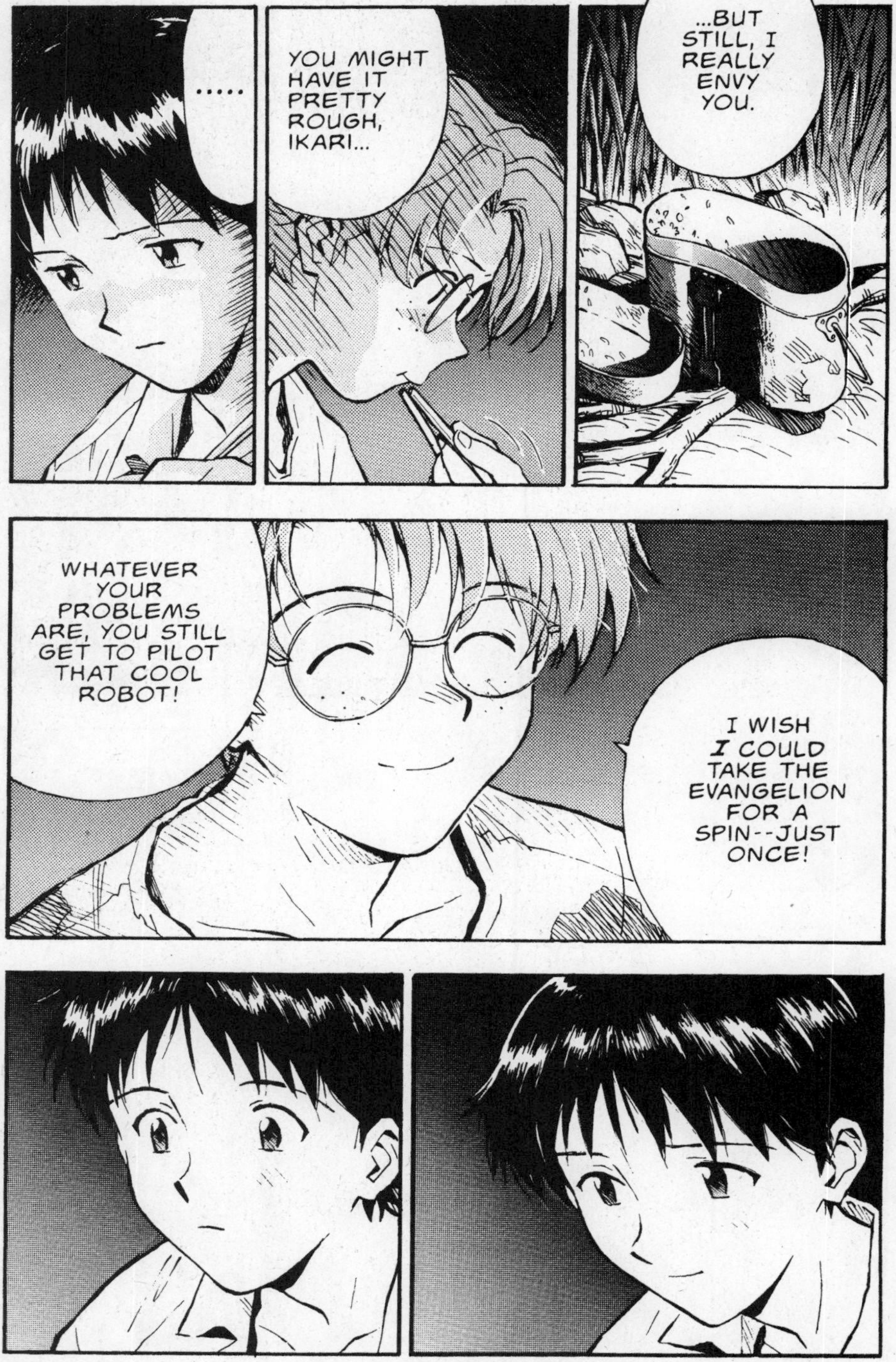
.....
YOU MIGHT HAVE IT PRETTY ROUGH, IKARI...
...BUT STILL, I REALLY ENVY YOU.
WHATEVER YOUR PROBLEMS ARE, YOU STILL GET TO PILOT THAT COOL ROBOT!
I WISH *I* COULD TAKE THE EVANGELION FOR A SPIN--JUST ONCE!

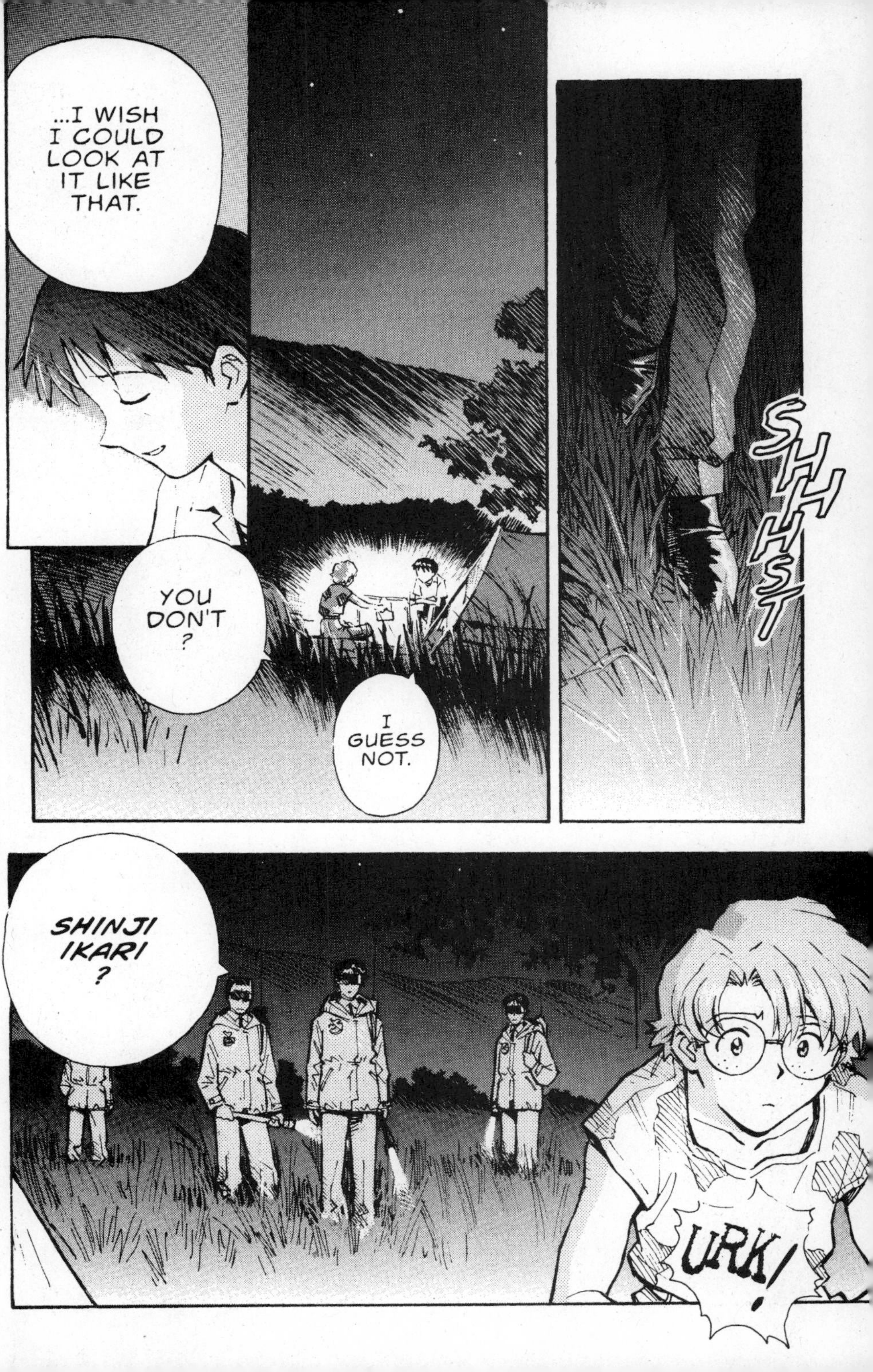
...I WISH I COULD LOOK AT IT LIKE THAT.
YOU DON'T ?
I GUESS NOT.
SHHHST
SHINJI IKARI ?
URK!

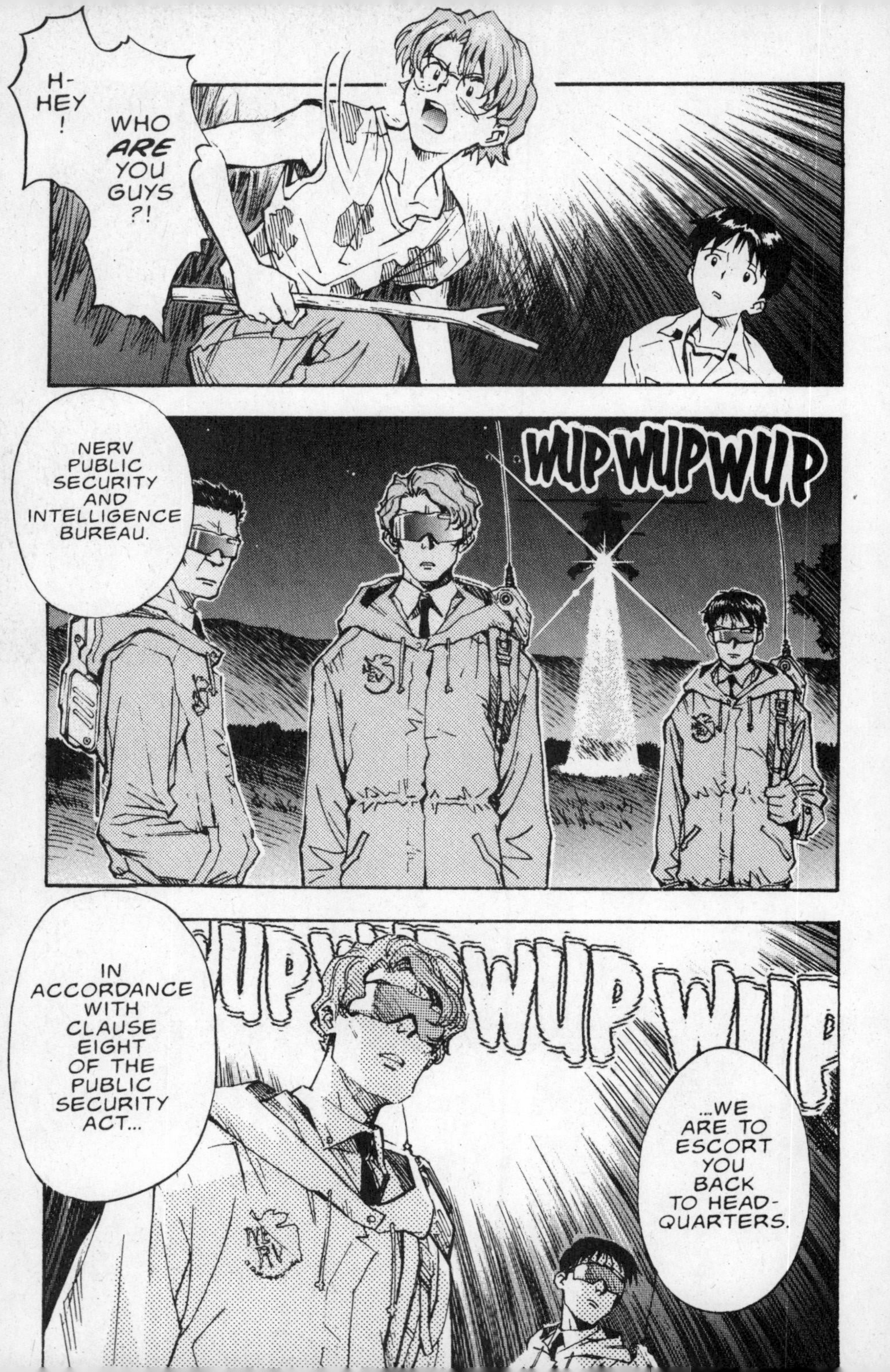
H-HEY!
WHO ARE YOU GUYS?!
NERV PUBLIC SECURITY AND INTELLIGENCE BUREAU.
WUP WUP WUP
IN ACCORDANCE WITH CLAUSE EIGHT OF THE PUBLIC SECURITY ACT...
WUP WUP WUP
...WE ARE TO ESCORT YOU BACK TO HEAD-QUARTERS.

IS THAT OK?

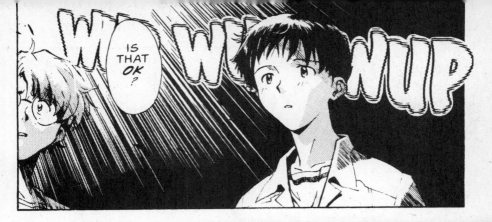

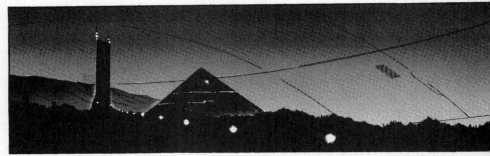

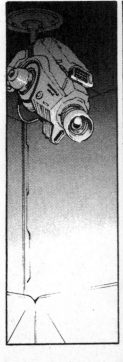

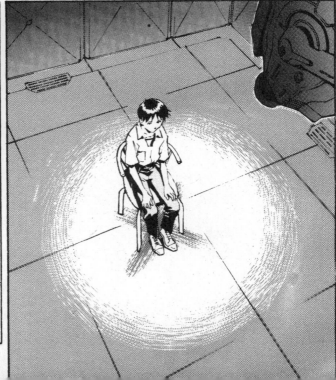

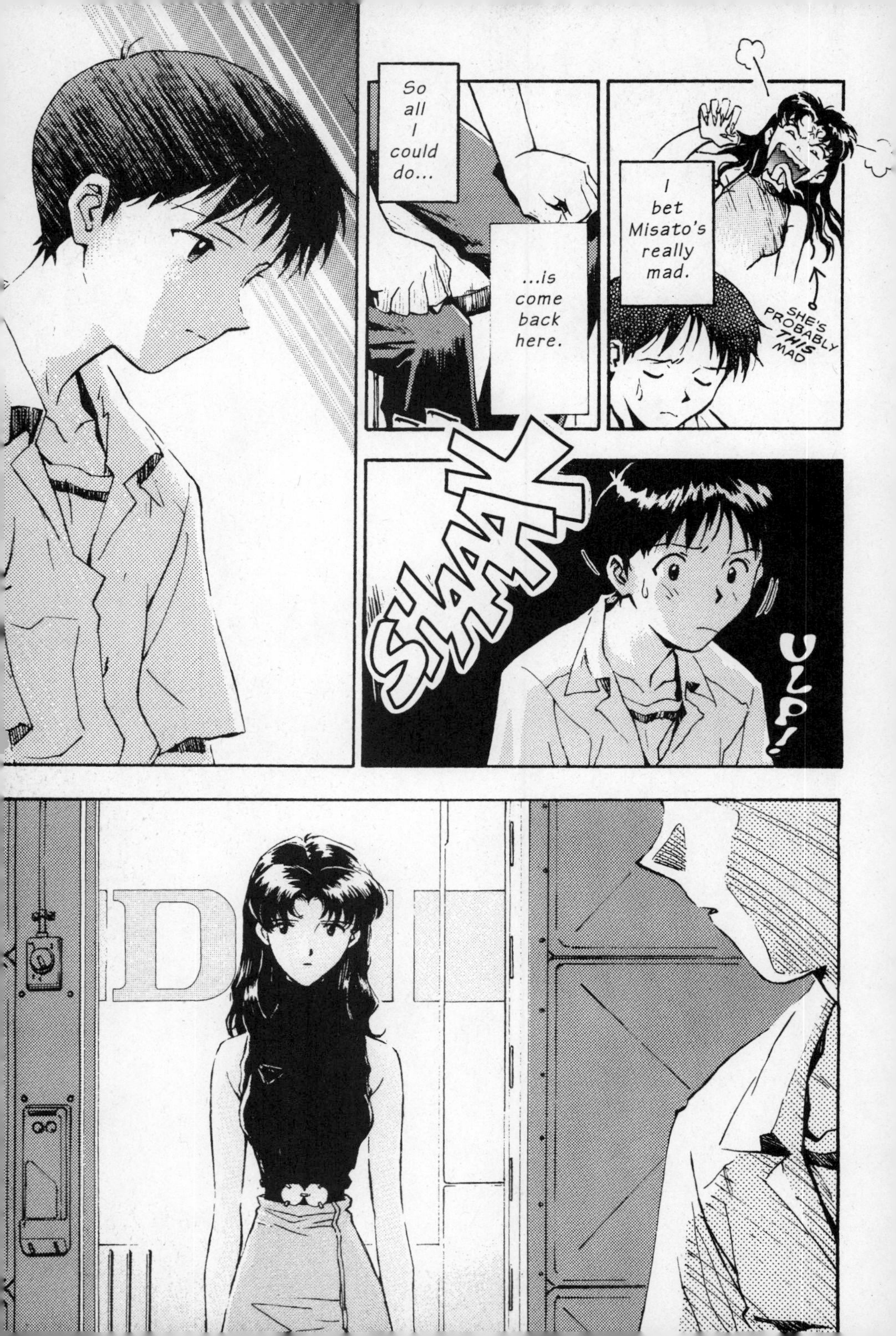
So all I could do...
...is come back here.
I bet Misato's really mad.
SHE'S PROBABLY THIS MAD
SHAAAK
ULP!

WELCOME BACK.

UH...

YEAH.

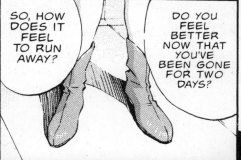

SO, HOW DOES IT FEEL TO RUN AWAY?

DO YOU FEEL BETTER NOW THAT YOU'VE BEEN GONE FOR TWO DAYS?

I'M...

...SORRY.

LET ME ASK YOU THIS...

DO YOU WANT TO BE AN EVA PILOT?

OR NOT?

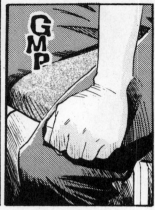

GMP

IT DOESN'T MATTER.

I TOLD YOU BEFORE, I DON'T PILOT IT BECAUSE I WANT TO.

BUT...

...EVEN IF I SAID I DIDN'T WANT TO, IT WOULDN'T CHANGE ANYTHING.

I'M THE ONLY PILOT YOU HAVE, RIGHT?

EVERYONE WOULD BE IN TROUBLE IF I DIDN'T PILOT IT, RIGHT?

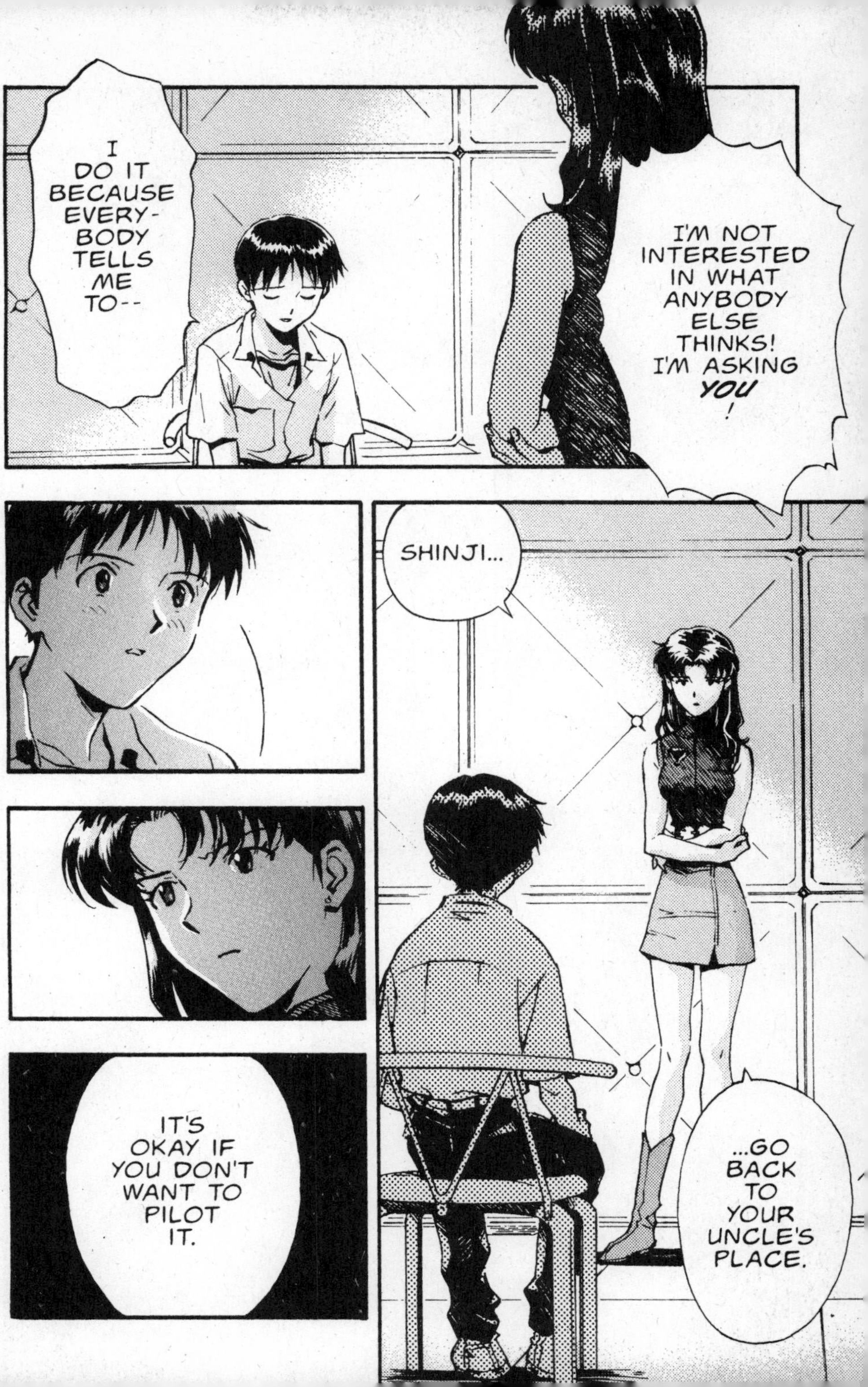
I DO IT BECAUSE EVERY-BODY TELLS ME TO--
I'M NOT INTERESTED IN WHAT ANYBODY ELSE THINKS! I'M ASKING ***YOU***!
IT'S OKAY IF YOU DON'T WANT TO PILOT IT.
SHINJI...
...GO BACK TO YOUR UNCLE'S PLACE.

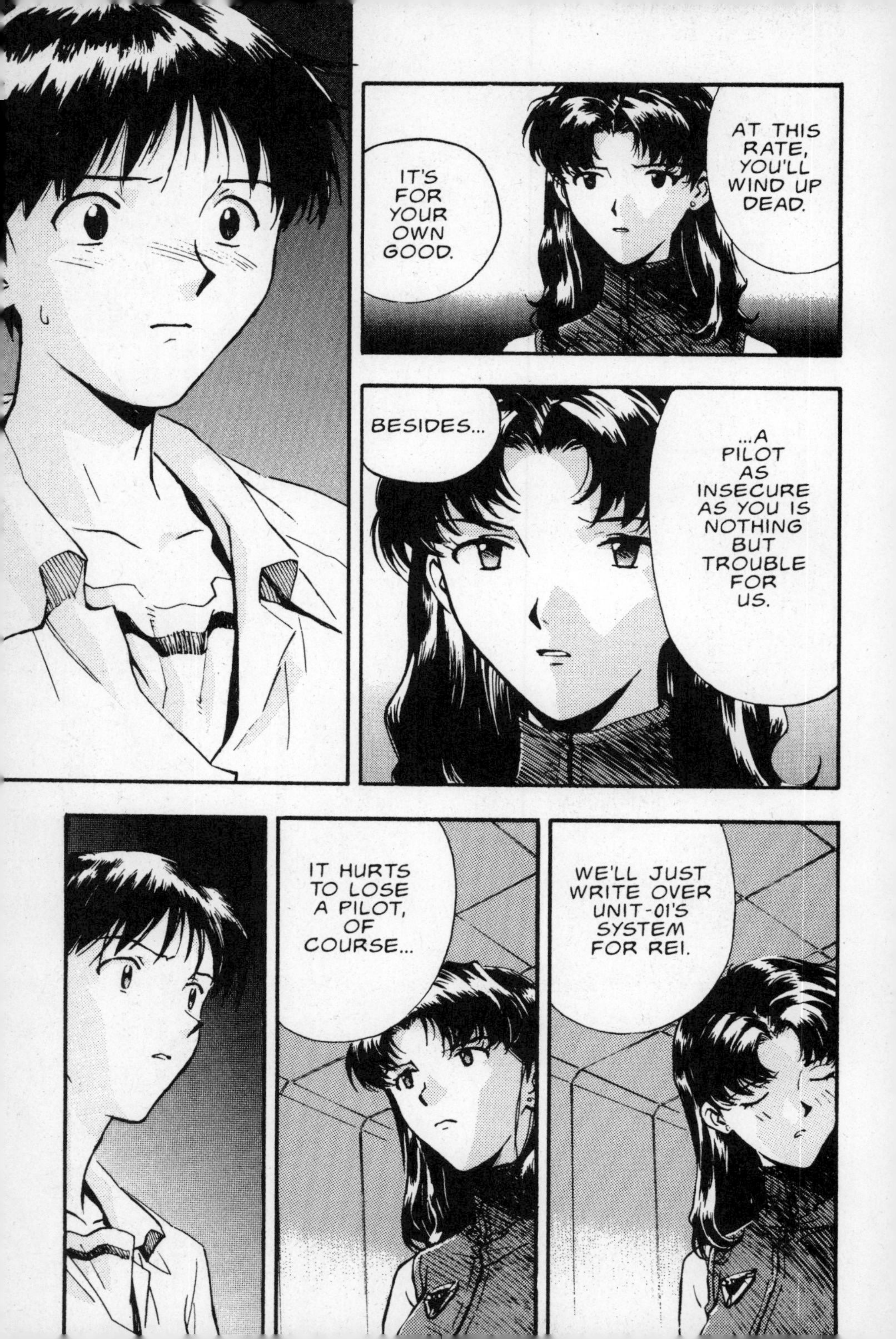
IT'S FOR YOUR OWN GOOD.
AT THIS RATE, YOU'LL WIND UP DEAD.
BESIDES...
...A PILOT AS INSECURE AS YOU IS NOTHING BUT TROUBLE FOR US.
IT HURTS TO LOSE A PILOT, OF COURSE...
WE'LL JUST WRITE OVER UNIT-01'S SYSTEM FOR REI.

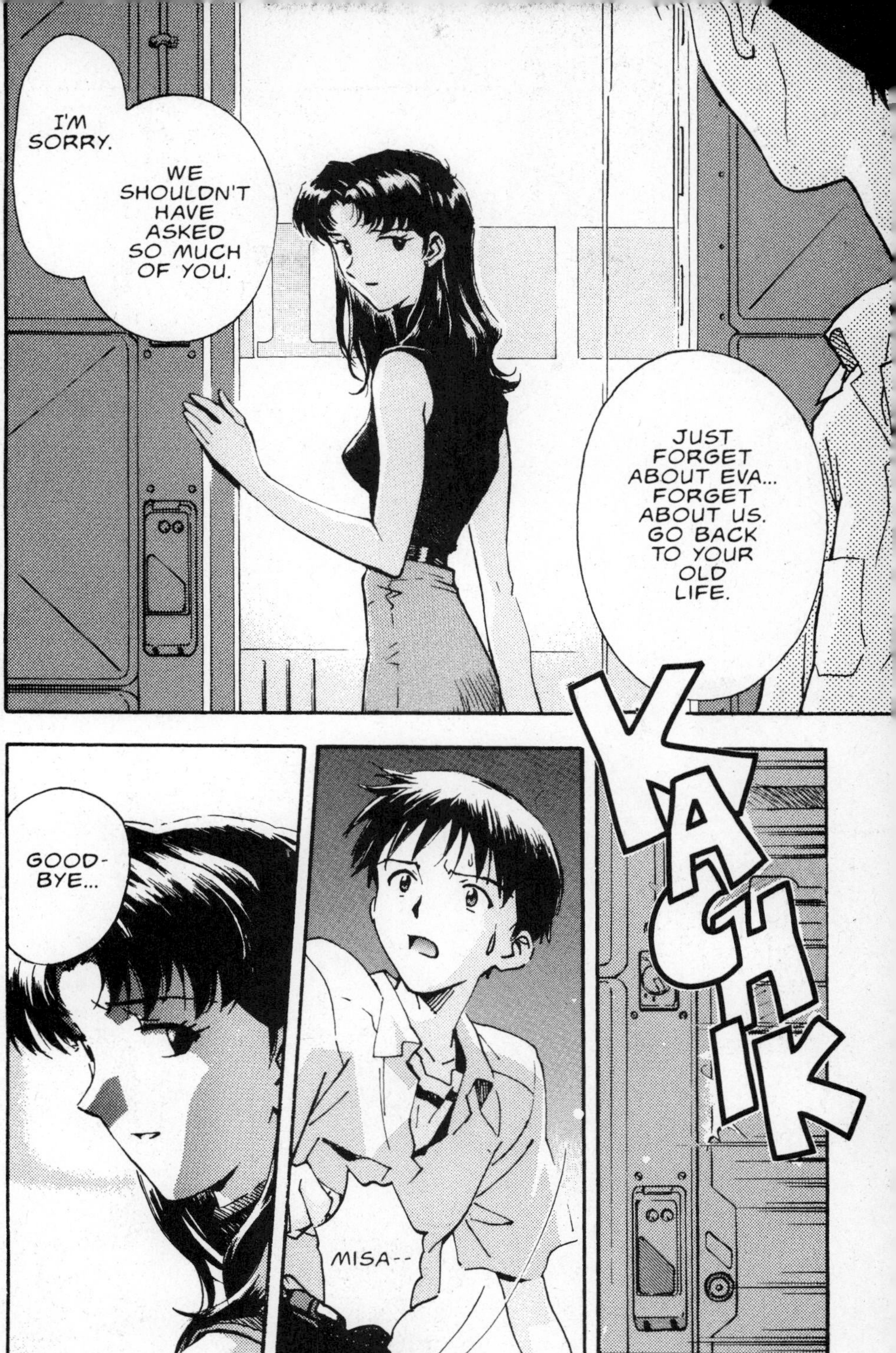
I'M SORRY.
WE SHOULDN'T HAVE ASKED SO MUCH OF YOU.
JUST FORGET ABOUT EVA... FORGET ABOUT US. GO BACK TO YOUR OLD LIFE.
GOOD-BYE...
MISA--
YACHIK

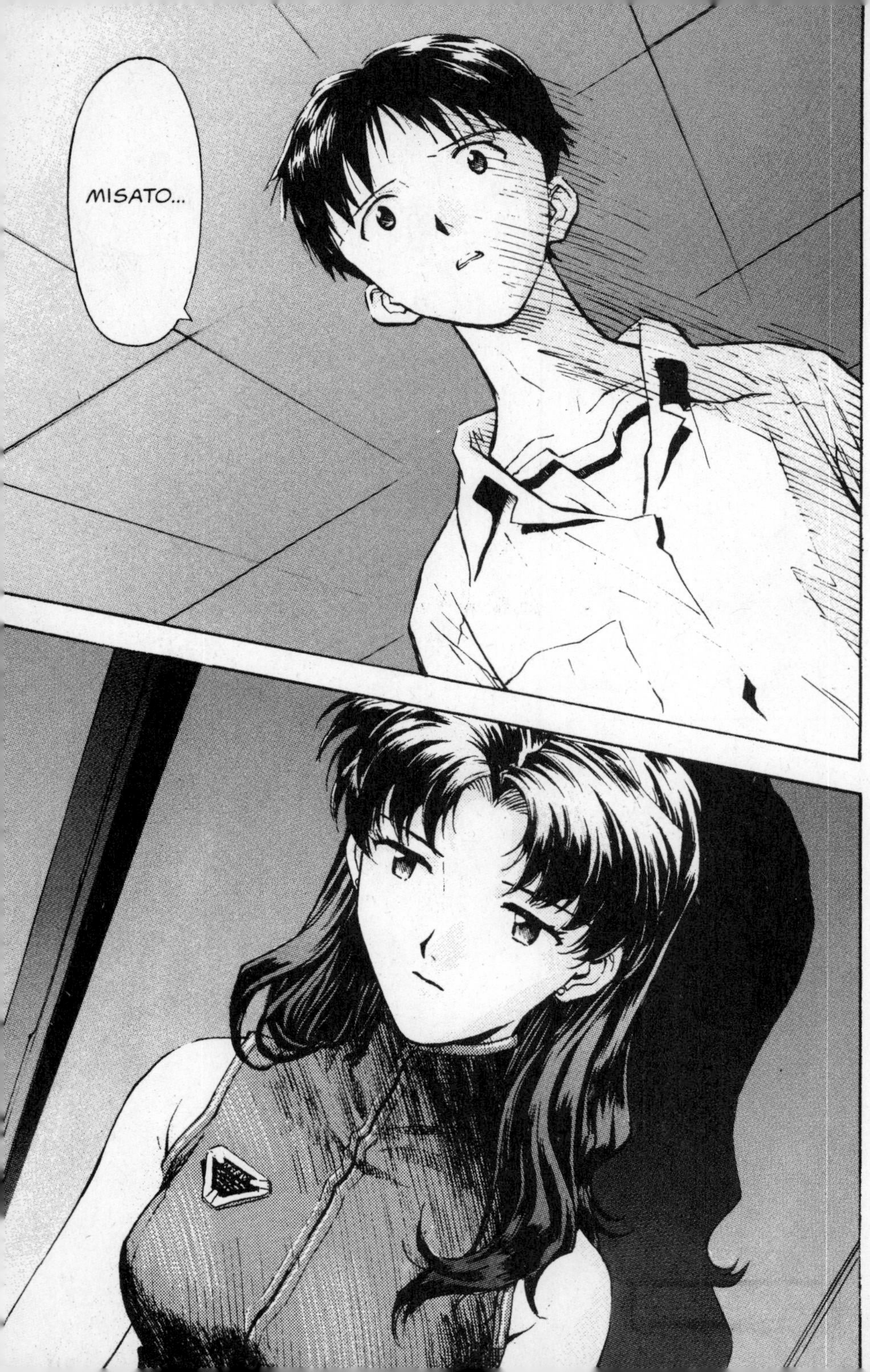
MISATO...

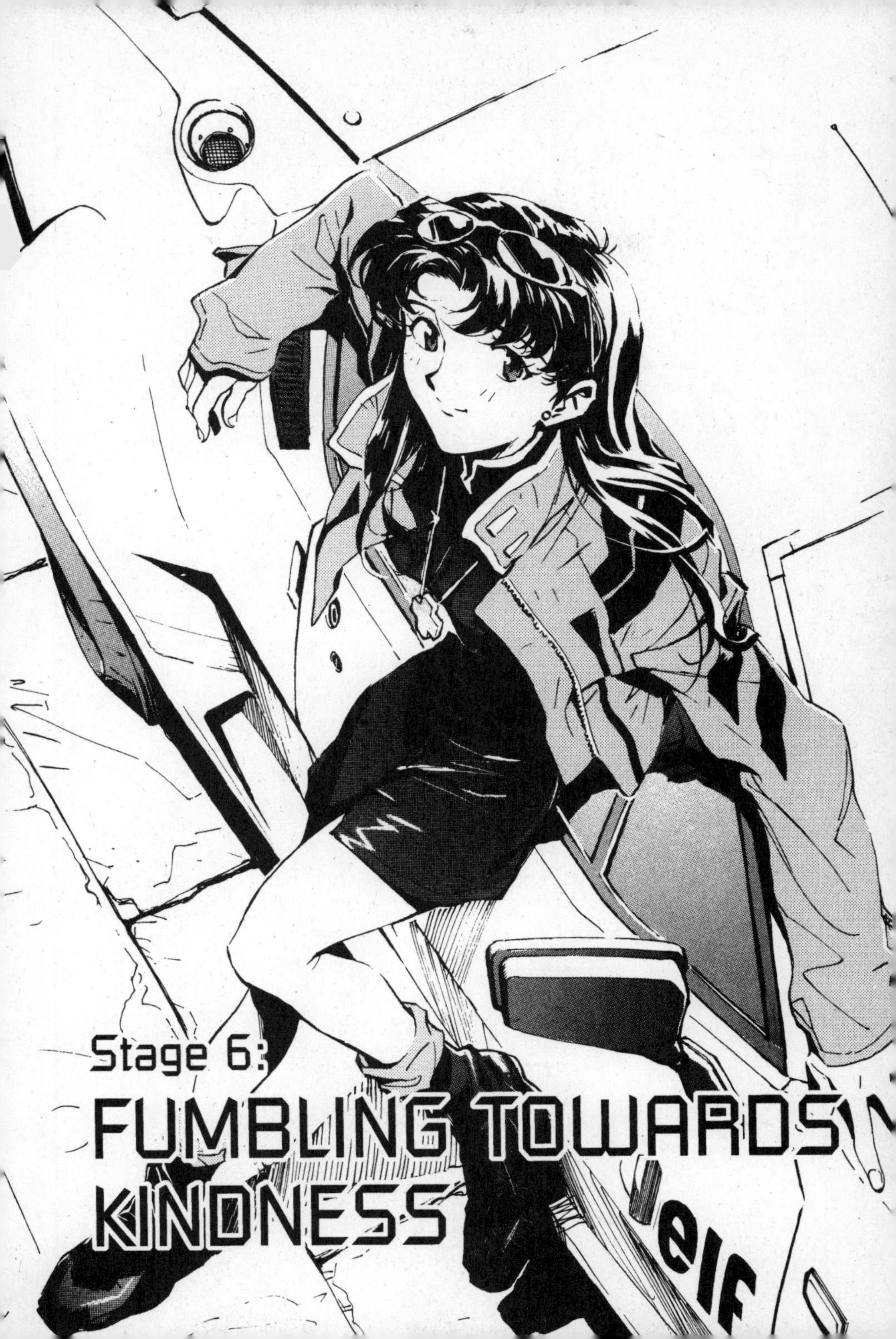
Stage 6:
FUMBLING TOWARDS KINDNESS

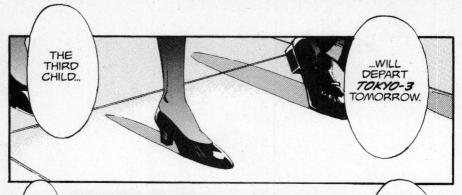

THE THIRD CHILD...

...WILL DEPART *TOKYO-3* TOMORROW.

I SEE...

ARE YOU SURE THIS IS ALL RIGHT?

BUT... THE MARDUK AGENCY HASN'T ANNOUNCED A *FOURTH CHILD* YET. WE DON'T HAVE A REPLACEMENT PILOT FOR UNIT-01...

THIS IS ONE OF THE SCENARIOS WE PREDICTED.

IT'S SIMPLICITY ITSELF TO FORESEE WHAT A PERSON WILL DO WHEN THEY'RE CORNERED.

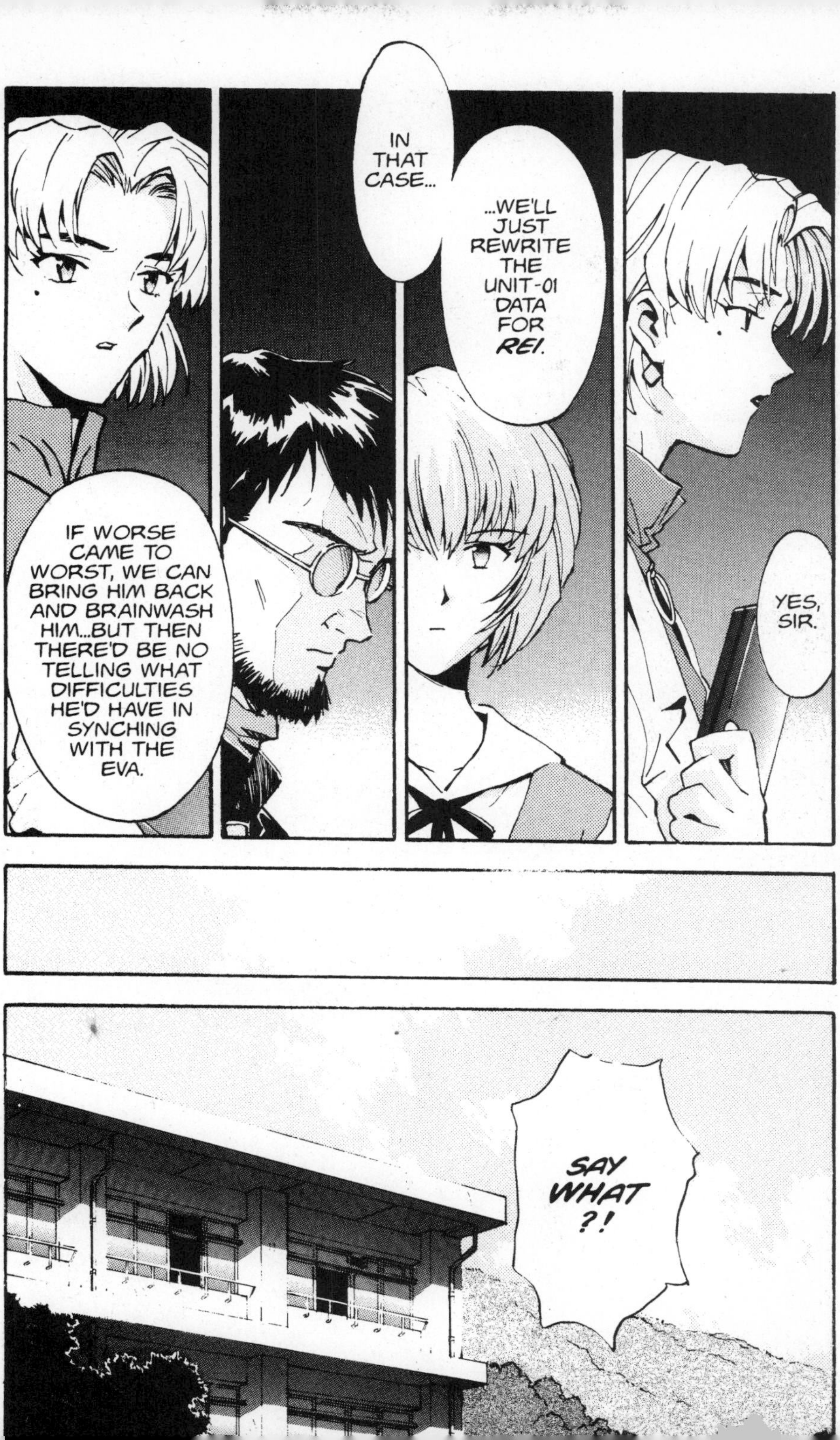
IF WORSE CAME TO WORST, WE CAN BRING HIM BACK AND BRAINWASH HIM...BUT THEN THERE'D BE NO TELLING WHAT DIFFICULTIES HE'D HAVE IN SYNCHING WITH THE EVA.
IN THAT CASE...
...WE'LL JUST REWRITE THE UNIT-01 DATA FOR *REI*.
YES, SIR.
SAY WHAT ?!

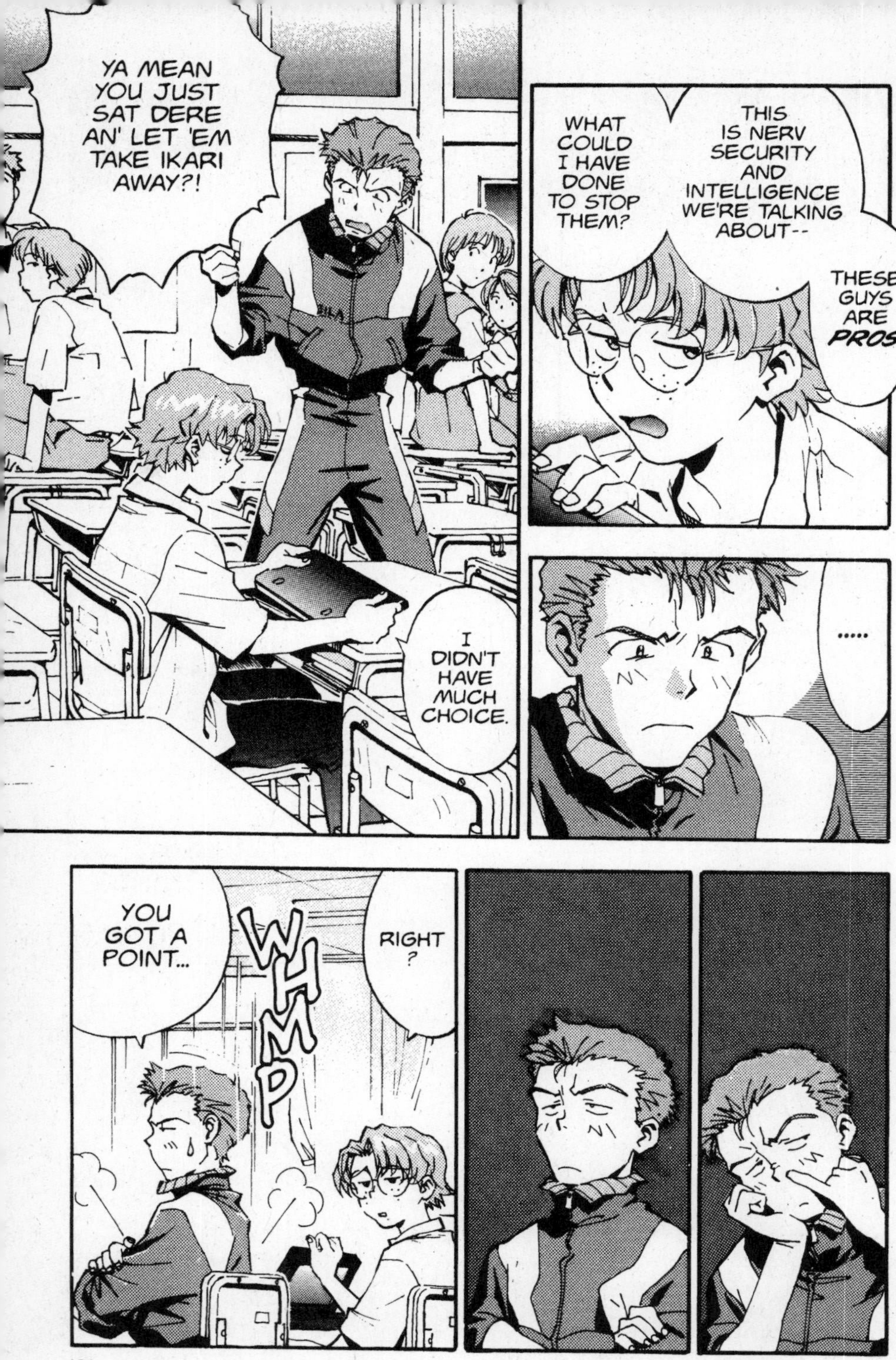
YA MEAN YOU JUST SAT DERE AN' LET 'EM TAKE IKARI AWAY?!
I DIDN'T HAVE MUCH CHOICE.
WHAT COULD I HAVE DONE TO STOP THEM?
THIS IS NERV SECURITY AND INTELLIGENCE WE'RE TALKING ABOUT--
THESE GUYS ARE *PROS*.
.....
YOU GOT A POINT...
WHMP
RIGHT?

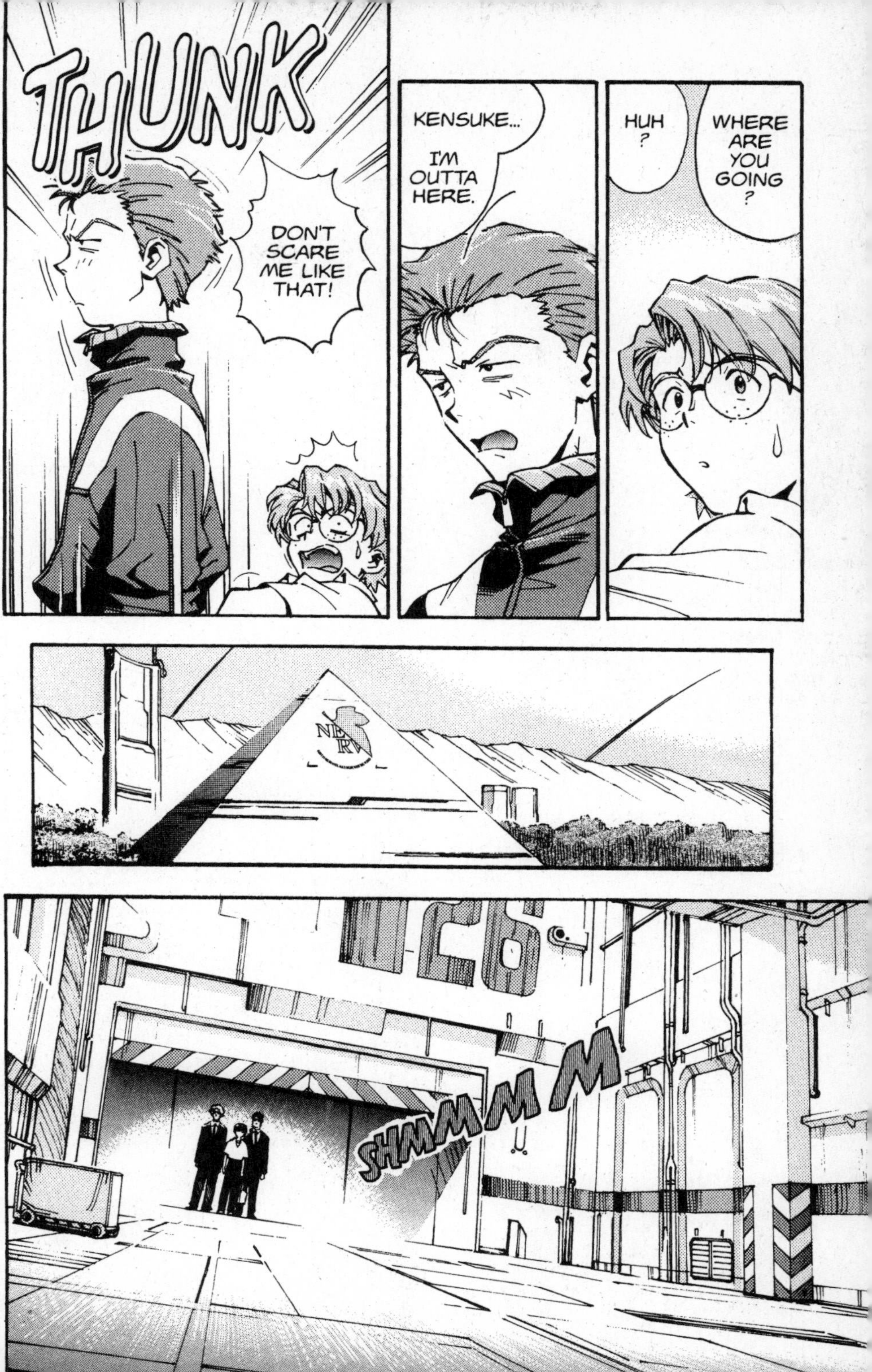
THUNK
DON'T SCARE ME LIKE THAT!
KENSUKE...
I'M OUTTA HERE.
HUH?
WHERE ARE YOU GOING?
SHMMMM

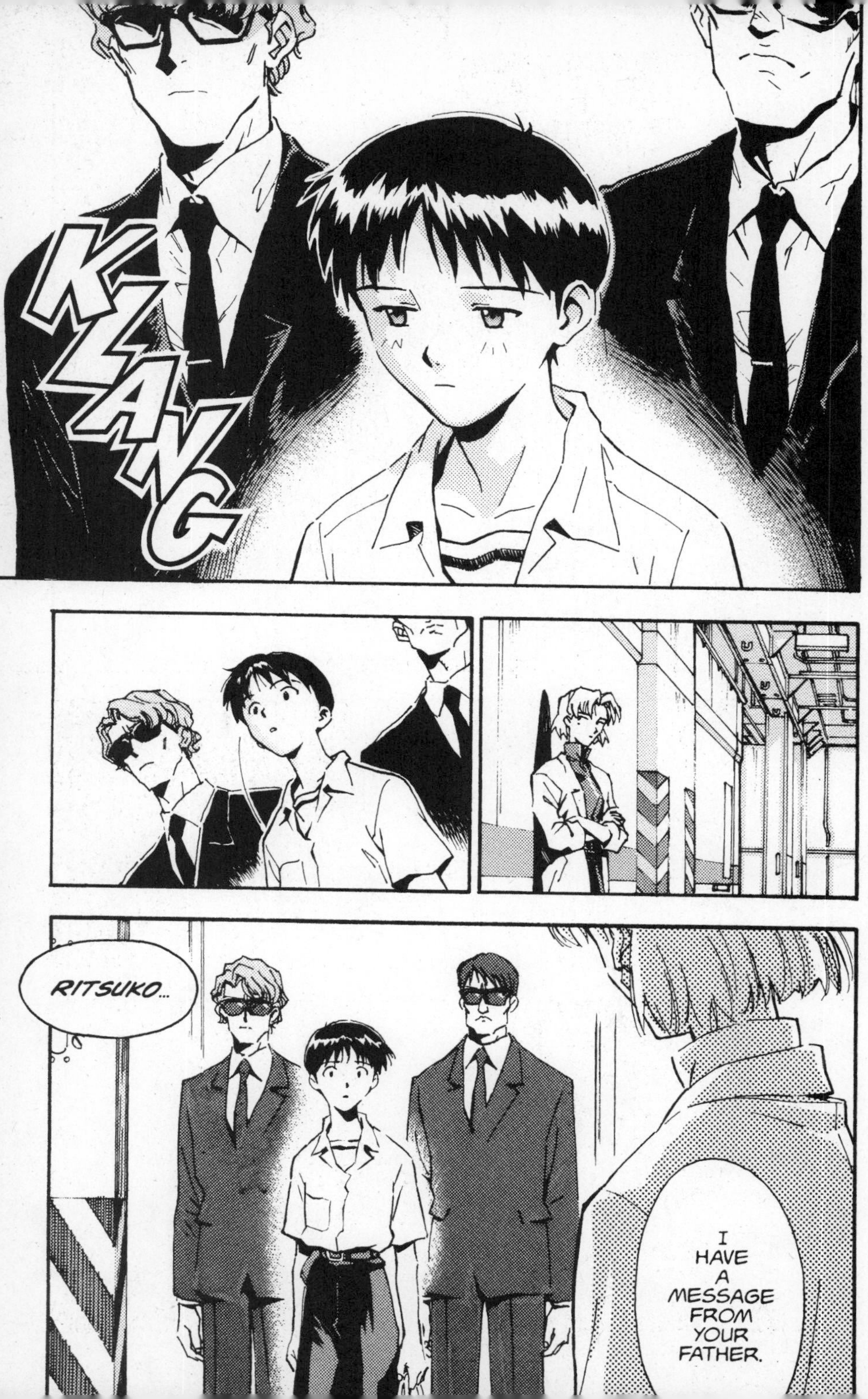
KLANG
RITSUKO...
I HAVE A MESSAGE FROM YOUR FATHER.

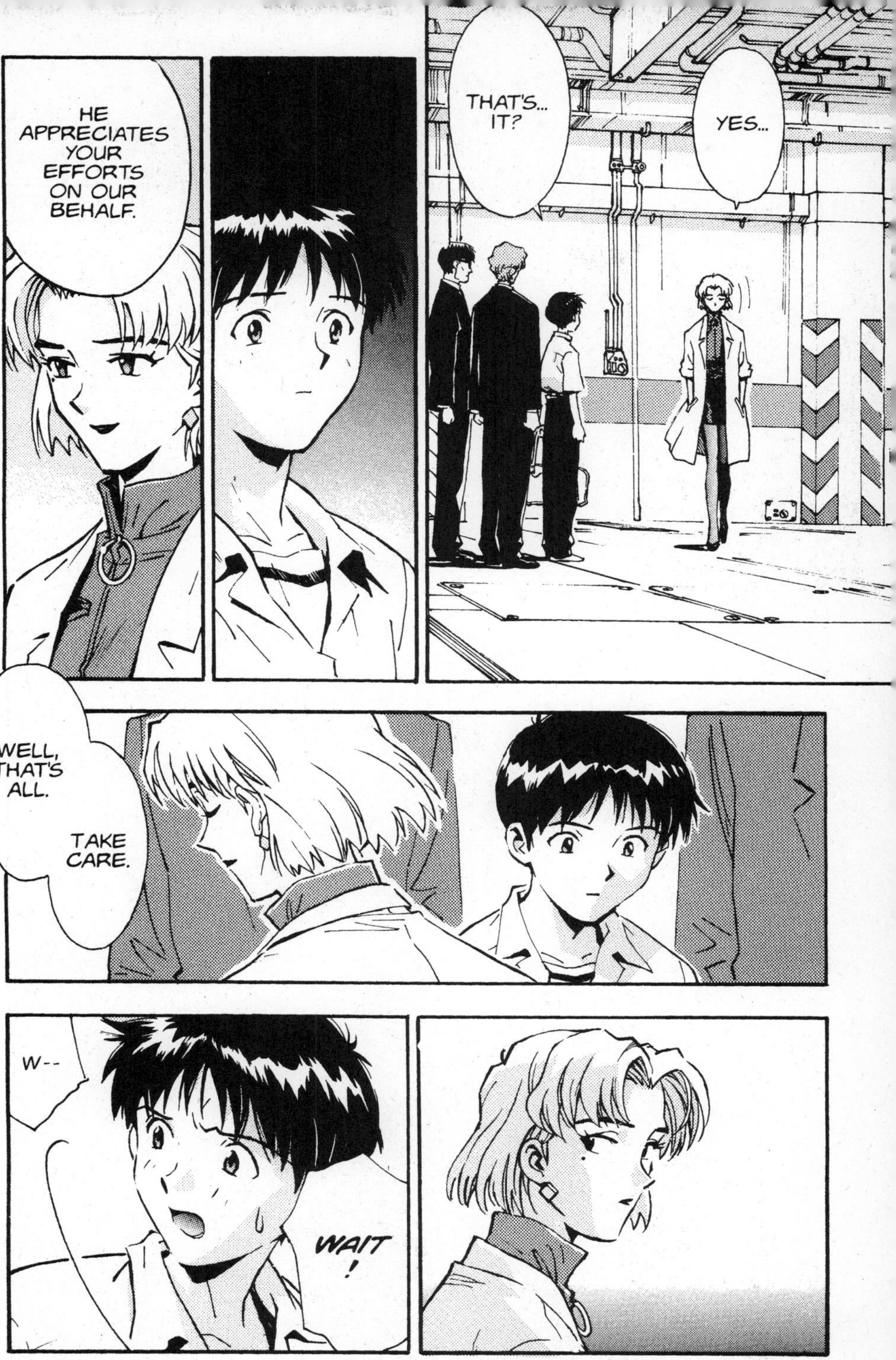
HE APPRECIATES YOUR EFFORTS ON OUR BEHALF.
THAT'S... IT?
YES...
WELL, THAT'S ALL.
TAKE CARE.
W--
WAIT!

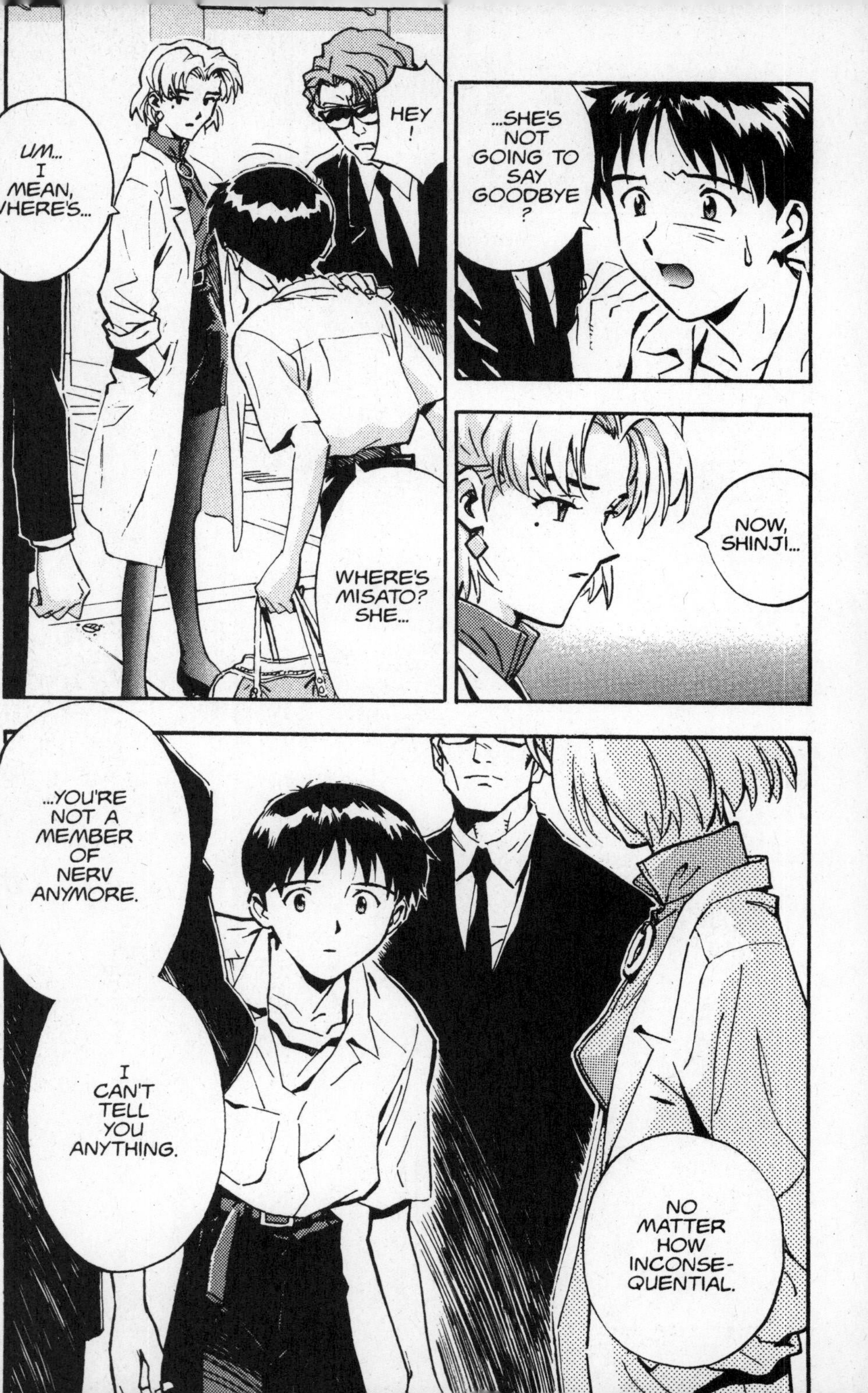
UM... I MEAN, WHERE'S...
HEY!
WHERE'S MISATO? SHE...
...SHE'S NOT GOING TO SAY GOODBYE?
NOW, SHINJI...
...YOU'RE NOT A MEMBER OF NERV ANYMORE.
I CAN'T TELL YOU ANYTHING.
NO MATTER HOW INCONSE-QUENTIAL.

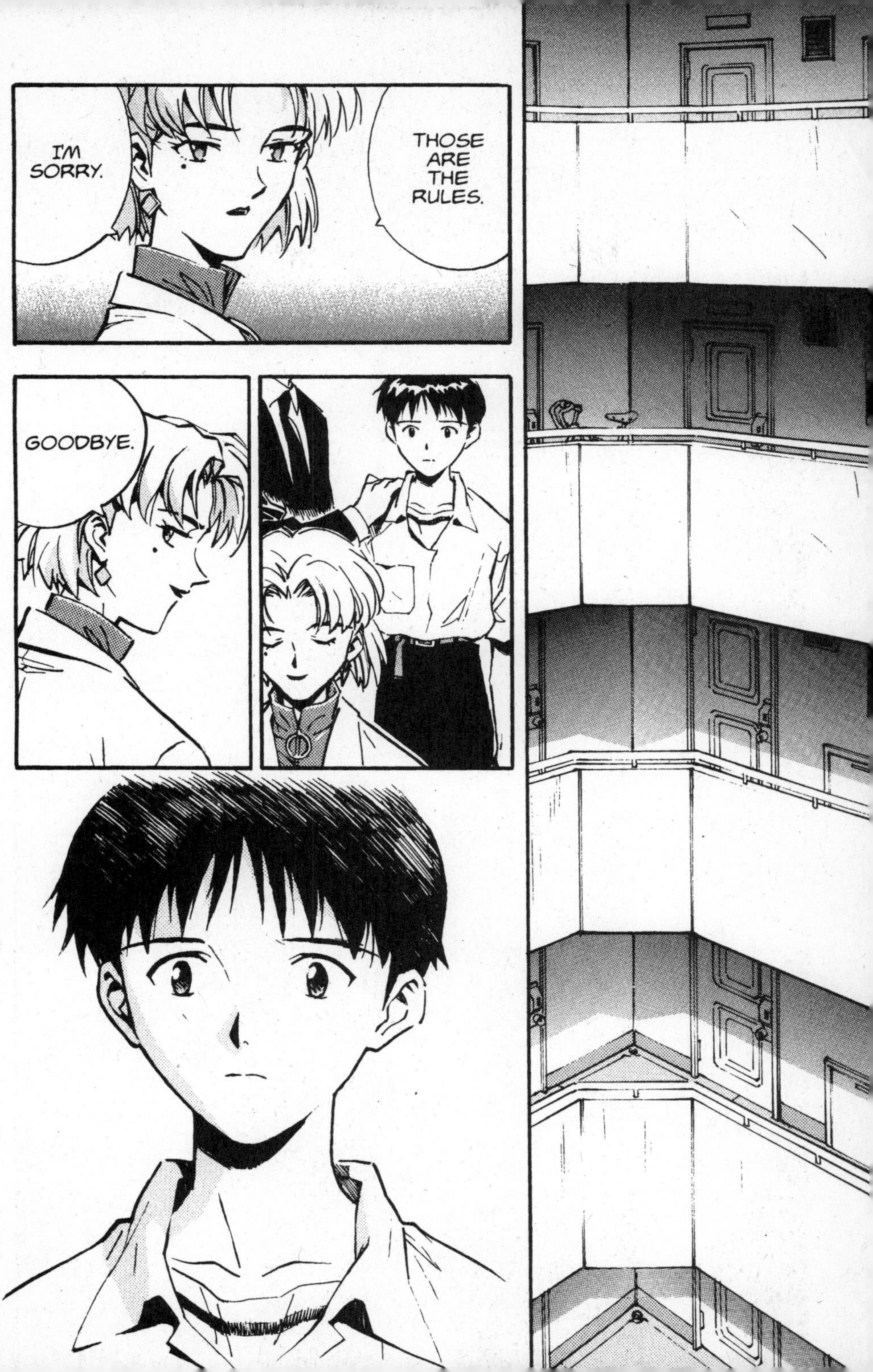
I'M SORRY.
THOSE ARE THE RULES.
GOODBYE.

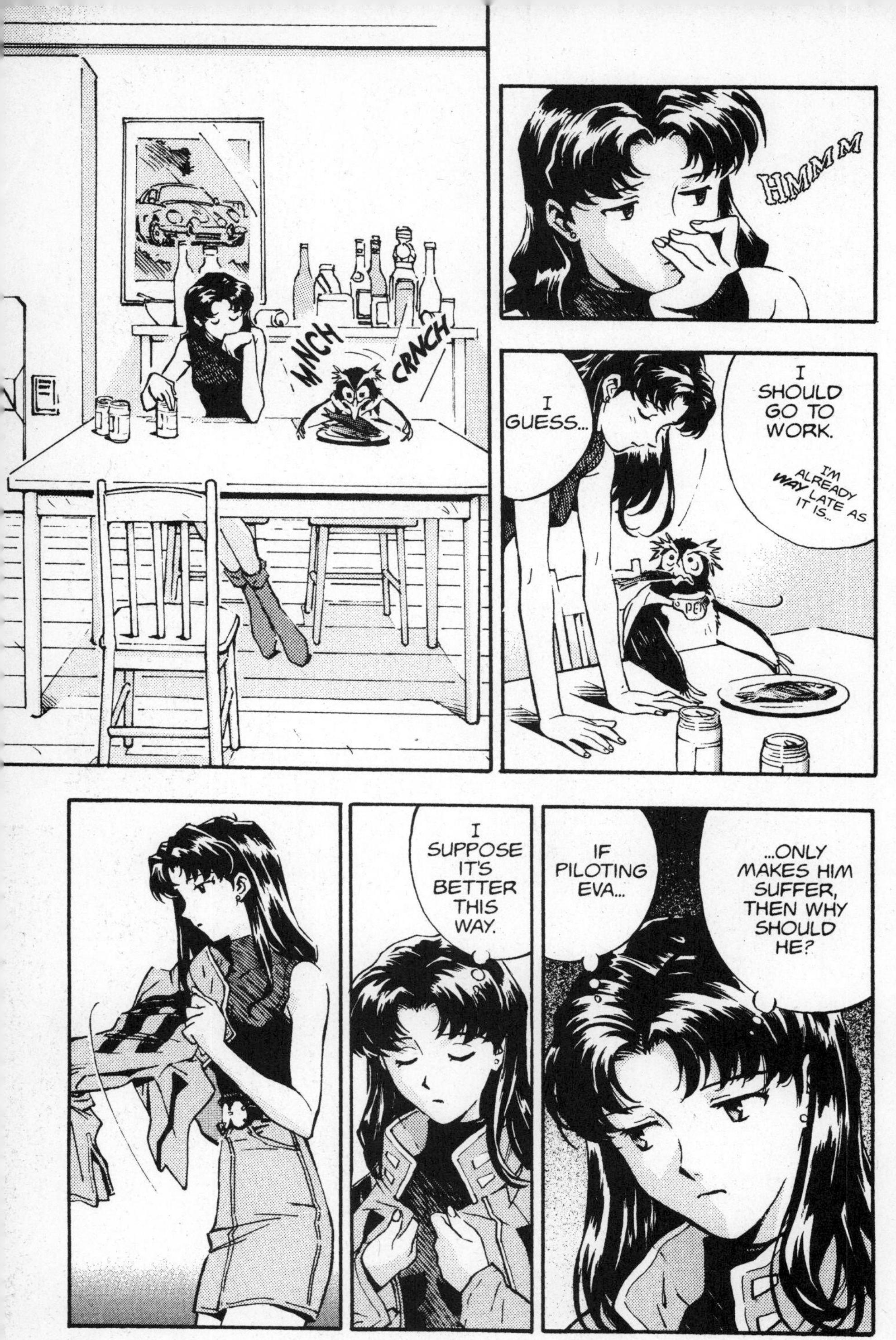
MNCH
CRNCH
HMMM M
I GUESS...
I SHOULD GO TO WORK.
I'M ALREADY WAY LATE AS IT IS...
I SUPPOSE IT'S BETTER THIS WAY.
IF PILOTING EVA...
...ONLY MAKES HIM SUFFER, THEN WHY SHOULD HE?

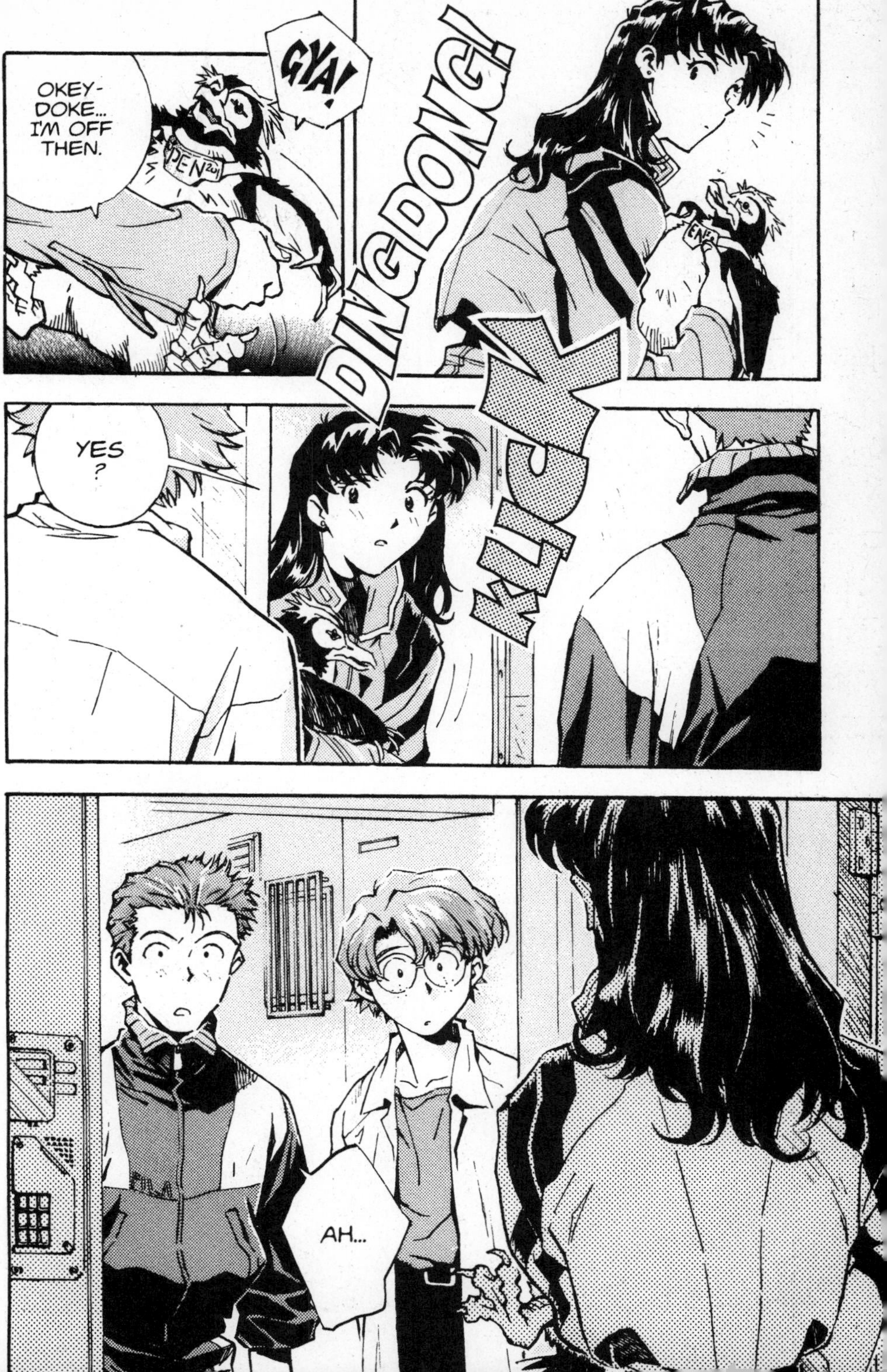

OKEY-DOKE... I'M OFF THEN.
GYA!
DINGDONG!
KLICK
YES ?
AH...

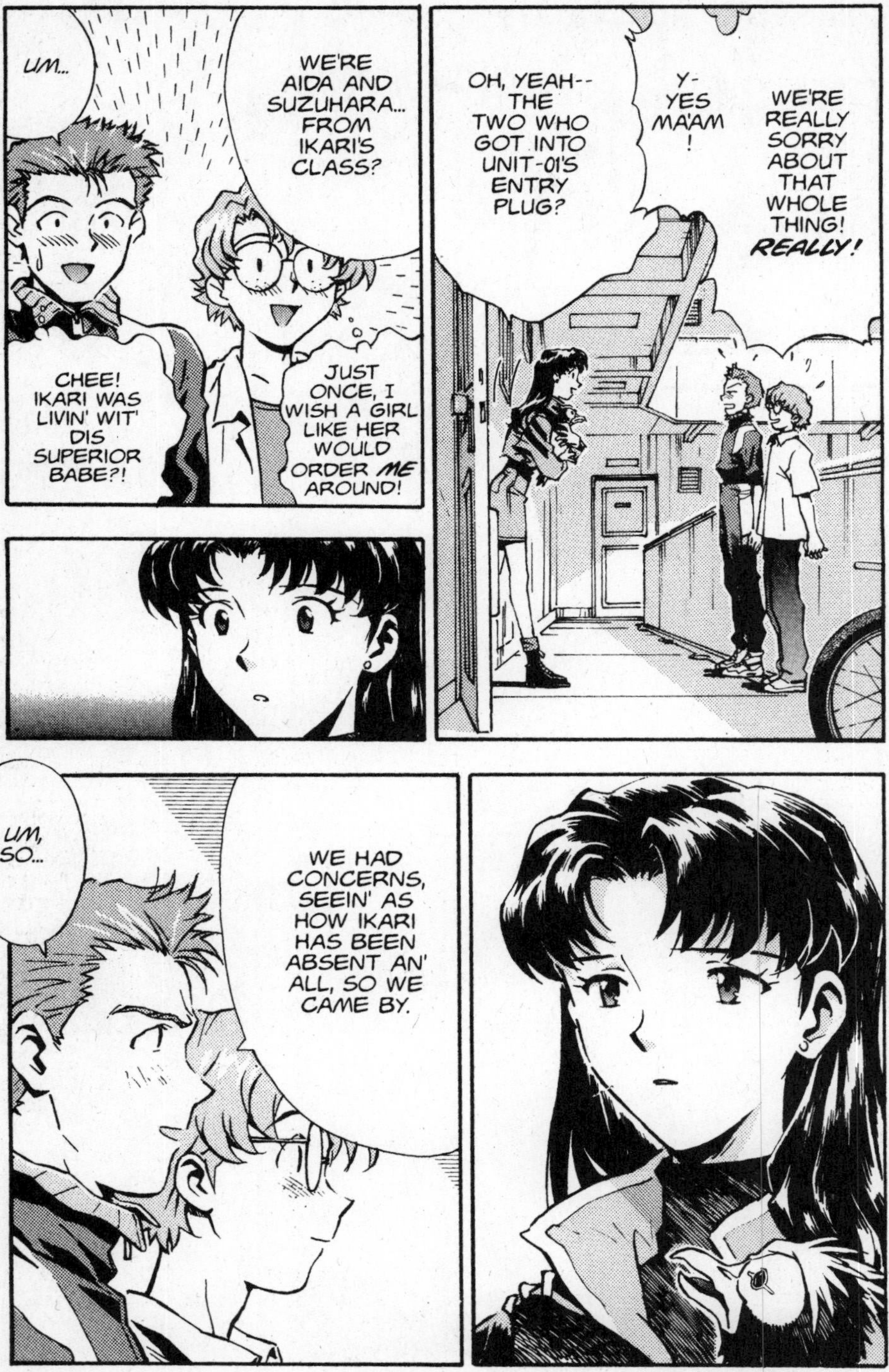
UM...
WE'RE AIDA AND SUZUHARA... FROM IKARI'S CLASS?
CHEE! IKARI WAS LIVIN' WIT' DIS SUPERIOR BABE?!
JUST ONCE, I WISH A GIRL LIKE HER WOULD ORDER *ME* AROUND!
OH, YEAH-- THE TWO WHO GOT INTO UNIT-01'S ENTRY PLUG?
Y-YES MA'AM!
WE'RE REALLY SORRY ABOUT THAT WHOLE THING! *REALLY!*
UM, SO...
WE HAD CONCERNS, SEEIN' AS HOW IKARI HAS BEEN ABSENT AN' ALL, SO WE CAME BY.

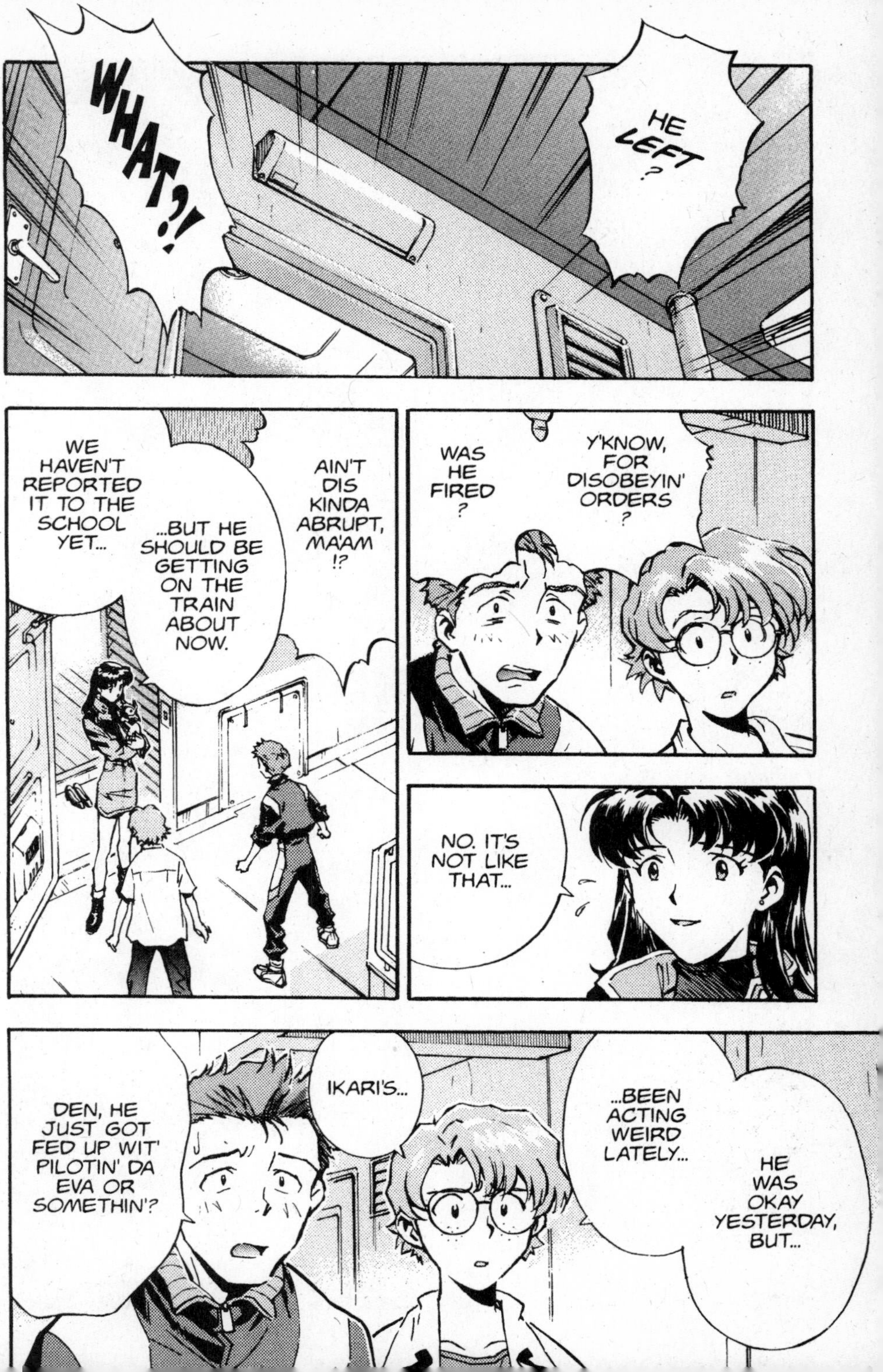
WHAT?!
HE LEFT?
WE HAVEN'T REPORTED IT TO THE SCHOOL YET...
...BUT HE SHOULD BE GETTING ON THE TRAIN ABOUT NOW.
AIN'T DIS KINDA ABRUPT, MA'AM!?
WAS HE FIRED?
Y'KNOW, FOR DISOBEYIN' ORDERS?
NO. IT'S NOT LIKE THAT...
DEN, HE JUST GOT FED UP WIT' PILOTIN' DA EVA OR SOMETHIN'?
IKARI'S...
...BEEN ACTING WEIRD LATELY...
HE WAS OKAY YESTERDAY, BUT...

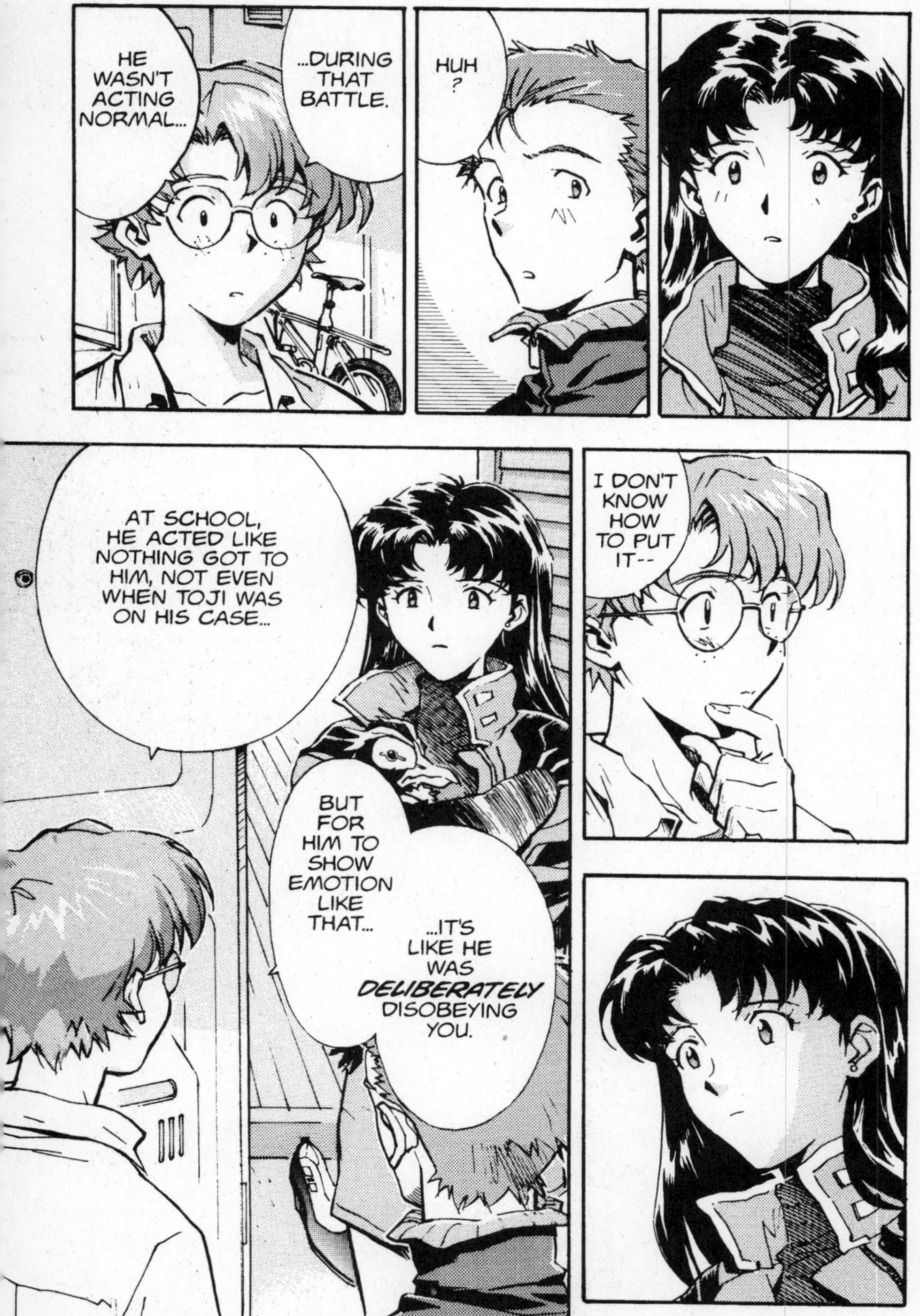
HE WASN'T ACTING NORMAL...
...DURING THAT BATTLE.
HUH?
AT SCHOOL, HE ACTED LIKE NOTHING GOT TO HIM, NOT EVEN WHEN TOJI WAS ON HIS CASE...
BUT FOR HIM TO SHOW EMOTION LIKE THAT...
...IT'S LIKE HE WAS DELIBERATELY DISOBEYING YOU.
I DON'T KNOW HOW TO PUT IT--

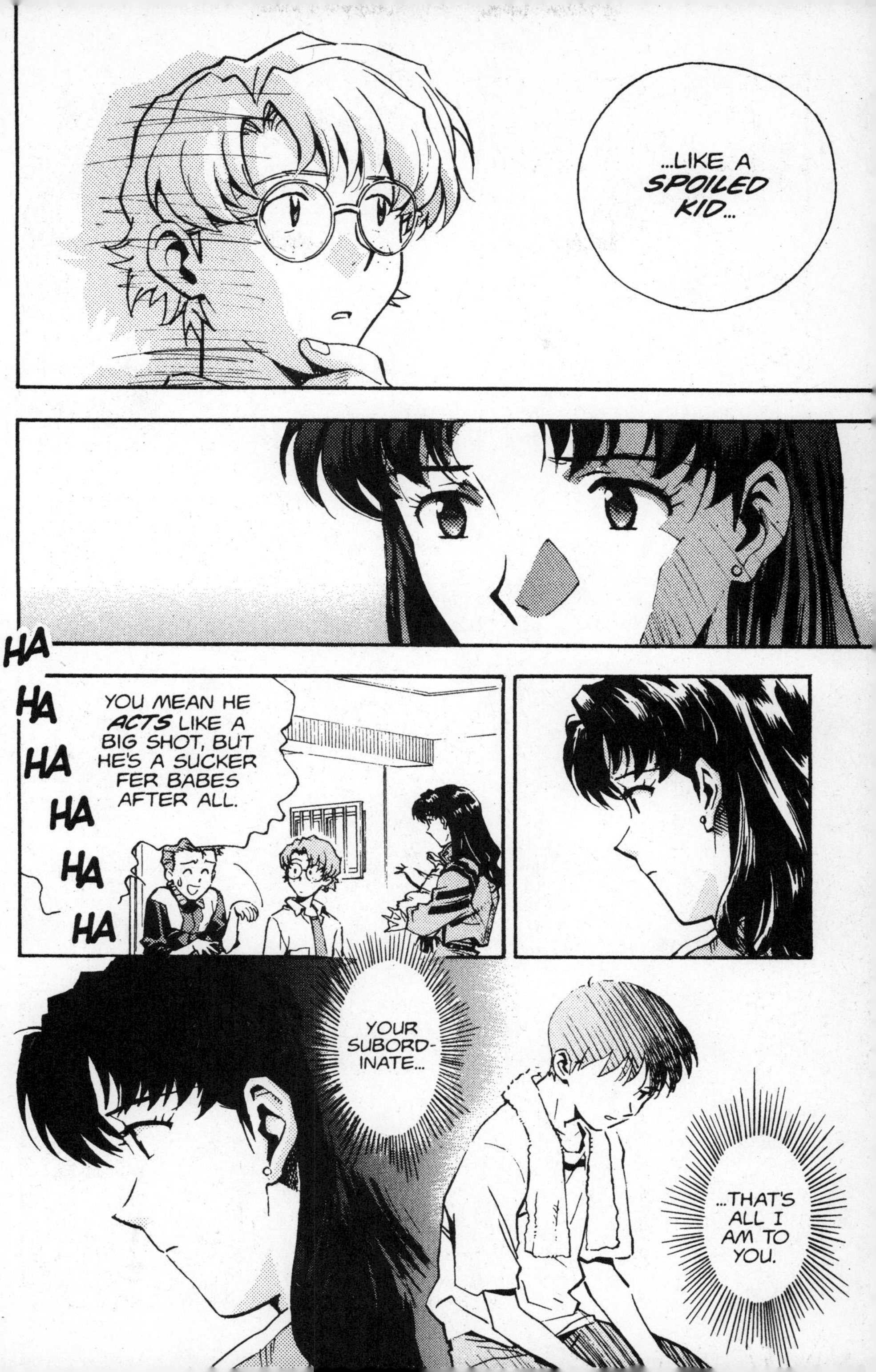
...LIKE A SPOILED KID...
HA HA HA HA HA HA
YOU MEAN HE ACTS LIKE A BIG SHOT, BUT HE'S A SUCKER FER BABES AFTER ALL.
YOUR SUBORD-INATE...
...THAT'S ALL I AM TO YOU.

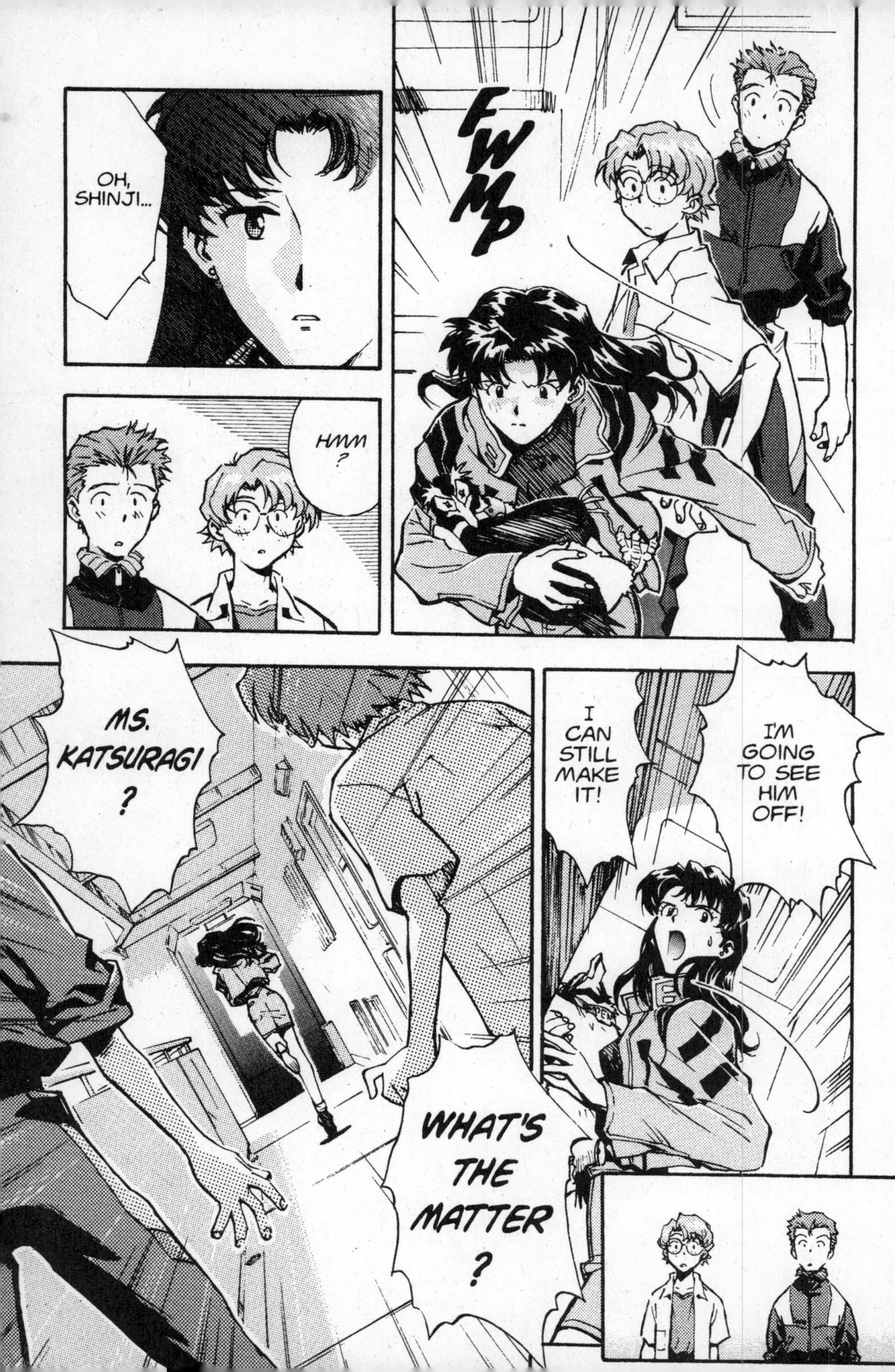
OH, SHINJI...
HMM ?
FWMP
MS. KATSURAGI ?
WHAT'S THE MATTER ?
I CAN STILL MAKE IT!
I'M GOING TO SEE HIM OFF!

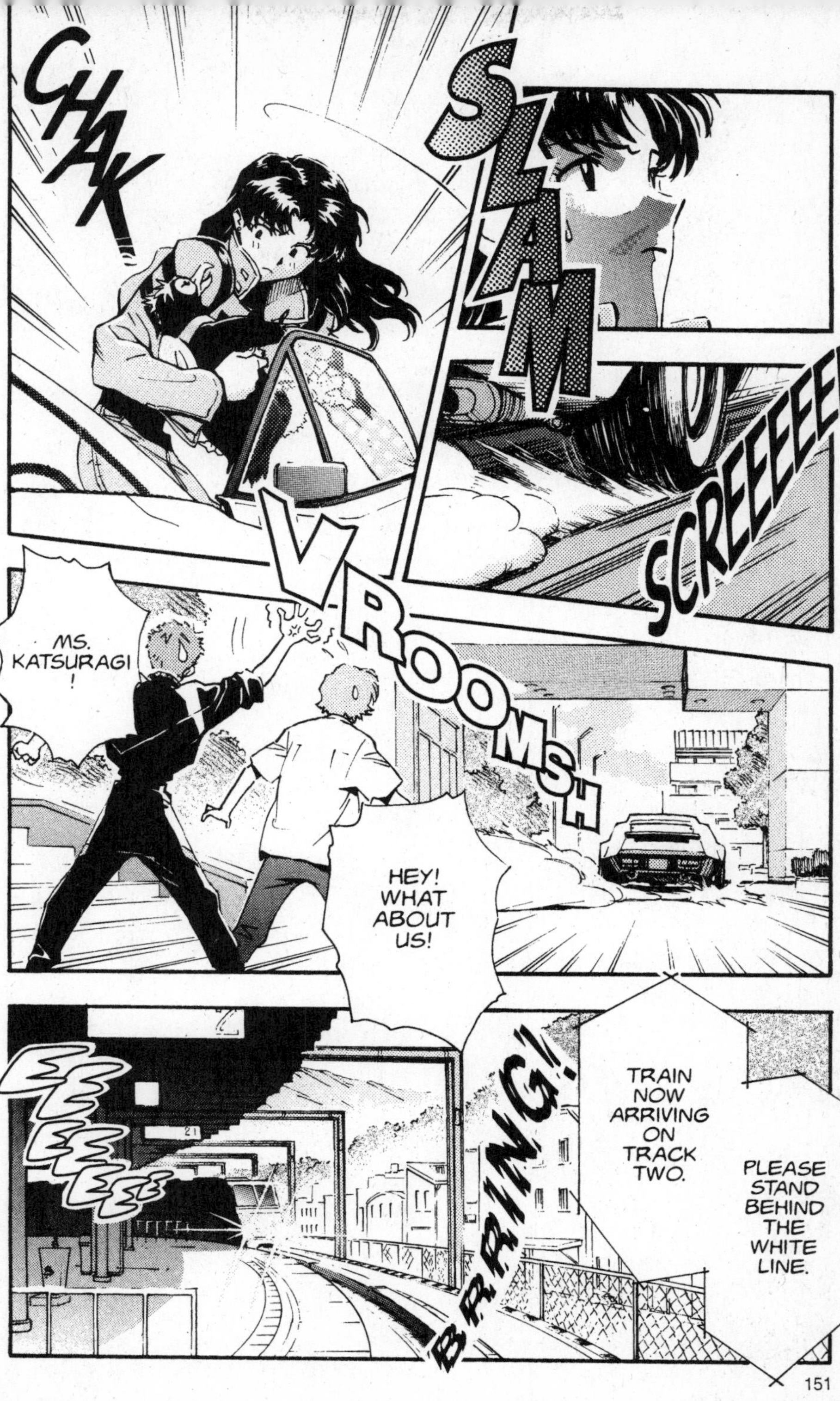
CHAK
SLAM
SCREEEEEE
VROOMSH
MS. KATSURAGI!
HEY! WHAT ABOUT US!
EEEEEEEEEEE
BRRING!!
TRAIN NOW ARRIVING ON TRACK TWO.
PLEASE STAND BEHIND THE WHITE LINE.

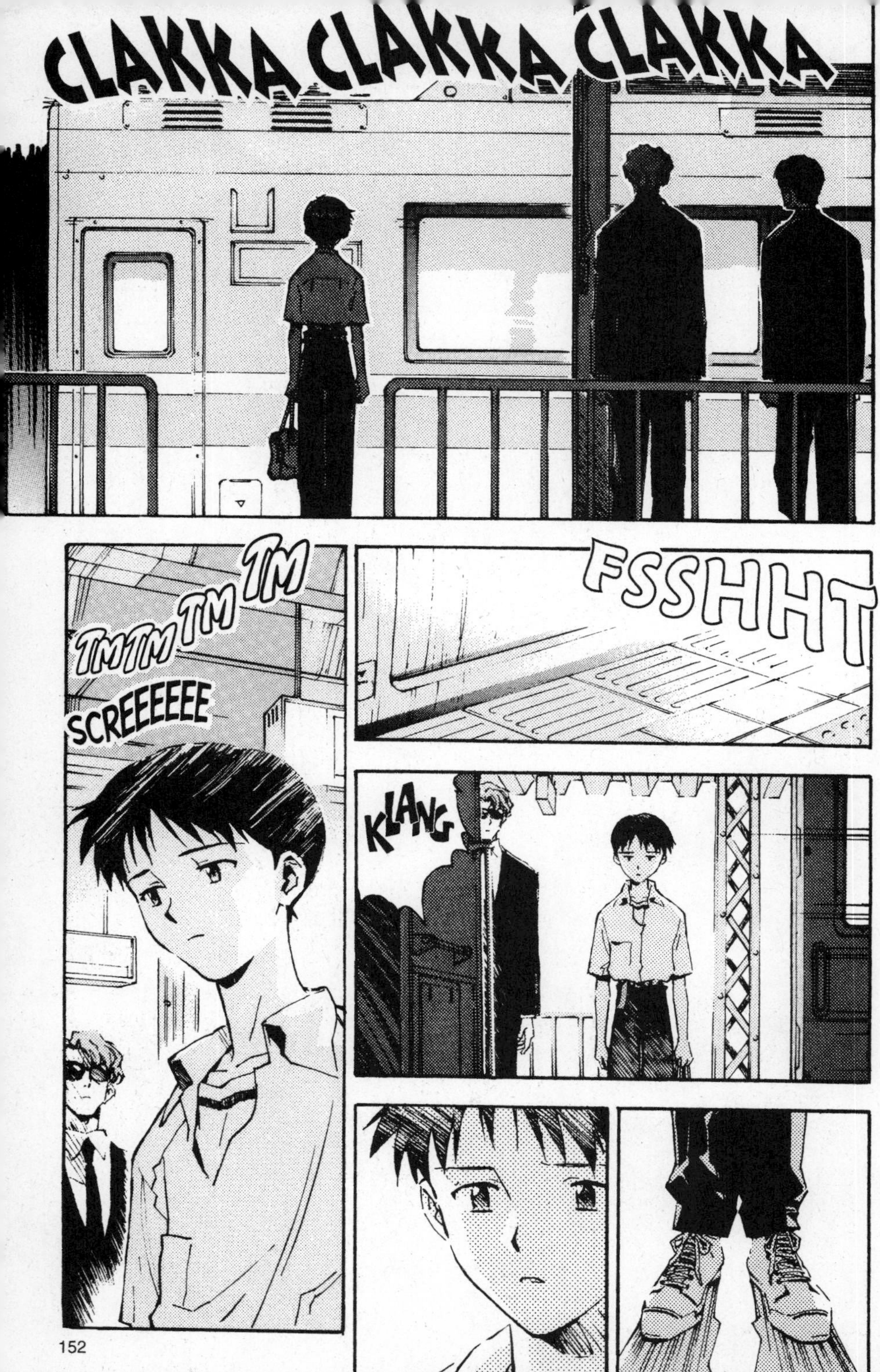
CLAKKA CLAKKA CLAKKA
TMTMTMTM
SCREEEEEE
FSSHHT
KLANG

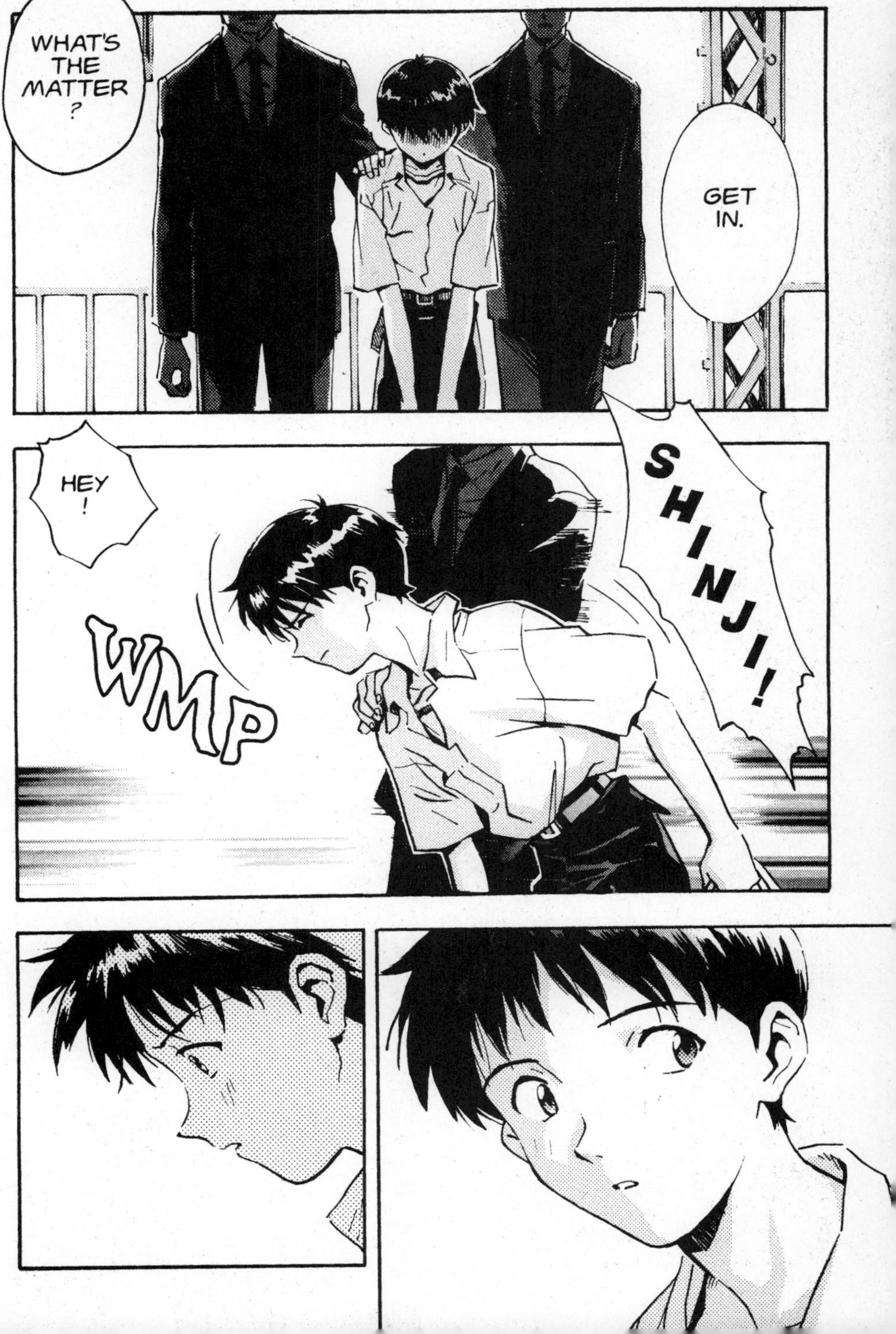
WHAT'S THE MATTER?
GET IN.
HEY!
WMP
SHINJI!

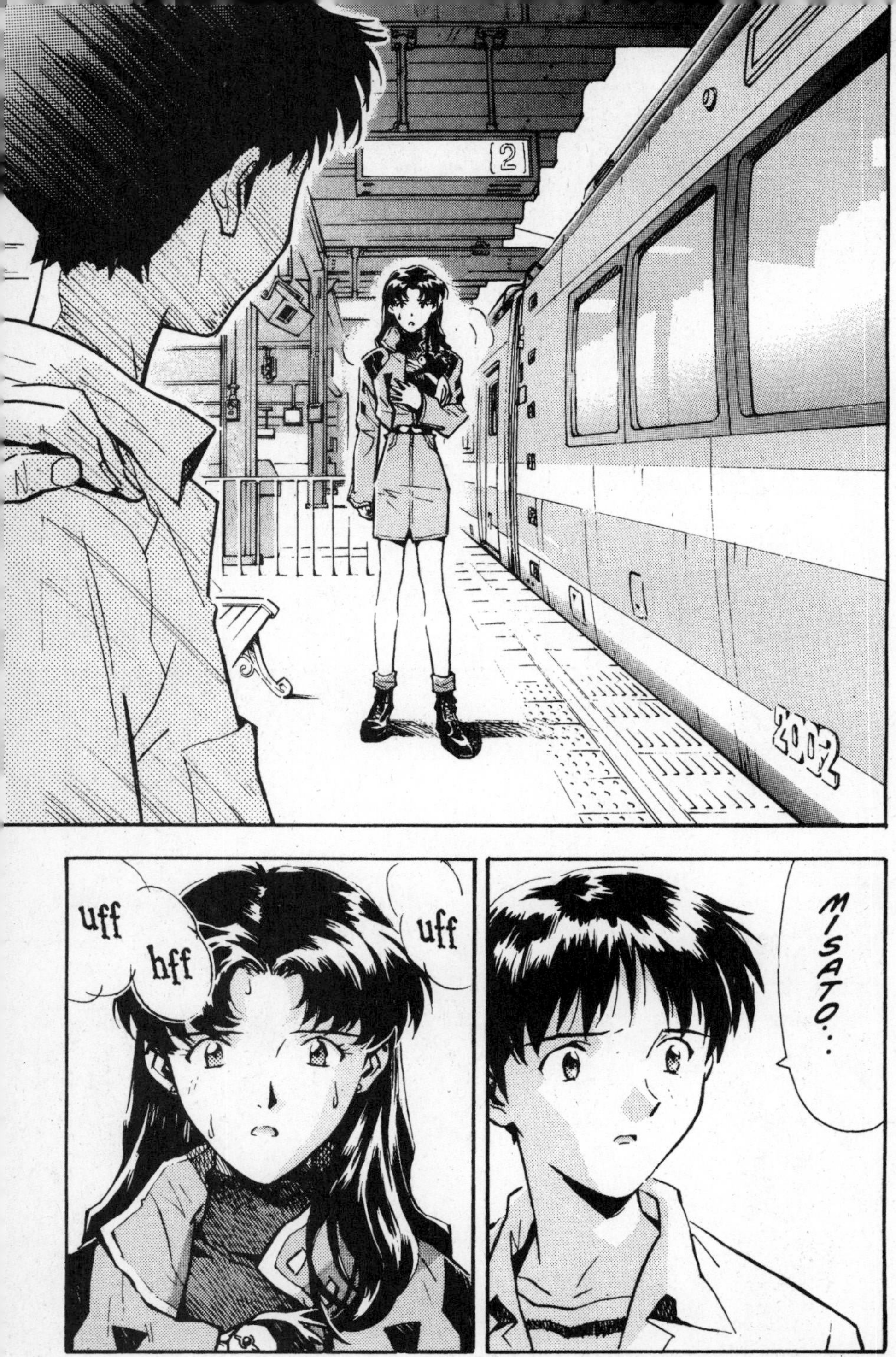
2
2002
uff
hff
uff
MISATO...

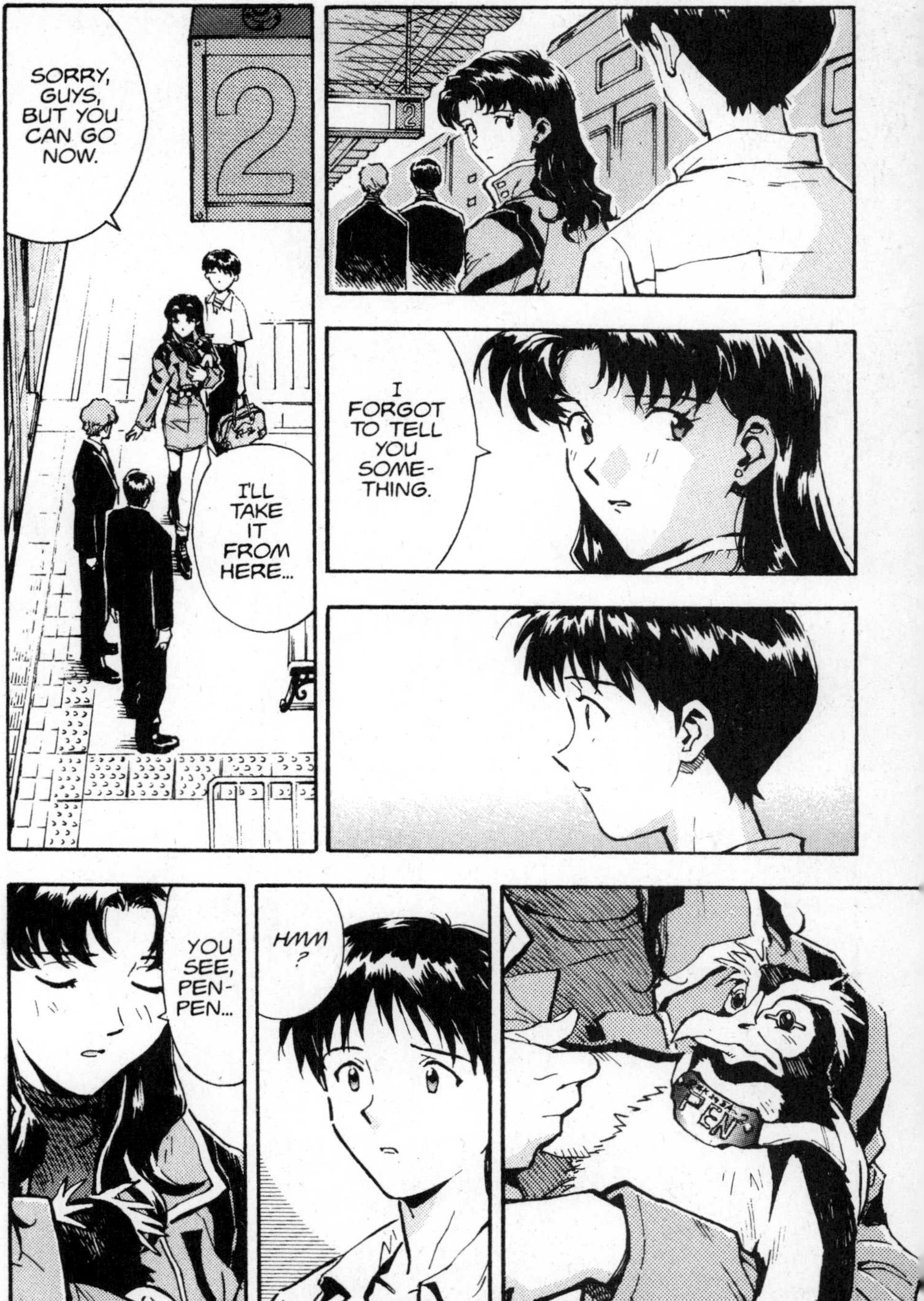
SORRY, GUYS, BUT YOU CAN GO NOW.
I'LL TAKE IT FROM HERE...
I FORGOT TO TELL YOU SOME-THING.
YOU SEE, PEN-PEN...
HMM ?
PEN

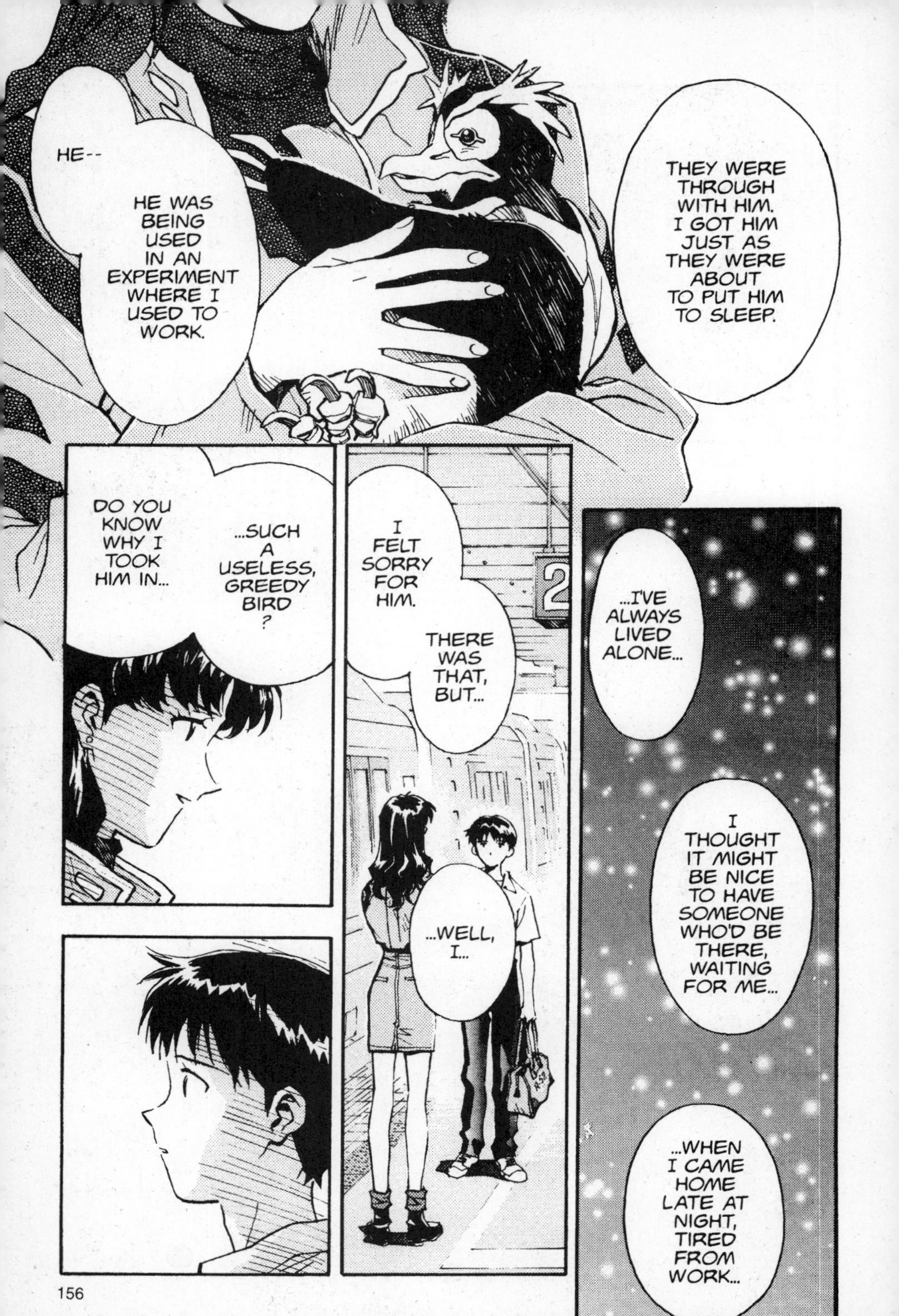
HE--
HE WAS BEING USED IN AN EXPERIMENT WHERE I USED TO WORK.
THEY WERE THROUGH WITH HIM. I GOT HIM JUST AS THEY WERE ABOUT TO PUT HIM TO SLEEP.
DO YOU KNOW WHY I TOOK HIM IN...
...SUCH A USELESS, GREEDY BIRD ?
I FELT SORRY FOR HIM.
THERE WAS THAT, BUT...
...WELL, I...
...I'VE ALWAYS LIVED ALONE...
I THOUGHT IT MIGHT BE NICE TO HAVE SOMEONE WHO'D BE THERE, WAITING FOR ME...
...WHEN I CAME HOME LATE AT NIGHT, TIRED FROM WORK...

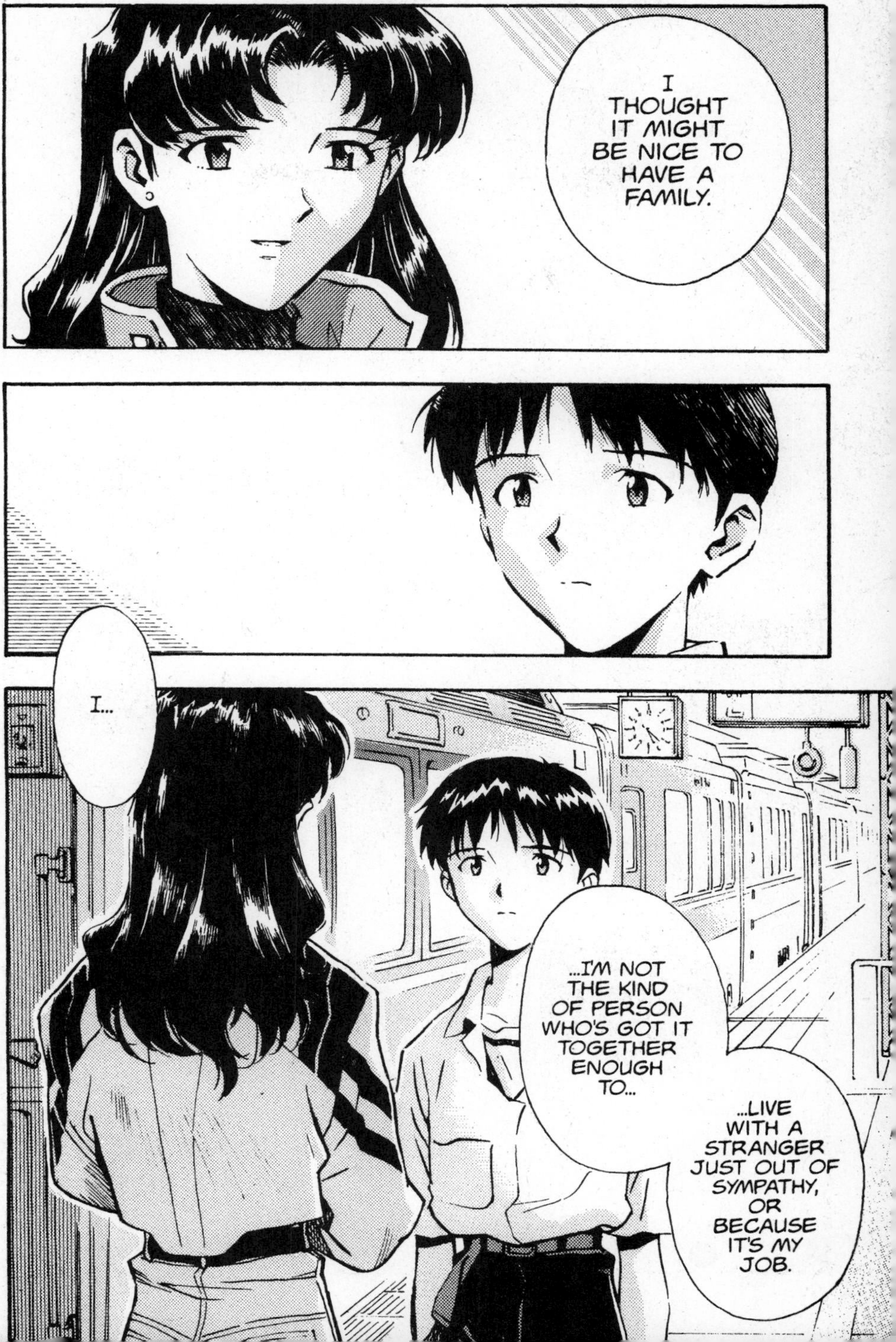
I THOUGHT IT MIGHT BE NICE TO HAVE A FAMILY.
I...
...I'M NOT THE KIND OF PERSON WHO'S GOT IT TOGETHER ENOUGH TO...
...LIVE WITH A STRANGER JUST OUT OF SYMPATHY, OR BECAUSE IT'S MY JOB.

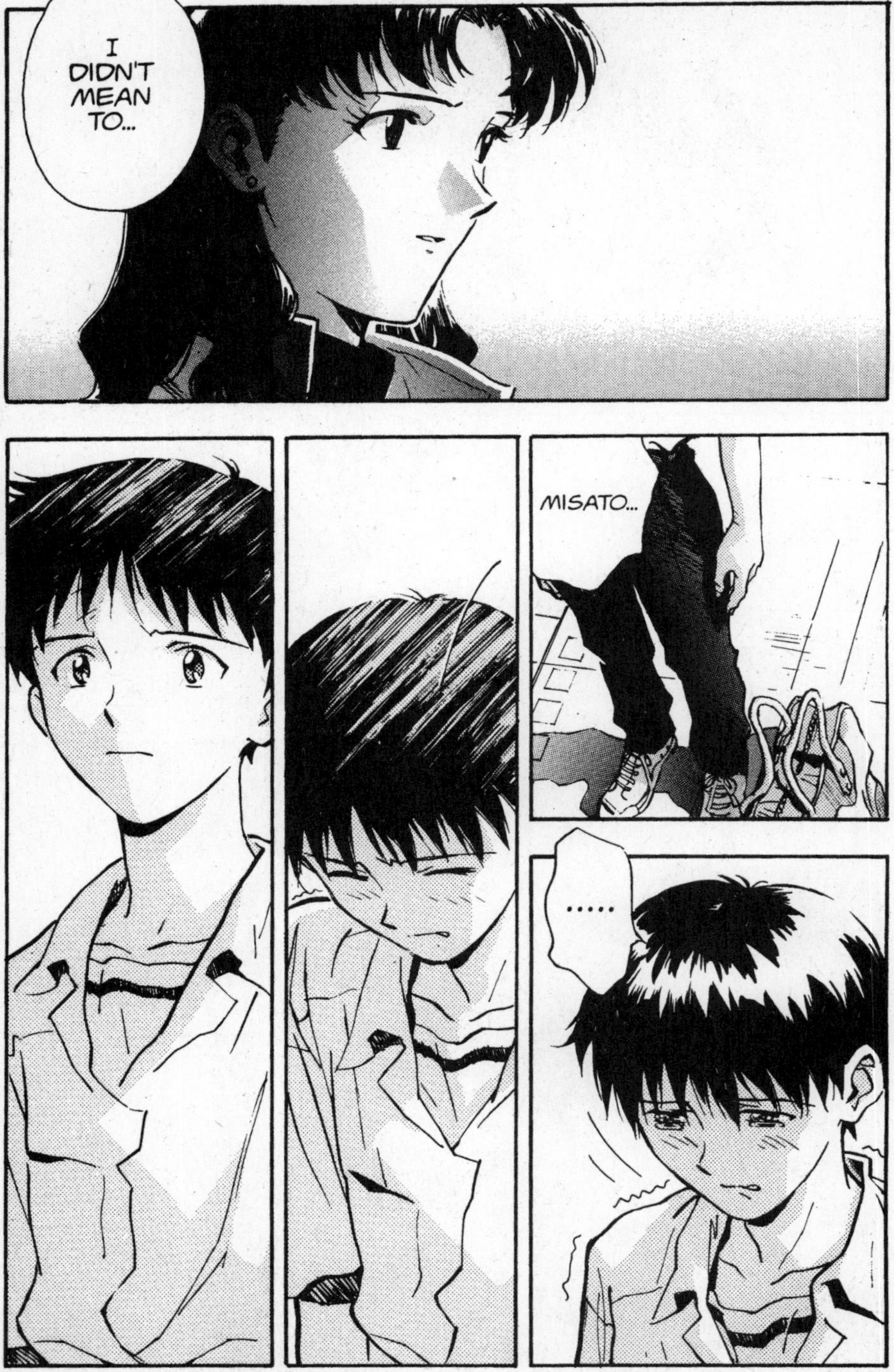
I DIDN'T MEAN TO...
MISATO...
......

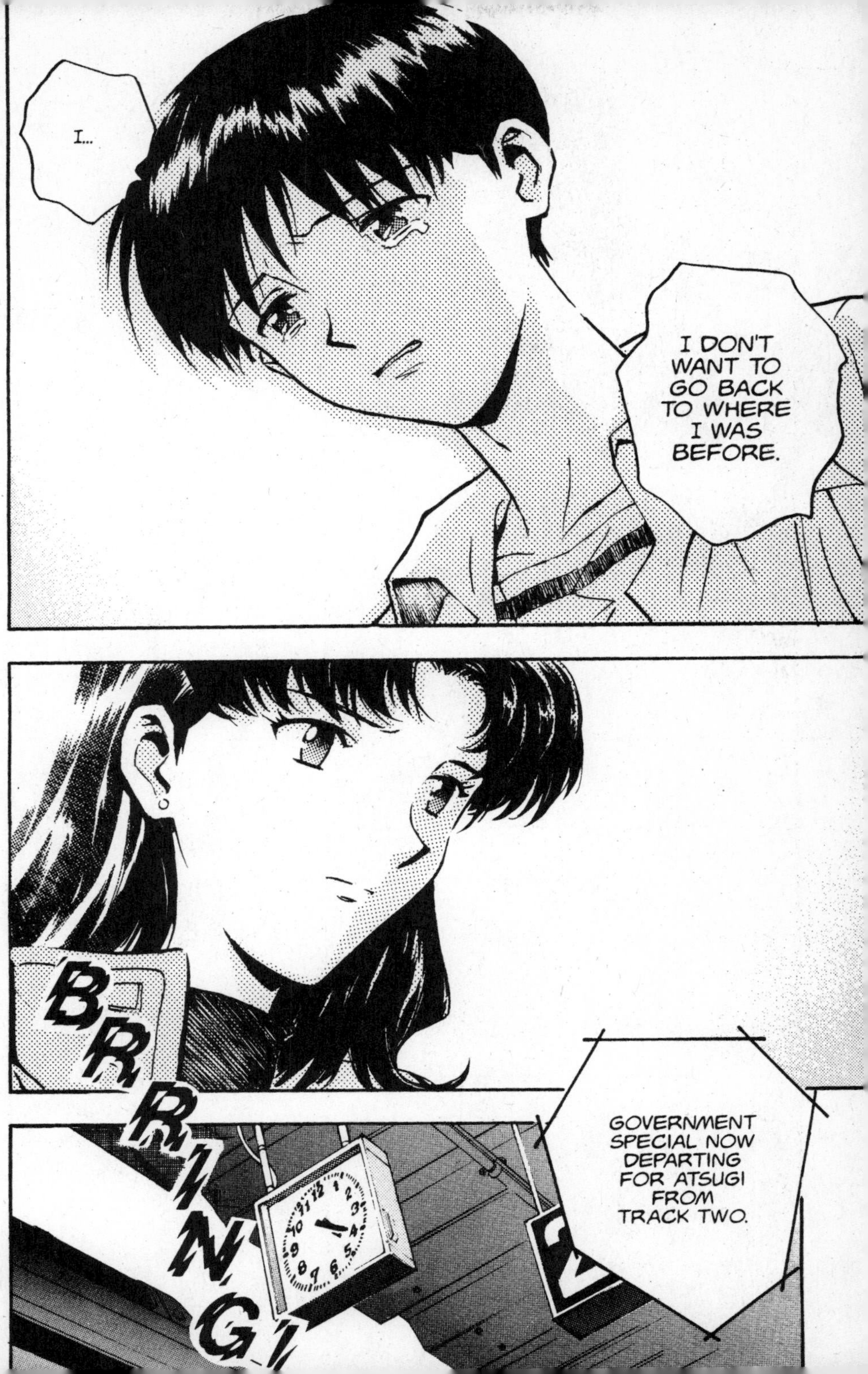
I...
I DON'T WANT TO GO BACK TO WHERE I WAS BEFORE.
BRRRING!
GOVERNMENT SPECIAL NOW DEPARTING FOR ATSUGI FROM TRACK TWO.

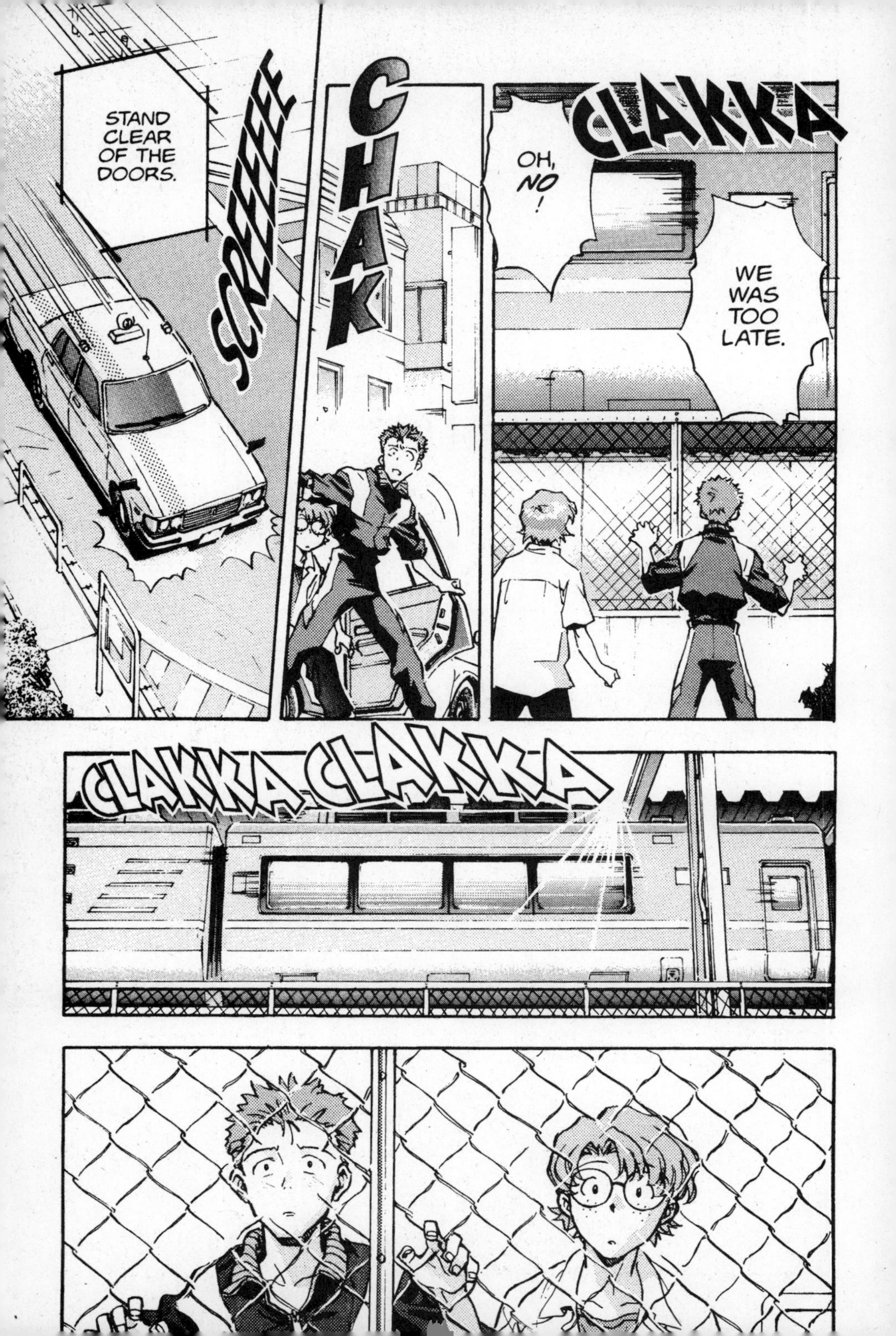
STAND CLEAR OF THE DOORS.
SCREEEEE
CHAK
CLAKKA
OH, NO!
WE WAS TOO LATE.
CLAKKA CLAKKA

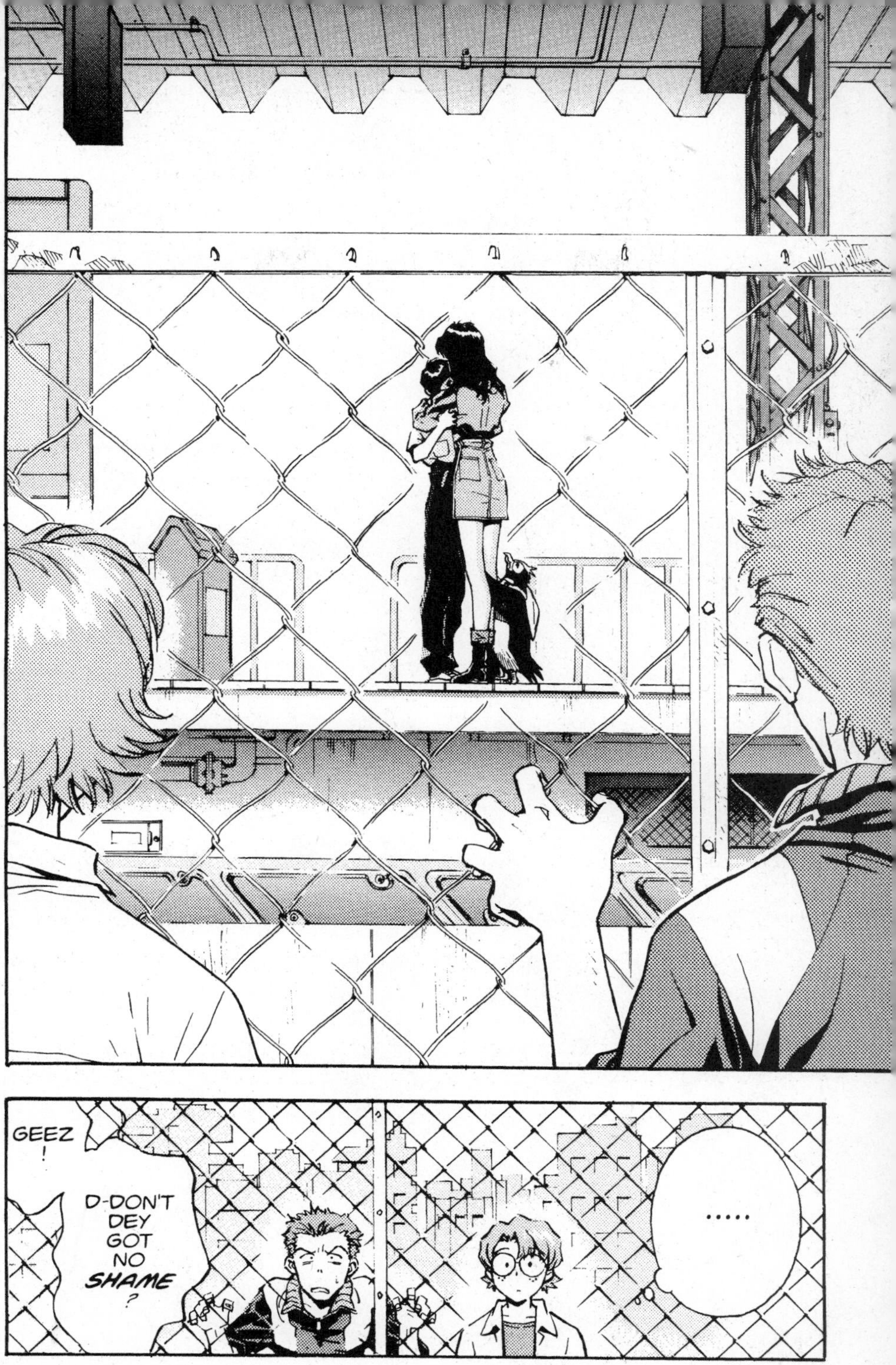
GEEZ!
D-DON'T DEY GOT NO SHAME?
.....

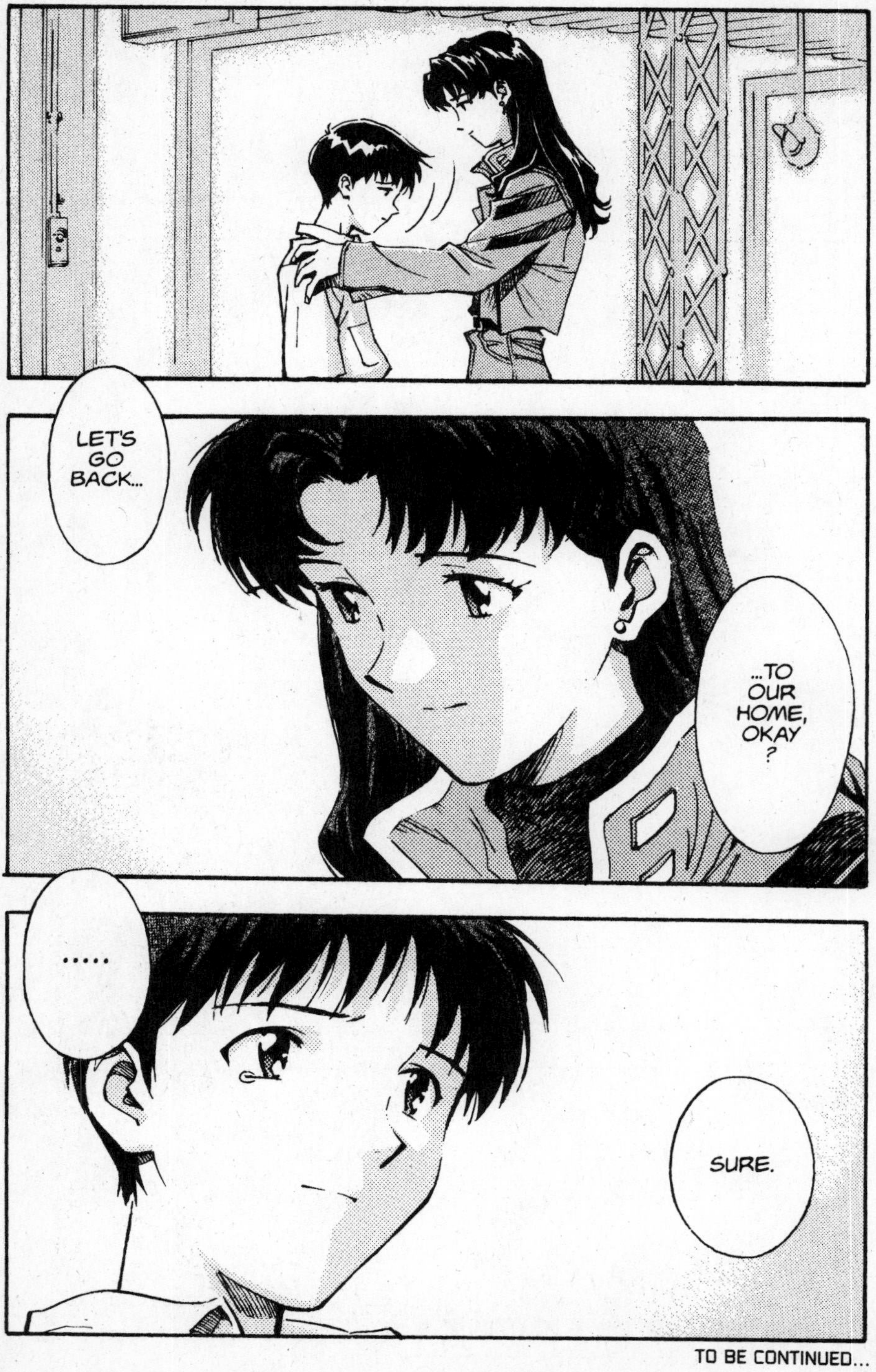
LET'S GO BACK...
...TO OUR HOME, OKAY?
......
SURE.

TO BE CONTINUED...

Manga Artist/Character Designer

My Thoughts at the Moment

(Translated By William Flanagan)

Over and above designing characters...

Q: You did the character designs for the animated version of *Evangelion*, and I'm sure that there were various points you paid special consideration to each character, so to start with, please talk about Shinji.

A: In a normal giant robot animated show the main character is noted for his enthusiastic battle spirit. And in *Eva*, the main character does pilot a giant robot, but Shinji is not noted for his enthusiasm, so I had to come up with a different heroic interpretation. Rather than a reflection of a hero, sort of a refraction of a hero.

Q: He's sort of a dry character.

A: He's a product of our era. I started out trying to create a character that would tap into the consciousness of today's anime fans.

Q: As a product of our era, you mean the attitude that, "My life is my own, and I'm not interested in the opinions of others," right?

A: He's a person who doesn't want to be interested in the opinions of others, but actually he's very interested. He's the kind of character who would encase himself in a shell of his own making.

Q: A sort of delicate character.

A: I wanted a sort of clean image that a woman tends to project. But also a character that is cold, unambitious—the type who would commit suicide, but can't bring himself to do it. It was my intention to create a wistful character who had given up on life.

Q: Did you have a model for his face?

A: Not particularly. The image of a hero in Japan is like *Ushiwakamaru*, the strong champion whom no adversity will affect. When you say "hero" in Japan, it conjures the impression of a man, just prior to middle age, accomplished at arms, with a burning spirit. Or maybe you think of a *bishonen* (beautiful young man). In the beginning I gave Shinji longer hair, so in the dramatic scenes, it could hide his face or wave in the breeze. But when I drew that, he looked a little too wild—and so delicate the slightest pressure would break him. So finally I tried for a look where you could see the forehead through the bangs, shorter hair—the look of a boyish young girl. Speaking in concrete terms, his eyes are a girl's eyes. I drew them exactly as I drew Nadia's [the heroine of Gainax's 1990 TV series *Nadia*, forthcoming in English from A.D.V. Films—ed.] eyes. He's a male Nadia, just as if I had given Nadia a masculine makeover. Lengthen the eyelashes and change the hair style, and you have Nadia.

Q: You don't draw characters out of any love of simplicity.
A: That's right. Our aim was to be the antithesis of all the giant robot animated shows around us. It's not a world where the wind blows through your hair while you declare your purpose in a booming voice. Especially in the past one or two years, this type of refractive, feminine character has not been seen. I wanted to tell the tale of a main character taken from my own life, so I designed a character straight from the more stoic part of myself.

Q: So instead of someone pushing you to draw, you added pieces of yourself to draw the characters.
A: I think that the theme of the animated version is that the main character's attitude changes little by little. I think that in the anime, Anno wrote the script in his own words, and that is why the change occurs. And the reason for the subtle changes between the animation and the manga is that Yoshiyuki Sadamoto is writing the script using Anno's characters. I think the anime is...I can't say cuter, but it has the feel of an honors student. The manga is a little more twisted...the feeling of a flunk-out. I think the reason behind this is that Anno was his class president in elementary and junior high schools, and flunking out was something he couldn't do, whereas I never had that problem. (laughs)

Q: You're saying that twisted sensibilities are a subtle difference?
A: According to Anno's thought process, a twisted person is one who puts on a cool face, but once you see the inside, you get to the crazy portion, just like all the young people today. My approach is the opposite. On the inside the characters are stoic and earnest, but the outside is twisted, just like a child. So I could never write the anime scripts in my own voice. My Shinji is quite a bit different than that. In the end it is his resistance, his refusal to listen to what Misato has to say, but he still makes the right decision. I think that approach is where our methods differ the most.

Q: What about Rei?
A: I played around with a character, Ukina, in a story I wrote a

long time ago in NEWTYPE called *Koto no Oni* ("The Ogre on the Desert Isle"). You take her, give her shaggy, bobbed, wolf-like hair, and you've got Rei. Really, I just played with her a bit—the way the eyes are drawn, the basic character is the same. Her character was locked in as translucent, like a shadow or the air. The kind of girl you can't touch. The girl you long for, but there is nothing about her that you can grab a hold onto.

Q: The same type of stance that Kensuke and Toji feel about Rei?
A: Even more distant. The first time you see Rei, she is all bandaged up. The group Kinniku Shojo Tai has a song called "Hotai de Masshiro na Shojo" ("The Girl White with Bandages"). When I heard that song, an image popped into my mind, and I drew Rei according to that. I thought, "I'd like to draw a girl like that." This girl who is fated to pilot a robot. I wanted to draw her even before I heard of Shinji. There were two things that went into the decision to make her eyes red: one is the fact that she didn't have enough outstanding features, and the second is from a business standpoint, the makers of the game wanted her differentiated from the other characters, but personally I think it turned out to have a great effect. She's so quiet you can only tell her character from her gaze and her facial expressions, so she leaves the impression of having a strong stare.

Eva in the Manga and the Anime

Q: Concentrating on the story, where do you think the biggest difference is between the manga and the anime?
A: Well I did write the script of the manga using the anime as a base. And at the moment, I think they're pretty much the same. I've made the story more compact. I think even if you rephrase a sentence into less words, you're still saying the same thing. But the manga does have a different approach. Maybe I should say it has a different choreography. The main point is that the anime has quite a few different people writing the continuity, for example when the assistant director, Mr. Tsurumaki wrote the continuity for a particular script, and when Masayuki wrote a continuity for the same script, it came out to be a completely different program. I think there's a difference there.

Q: There are the differences of format. You can't draw a manga in the same way you would animate a show.
A: And that's the reason I tend to change the script entirely. I pick and choose what is easier to say in manga. The anime became a craze among the fans, and I wanted to lower the